D1613431

THE
EMPTY
EDEN

THE EMPTY EDEN

TEXT
MERVYN DYKES

PHOTOGRAPHS
HANS STROHHACKER

NORTH-WEST BOOK CO. LTD.

Canadian Cataloguing in Publication Data

Dykes, Mervyn.
    The Empty Eden

Includes bibliographical references.
ISBN 0-9694257-0-8

      1. Endangered species — Africa. 2. Wildlife conservation —
Africa. 3. Man — Influence on nature — Africa. I. Strohhacker,
Hans J. (Hans Juergen), 1939-   . II. Title.

QL84.6.A1D94   1990   333.95'416'096   C89-091604-7

Concept and design: Hans J. Strohhacker

Senior editor: Elaine Jones, Vancouver

Typesetting by: PolaGraphics
         1201 West Pender Street, Vancouver, B.C.
         Canada V6E 2V2

Maps by: Weller Cartographic Services Ltd.
         6268 129th St., Surrey, B.C.
         Canada V3W 8H5

Colour separations: B.K. Trade Colour Separations Ltd.
         16652 - 117 Avenue, Edmonton, Alberta
         Canada T5M 3W2

Printed on 100 lb. Lustro Gloss acid-free paper by:
         Quality Color Press Inc.
         17612 - 103 Avenue, Edmonton, Alberta
         Canada T5S 1J9

Bound by:
         North-West Book Company Ltd.
         8115 - 132nd Street, Surrey, B.C.
         Canada V3W 4N5

Foreword

The evening breeze wafted across the open plains of the Serengeti, carrying the sweet scents of herbs and grasses up to my hiding place atop one of the numerous kopjes that studded the sea of grass like rocky islands.

Although I was enjoying the breeze, most of my attention was focussed on two young male lions under the umbrella of a lone acacia tree as they stirred and prepared to rise from their afternoon nap. Then, as I watched their slow preparation for the evening hunt, I became aware of a new scent.

At first it was very faint, but it grew in strength, mingling with the smells of the herbs. I recognized it long before I caught my first glimpse of the newcomers. Elephants.

The first to appear were two youngsters that burst from behind a huge rock on my right. They were just like children, running ahead of their family to go exploring. Not far behind them was a gigantic adult with gleaming white tusks — obviously one of the leading females, perhaps even the matriarch of the herd.

As more and more elephants came into view, I started to count. The seemingly endless procession reminded me of the long trains that carry coal from the Interior to the coast back home in British Columbia. I counted more than eighty elephants. The only sounds of their awesome progress were the rumblings of contentment that rolled from their massive chests as they slipped through the tall, yellow grass in the fading light of that February evening.

This was the Africa that I had come to photograph for a book on Africa's wildlife, a lifelong dream that was finally becoming reality. But was it reality?

Once there were no elephants in the Serengeti. Now there are thousands seeking sanctuary from the most deadly of all predators — man. The wanton killing of Africa's wildlife and the destruction of its habitat that I witnessed during my first six weeks on that continent had filled me with a sense of horror and disgust.

The concept of this book changed during those early days in Africa. The story of Africa's struggle to preserve its wild heritage became the focal point of the book and inspired its title, *The Empty Eden*.

The plight of Africa's wildlife is mirrored in all wild places throughout the world. Finding solutions in Africa will help every other country. But time is running out.

Once our planet seemed set to roll on, unchanged forever. It was too big for man to harm; its resources inexhaustible; its wealth beyond counting. But in the space of a few decades we have been forced to accept that there are limits.

We now acknowledge that we live in a closed environment, and we realize that if we continue to pollute the Earth, we too may die.

There is no more room for doubts, or excuses, because the dying has begun already. We have fouled the oceans and poisoned the air we breathe. We are cutting down the forests that could purify this air. We have taken a terrible toll of the plant and animal life with which we share this planet. We have been thoughtless, selfish and short-sighted. Now we face our reckoning.

By the end of this century a great part of creation will have been destroyed or brought to the brink of destruction at the hands of man. Between the time I write this and the year 2000, many thousands of plant and animal species could become extinct. Some have suggested that the rate of extinction might be as great as one an hour.

We look back to the passing of the dinosaurs and ask how such a great disaster could have occurred. Yet we stand now indicted as the culprits of a disaster which is potentially greater.

In Africa, my friends the elephants and rhinos are falling victim to killers — greedy humans who are abusing the power they hold over the animals.

Superior intelligence does not grant us the right to take the lives of lesser creatures. On the contrary, our knowledge and understanding place an awesome responsibility on our shoulders — to be the keepers of life. Only when we recognize this and are willing to make the necessary sacrifices can the healing of life on Earth begin. The right to life that man has enshrined in religions and constitutions must now embrace all creation.

Are we capable of meeting this challenge? The way we treat our fellow human beings gives ample cause for doubt. Our deeds range from the enslavement of our brothers in the past to outright genocide in recent history. Faced with such doubts, we must search out and cling to the positive achievements that have sprung from the goodness of the great men and women of the past. We must rehabilitate ourselves and learn to

Page   CONTENTS

◁ Victoria Falls.

believe in the goodness of the human race.

We have the ability to reverse the trends that threaten the very life of Spaceship Earth. Thousands of scientists and philosophers the world over already search for answers to the mysteries of life and our place in the universe. Our nature compels us to ask these questions and seek answers to the unknown. But have we come so far only to defeat ourselves?

This must not be allowed to happen. Solutions can be found. We must formulate them and work towards implementation.

One of our first priorities should be the establishment of an international authority to deal with global pollution. Disasters such as the Chernobyl nuclear power plant accident and the *Exxon Valdez* oil spill belong in front of international courts of law, free of interference and protectionism. They are crimes against humanity.

To help deal with disasters of this magnitude, an international fund could be established. All countries and corporations dealing with potentially hazardous commodities would contribute to this fund, which could not only finance clean-ups but aid research and development.

Mankind is busily engaged in space programs and extending its influence to other worlds. The value of space research cannot be denied, but we must also question our priorities. Before continuing our quest for life on other planets, it is imperative that we halt the destruction of life on our own.

In the words of astronomer Carl Sagan: ''Our loyalties are to the species of this planet. We speak for Earth. Our obligation to survive is owed not just to ourselves, but also to that cosmos, ancient and vast, from which we spring.''

Hans Strohhacker
Surrey, British Columbia
Canada.
March, 1990.

CHAPTER ONE
ELEPHANTS: "The Animal Most Like Man"

She looked rather like everyone's favourite grandmother as she bustled across the lawn in front of her home in Nairobi National Park, heading for an open area in front of a sturdy wooden shed. As soon as she reached it, she stopped and stood motionless, the light breeze occasionally riffling strands of her greying hair.

Like parents and grandparents everywhere, Daphne Sheldrick was listening for the first sound of her youngsters coming home, and she seemed the slightest bit worried because they were later than usual.

"They should be here any moment now," she said. "They have their milk the same time every day." An anxious hand began to smooth the front of her dress. Beyond the oasis of her immediate domain stretched the pale yellow grass of the park, studded by occasional trees and patches of bush. There were wild animals out there, including lions whose roars were sometimes heard in the city of Nairobi, which sprawls close to the borders of the park.

Suddenly, she looked up. "Here they come!"

Two young elephants exploded around the side of the shed, pursued by their handlers, grinning and shouting behind them. Like excited children, the four cavorted about on the lawn until one of the elephants broke away from the group and rushed up to Daphne Sheldrick, its whole bearing still suggesting high spirits. At the last moment the youngster stopped directly in front of her. Its mood changed instantly. Moving very slowly now, it stretched out its trunk and, with great gentleness, stroked the upper part of her left arm two or three times. Sheldrick's right hand touched its head in an answering caress. For a few seconds they remained in contact and then, as though unable to restrain its mischief any longer, the elephant wheeled away to rejoin the mad whirl on the lawn.

I could interpret what had happened in only one way. I had seen an expression of endearment between two species — one a human being and the other, technically, a wild animal. It was a beautiful, priceless moment and one of the strongest images I would take away from Africa.

Daphne Sheldrick is known for her belief that there are many emotional and intellectual similarities between elephants and human beings. Earlier, she had explained her views to me at great length and with considerable eloquence. Although I was sympathetic, I remained unconvinced until that moment on the lawn. The message couldn't have been clearer if the elephant had called out in English: "Hi, Mom. I'm home!"

Sheldrick has been a foster mother to orphaned animals of many species. Quietly and efficiently she has seen to their physical needs; and just as matter-of-factly, she has healed emotional wounds as well. Somehow she has been able to provide the love and companionship which are part of daily life in an elephant herd without making the animals so tame they can no longer survive in the wild. She has taken elephant orphans as young as three weeks and helped them thrive, something no one had done before. The two irrepressible elephants on her lawn, for instance, were only babies when their mothers fell victim to that plague of modern Africa — poachers' bullets. Without her help, the babies would have certainly died — from starvation, if somehow the predators missed them.

"It has always been considered impossible to hand-raise African elephants," said Sheldrick. "The fat of elephants' milk is so unlike that of the cow that to feed any form of cow's milk fat to a baby elephant is to seal its death. Yet elephants also require a lot of fat in their diet. They cannot go longer than three hours between feeds, so must be fed every three hours, day and night, for at least eighteen months."

The key to her success is SMA Goldcap (S 26) a powdered milk formula imported from the United Kingdom. To this she adds extra glucose, B and C vitamins, minerals, calcium, salt and — later on — cereals. By the time a calf is nine months old, it will be consuming upwards of fifty-five pints of milk every twenty-four hours.

"Of all the wild animals, elephants are the most difficult, the most demanding and the most delicate [to nurture], for they are very human in their intelligence and sensitivity," she said. "Above all, they require a great deal of genuine and sincere loving. They must be happy in order to thrive and in order to be happy, they must be fond of their attendants, yet not so fond of anyone that they will miss his absence and go into a decline. They must never be left unattended, even at night, and they require mental stimulation as well in the form of playthings and varied surroundings. Initially, they must be fed beneath a tent, or tarpaulin — something large overhead to replace the form of their mother . . ."

Daphne Sheldrick's fund of knowledge about the domestic affairs of elephants and her theories about what motivates them have been built up during many years of first-hand experience.

"I've raised most animals, from dik-diks to elands, buffaloes, rhinoceros and elephants and many more of them," she told me. "But of all the animals I've raised the elephants are the most human in their intelligence and emotions.

"I think that will be authenticated by the scientists. I'm just a lay person, but I've probably had more practical experience with elephants than anyone else alive.

"I've known them for many, many years. I've raised them from infancy and I've followed their lives right into adulthood.

"We [she and her late husband, David, who died in 1977] were also in the Tsavo National Park [in southern Kenya] for thirty years. My husband was the founder warden in that case, so I've seen it all. I've seen them die during droughts. I've seen the terrible poaching and all that sort of thing that's gone on and now I feel that elephants, of all things . . . we should just give them a place to live. I think that really is an international obligation, because the protection of elephants in the field is, in the present circumstances, beyond the capability of the local government.

"The threat to elephants now, with automatic weapons and so on, is so sinister that there are no local forces at the moment that are competent to deal with it — not even the army."

Daphne Sheldrick is the chair and a trustee of The David Sheldrick Wildlife Trust, a volunteer organization established in memory of her husband, which works to preserve wildlife, particularly in the Tsavo National Park. A fearless and articulate campaigner for elephants, rhinos, and other endangered species, she has toiled tirelessly for years with the myriad small tasks and administrative challenges that are hidden behind the Trust's more public achievements. In the process, she has earned the respect of scientist and amateur alike.

She faces, unflinchingly, the vision of an awful future: the very real possibility that Africa's gift to the world — some of the most beautiful and diverse animal and plant species on our planet — may not survive with us into the next century. In fact, the elephants and the rhinos may go down in the next ten years. And they are not alone. Primates, predators, ungulates, birds, reptiles, plants — all have representatives on the lists of endangered species.

I came to Africa believing that my researches had given me a good grasp of the wildlife situation. All I was going to do there was gather up-to-date information from people in the field and round out whatever I wrote by capturing some of the local colour, including that almost mystical thing that people talk about as the essence of Africa. What I found was an education. Within the first week that intellectual appreciation was shaken till it rattled. During the next few weeks, it became mixed with liberal doses of anger, and now this compound burns away in steady outrage at what we have done and are still doing to the animals.

Have I become as ''emotional'' as Daphne Sheldrick? I hope so. And, like Daphne Sheldrick, I make no apologies for it. The information in this and succeeding chapters must be felt as well as thought about. The scientific information is there for those who want it — and so is a message. In wasting the lives of Africa's animals and plants, we are altering our planet in ways that almost certainly will turn against us.

We can no longer live in isolation. If we lose the animals and forests of Africa and South America, we may lose everything. We may be the final casualties of our own carelessness. Already, we stand among the ranks of species that are on the list of the merely ''threatened,'' as opposed to the ''endangered.'' We are prime candidates for a deadly promotion. Our own survival depends on how well we treat the plant and animal life forms around us.

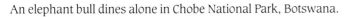

An elephant bull dines alone in Chobe National Park, Botswana.

THE INESCAPABLE PROBLEMS, THE DIFFICULT SOLUTIONS

Photographer Hans Strohhacker had been to Africa before and his experiences led directly to this book, but even that didn't make him immune from shock. One morning when we were staying at Salt Lick Lodge south of Tsavo and just north of the Tanzanian border, he returned from a game drive in a sombre mood. Barely five minutes from the lodge he had found the butchered remains of an elephant. Poachers had shot it and hacked out the tusks with a chainsaw.

Who would do such a thing? Why? The answer is one our profit-seeking society should have no trouble understanding: it pays.

The World Wide Fund for Nature (WWF), which assembles prices from a variety of legal and black-

One of the saddest sights in modern Africa, the mutilated carcase of an elephant left behind by poachers. These remains lie near Salt Lick Lodge in southern Kenya.

market sources, claims that ivory sold for US$7.44 per kilo in 1970. That figure jumped twelve-fold to US$100 per kilo in 1987. Other sources recorded prices of up to US$300 a kilo, a global trade worth about US$300 million a year. Today ivory is literally worth its weight in silver.

International trade records show that about three hundred tonnes of uncarved elephant tusks were exported legally by African countries in 1986. But a 1987 meeting of CITES (the Convention for International Trade in Endangered Species of Wild Fauna and Flora) claimed that such a figure represents only 26 per cent of the ivory that actually leaves Africa. About twelve hundred tonnes go out each year under faked documents or in mislabelled containers to satisfy consumer demand. Obviously, poaching is excellent business, and those who buy ivory products have helped make it so.

While poaching is not the only thing humans are doing to cause Africa's animals to die by the thousands every year, it is the most visible and the most dramatic. Far more insidious is the loss of animal habitat due largely to the rapid increase in the human population. There are now more than 615 million people in Africa — about one-eighth of the world's total — and this wave of humanity is swelling at a much faster rate than in other parts of the globe.

Reliable figures are difficult to obtain in Africa. Some countries have never conducted a census. But estimates from various economic studies indicate that the population has skyrocketed upward from about 300 million in 1969 and 457 million as recently as 1979. Land is being gobbled up at an equally alarming rate for farms, settlements, factories, roads, and other requirements of civilization.

As the human wave ripples outward from the main population centres, the animals lose access to food and water. They are stripped of shelter and concealment as the bush and scrub go down. Their traditional migratory routes are cut by highways and railroads, leaving them exposed to influences from which they were once able to retreat. No longer can the animals move about freely to take advantage of seasonal variations in food and water supplies. Increasingly, domestic livestock gets first chance at the already meagre resources. What is more, poor human pastoral and farming techniques are hastening the spread of deserts.

While it is clear that some of the problems faced by Africa's human and animal populations are connected and can be resolved concurrently, human needs are usually given priority whenever a choice is made.

This book urges two paired and parallel courses of action. First, we must stop the poachers. Second, in this vast continent, let us find places where wildlife can be allowed to come first. To make these plans happen, we must provide greater international support to national governments.

There are sound economic reasons for this course. Much of Africa's tourism is prompted by the desire of international visitors to see Africa's fabled animals, savannas, and jungles in person. Both the poachers and the plundering of the land work against Africa's economic interests.

Poaching gives short-term rewards in dollars. Stopping poaching and preserving unique plants and animals will give long-term rewards in survival. While not all poaching is for economic gain, it is this aspect that is causing greatest concern.

In only six years, more than a third of the elephants have gone. What will the next six years bring? At this rate, the extermination of elephants in the wild is frighteningly close. Of course, some, the "last" elephants, will manage to hide out for years, but one of the greatest sights on Earth, a huge herd of elephants on the march, may be gone forever.

Elephants crossing a road in Chobe National Park, Botswana. This intrusion by man is relatively gentle, but elsewhere highways cause serious problems by cutting animals' traditional migration routes.

A long file of elephants on the move near Salt Lick Lodge, which borders Tsavo National Park in Kenya.

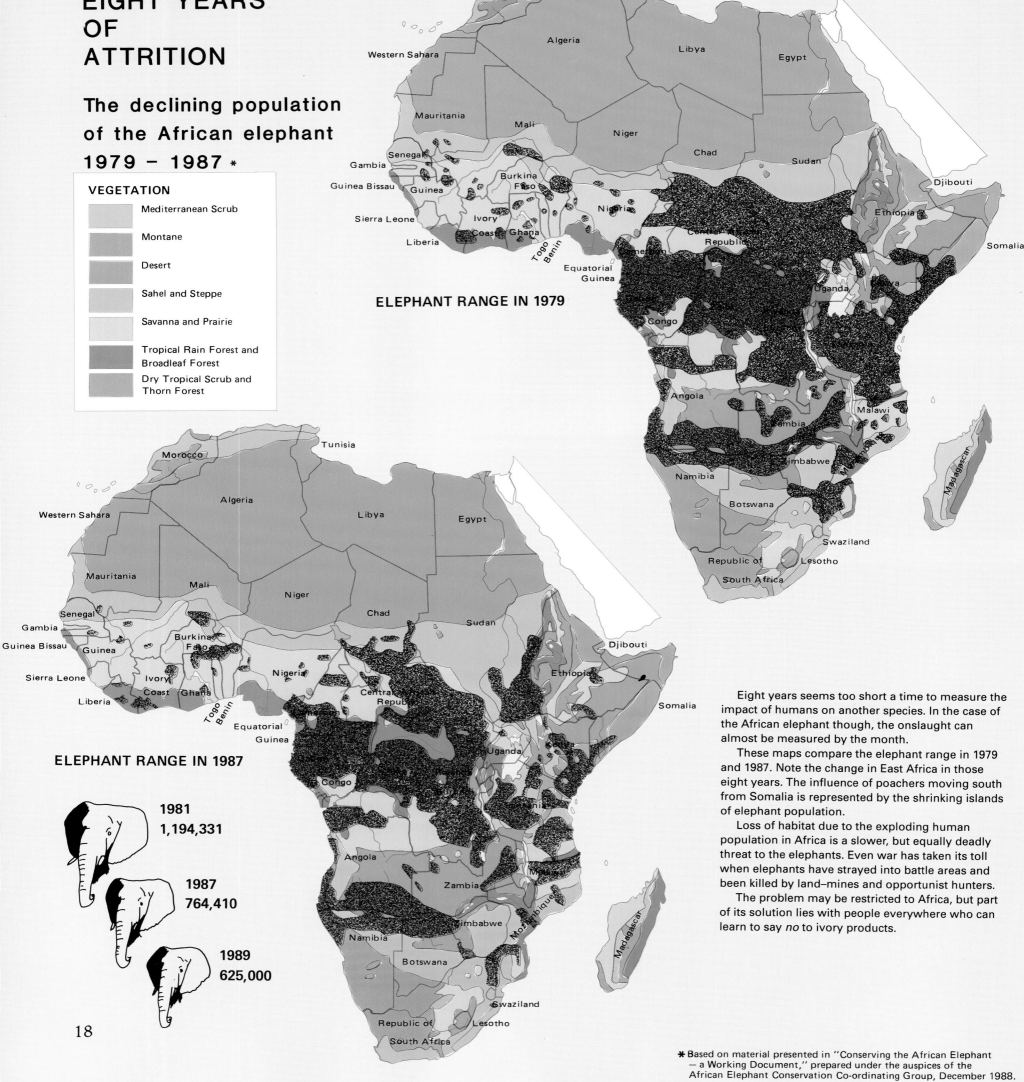

EIGHT YEARS OF ATTRITION

The declining population of the African elephant 1979 – 1987 *

VEGETATION

- Mediterranean Scrub
- Montane
- Desert
- Sahel and Steppe
- Savanna and Prairie
- Tropical Rain Forest and Broadleaf Forest
- Dry Tropical Scrub and Thorn Forest

ELEPHANT RANGE IN 1979

ELEPHANT RANGE IN 1987

1981
1,194,331

1987
764,410

1989
625,000

18

Eight years seems too short a time to measure the impact of humans on another species. In the case of the African elephant though, the onslaught can almost be measured by the month.

These maps compare the elephant range in 1979 and 1987. Note the change in East Africa in those eight years. The influence of poachers moving south from Somalia is represented by the shrinking islands of elephant population.

Loss of habitat due to the exploding human population in Africa is a slower, but equally deadly threat to the elephants. Even war has taken its toll when elephants have strayed into battle areas and been killed by land–mines and opportunist hunters.

The problem may be restricted to Africa, but part of its solution lies with people everywhere who can learn to say *no* to ivory products.

✱ Based on material presented in "Conserving the African Elephant — a Working Document," prepared under the auspices of the African Elephant Conservation Co-ordinating Group, December 1988.

ELEPHANT POPULATIONS

Country by Region	1981	1987
WEST AFRICA		
Benin	1,250	2,100
Burhina Faso	3,500	3,900
Ghana	970	1,100
Guinea	800	300
Guinea-Bissau	0	20
Côte d'Ivoire	4,800	3,300
Liberia	2,000	650
Mali	780	600
Mauritania	40	20
Niger	800	800
Nigeria	1,820	3,100
Senegal	200	50
Sierra Leone	500	250
Togo	150	100
Sub-total	17,610	16,290
CENTRAL AFRICA		
Cameroon	5,000	21,200
Central African Republic	31,000	19,000
Chad	?	3,100
Congo	10,800	61,000
Equatorial Guinea	?	500
Gabon	13,400	76,000
Zaire	376,000	195,000
Sub-total	436,200	375,800
EASTERN AFRICA		
Ethiopia	?	6,650
Kenya	65,056	35,000
Rwanda	150	70
Somalia	24,323	6,000
Sudan	133,727	40,000
Tanzania	203,900	100,000
Uganda	2,320	3,000
Sub-total	429,521	190,720
SOUTHERN AFRICA		
Angola	12,400	12,400
Botswana	20,000	51,000
Malawi	4,500	2,400
Mozambique	54,800	18,600
Namibia	2,300	5,000
South Africa	8,000	8,200
Zambia	160,000	41,000
Zimbabwe	49,000	43,000
Sub-total	311,000	181,600
TOTAL	1,194,331	764,410

THE URGENCY

Consider these figures:

● Africa's elephant population is being cut by half every ten years. In some areas, the losses in the last decade have exceeded 90 per cent.

● Elephants were once numbered in the millions. In 1987, there were only 764,410 left, and poaching was taking about 150,000 animals a year.

● Between 1981 and 1987 the elephant population fell by 36 per cent.

Where do these figures come from? The task of counting elephants in Africa is daunting. Usually it is done from the air, using a grid search pattern and photographs, but there is always an element of informed guesswork. Many of the elephants remain invisible. They are either forest dwellers, or have been forced into the more remote regions by human population and poaching pressures, so some allowance must always be made for the hidden component of the population.

No matter how accurate a count may be, only one fact is certain. By the time the survey is completed, there will be fewer elephants than when it started. For example, when I obtained the total of 764,410 elephants from the WWF in November, 1988, I was told it was the latest available. By January, 1989, I had been given a new figure of 625,000.

In December, 1988, the African Elephant Conservation Co-ordinating Group, in conjunction with several other organizations, issued a report entitled *Conserving the African Elephant: A Working Document.* It compares elephant populations in 1981 and 1987, with the caution that some of the 1981 estimates for Cameroon, Congo, Gabon, and possibly Botswana, are now thought to have been underestimates. The apparent "increases" in the 1987 population are therefore misleading. They actually result from underestimates in 1981 (when a total of 1,194,331 was recorded) and more rigorous research on the density of forest elephants in 1987.

In contrast, the report continues: "Many of the dramatic declines are certainly real, for instance in Central African Republic, Zaire, Sudan, Somalia, Kenya, Tanzania, Zambia, and Mozambique. In each of these cases, the declines are the result of poaching, contrary to government intentions. Only in Zimbabwe has there been a managed reduction in elephant populations, to prevent habitat damage and human-elephant conflicts."

Let's look at Kenya — a corner of the continent where we might expect to be optimistic about the future of the elephants. Kenya is considered the flagship of democracy in Africa, a country that has made the transition from colonial rule to independence with relatively little trauma. Advanced in conservation as well, it banned trophy hunting in May, 1977. In 1975, it had 120,000 elephants. In 1988, it had fewer than 20,000. One 1975 survey estimated the poaching level at between 10,000 and 20,000 elephants a year. Checked by tougher anti-poaching measures, this rate of slaughter slowed until the early 1980s. Since then, it has continued to creep inexorably upward.

In September, 1988, *The Weekly Review* in Nairobi reported that a new aerial count in Tsavo National Park confirmed the massacre of five hundred elephants since February — nearly three a day for six months. Discouraged conservationists claim that this rate, much lower than the levels reported in the mid-1970s, is not due to better anti-poaching measures so much as to elephants now being harder to find.

But what about the national parks and reserves that dot Africa? Terrifyingly, these preserves, intended as sanctuaries, have only let the poachers know where they can find a better supply of the animals than elsewhere. For the greedy and unscrupulous, the animals are walking banks waiting to be robbed. Species that survived in the wild for thousands of years have been brought to their knees in a few decades.

Furthermore, the protected grasslands are an invitation that the poverty-stricken neighbours of these parks cannot resist. Unbelievably, the most numerous animals within some park boundaries are domestic goats and cattle.

The safari tours can still show you plenty of wild animals, but increasingly these are in "artificial populations" maintained in a kind of storefront for tourists whose contributions to national coffers are vital.

In recognition of the problems, the parks are patrolled. But gun battles between rangers and poachers are now accepted as "normal" occurrences,

with deaths on both sides. In fact, the poachers are usually better armed than the rangers and are so ruthless they have fired on tourists who might be witnesses or provide extra booty.

The plight of elephants — and that of other wildlife — has become so desperate that conservationists no longer talk of preserving the present numbers. This is beyond their resources, and quite simply there isn't time. Instead they are working urgently toward establishing baseline populations — minimum levels needed to maintain a species. For the Earth's last 625,000 elephants, the baseline is around 200,000. That means we can "afford" to lose almost half a million elephants. But can we? It is a desperate rearguard action.

What is your image of Africa? If you are like most Westerners, Africa is its wildlife: endless grasslands and jungles swarming with innumerable animals of all kinds. That image begins in the nursery, where the alphabet is learned to chants of "E is for elephant . . . L is for lion . . . Z is for zebra." Africa and animals are synonymous.

The result has been a warm feeling toward Africa — and a false sense of security. Ask almost anyone if they are in favour of conserving Africa's wildlife and the answer will be a quick "yes." Ask them what they are doing personally for the cause and the likely response will be puzzlement. Surely there are so many animals in Africa that they could never be in danger of extinction? Surely if a problem does exist, the Africans can take care of it?

The Africa they see is one which does still exist, but is rapidly becoming a façade maintained for tourists and their dollars in the controlled environments of the more secure national parks. The very day Hans discovered that mutilated elephant I was back in the lodge writing my impressions of the morning in my journal.

This is what I wrote:

Fingers of early morning sunlight poked and prodded into the folds of the hills south of Kenya's Tsavo National Park. In the twin lodges of Salt Lick and Taita Hills, the first of the camera-toting tourists were laughing and joking as they jockeyed for the best seats in their safari mini-buses. The drivers were good-humoured too as they called to each other and organized their charges.

A lioness, lying half-concealed in a clump of bushes near Salt Lick Lodge, pretended to be annoyed when two of her cubs alternately pounced on and chewed her ropey tail. Birds arced down to artificial water holes that had been sited carefully to give lodge guests a view of the wildlife. A trio of elephants ghosted by in the half-light and two young impala bucks rattled heads in the early rites of puberty . . . .

I now believe that these images, so typical of tourist brochures, can be dangerous. They imply that everything is still all right with the world of Africa's animals. They also help establish an ambivalence toward Africa among Westerners. Although this warm feeling for Africa's wildlife has been bred into whole generations, Africa is seen as an exotic vacation, a faraway fantasy place that has little to do with our daily lives.

THE ELEPHANTS: OUR KIN

One of the greatest tragedies — and perhaps one of the least recognized — is that, if elephants die out in the next ten years, we will never have known them properly. In spite of our centuries of association with elephants, we still know remarkably little about them. Circuses, zoos, movies and books have left us with the impression of familiarity, but the level of knowing has been very shallow. As in the case of dolphins and whales, the true worth and intelligence of elephants have long gone unrecognized.

My first encounter with elephants in the wild came when Hans and I visited Amboseli National Park — another of the cluster of reserves in southern Kenya, near the Tanzanian border. During an early morning photographic expedition we spied a file of about a dozen elephants heading for water. We drove ahead of them several hundred metres and parked in their path to get photographs.

Knowledge of sources of water and food are essential to survival. Poachers, who kill older elephants for their impressive tusks, also remove a store of information which increases the death toll among younger animals.

This string of elephants at Amboseli National Park in Kenya is about to provide us with our closest encounter. They passed by within two metres of us, en route to water.

Both of us clicked steadily — me from the driver's seat with a hand-held 35mm camera and Hans shooting through the roof hatch of the combi van with a larger-frame camera mounted on a tripod. Suddenly I realized that I didn't need my telephoto lens any more. The elephants were much closer, walking directly toward us with long, easy strides that seemed slow, but covered ground quickly. What if they didn't stop? What if, in their single-minded progress toward water, they brushed the combi aside and left us in a mangled heap? I had no doubt that they could do it.

While such thoughts were racing through my mind I was still snapping away furiously, but subliminal instincts for self-preservation made sure that the van's engine was running and all was in order for a hasty retreat. My film came to an end; and with fingers that seemed as thick and clumsy as sausages, I started to rewind it. In my haste I opened the back of the camera too soon and exposed at least a third of the roll — the part containing the best of my close-ups.

By this time the elephants were barely five metres away and showed no sign of turning aside. Desperately I tried to reload but couldn't make the film feed properly. By then it was too late anyway. The shadow of the lead elephant fell on me, and I looked up to see her swerve just enough to miss the van, leading the others past. I sat in awe, my camera forgotten, as the parade of elephants swung by with strides as slow and deliberate as someone trying to walk underwater, but which took them out of sight in less than a minute.

I know that old Africa hands may think this experience rather trivial compared with some of their own; but to me, barely a week from suburbia, it was marvellous. I was humble enough to admit that it was not a real encounter. The elephants had hardly bothered to notice us. But I will never feel the same way about elephants again. My casual assumptions about the superiority and central importance of my own species received a salutary and permanent jolt. This is a lesson I would earnestly desire for every other human being who has not learned it already.

23

The African elephant, *Loxodonta africana*, has two subspecies — the savanna elephant (subspecies *africana*) and the forest elephant (subspecies *cyclotis*). The savanna elephant is the larger of the two, a mature female usually standing 2.5 metres high at the shoulder, with males averaging 3.1 metres. The female is likely to weigh 2,700 to 3,500 kilograms and the male a whopping 4,500 to 5,300 kilograms. The overall length of a large male from trunk to tail can be as much as nine metres. Both species have large ears which have several uses besides hearing. For example, the ears may help prevent overheating. They are relatively thin and blood passing through them cools by several degrees before returning to the rest of the body. Also, when the ears are fully extended during confrontations, the elephant is an awesome sight head-on, appearing to treble in size.

Forest elephants average about sixty centimetres shorter in height than the savanna subspecies, with the differences in bulk between males and females being less pronounced. Their tusks are more slender than those of the savanna elephant and are either straight or only slightly curved. While the savanna elephant's tusks point forward, those of the forest elephant grow downward. Its range is the equatorial forests of the central African basin and West Africa. However, a certain amount of hybridization occurs over large areas of Africa where forests and savannas merge.

The earliest known ancestor of the modern elephant is *Moeritherium*, an animal which lived about twenty-five million years ago and was the size of a large pig. Remains of this species have been found at Lake Moeris, near El Fayyum in Egypt.

Modern elephants and the now-extinct mammoths are believed to have evolved about five million years ago. While the cause of the extinction of mammoths is still a matter of debate, climatic change and over-hunting by human beings have been implicated in various studies. This sounds an ominous warning because these are two of the most serious threats facing the elephant today.

Harried, embattled, but still defiant, this old warrior bears the scars of his advanced years proudly in Kruger National Park, South Africa. In areas that are not so well protected, it is now rare to see elephants of this age.

Enjoying the waters of the Chobe River, Botswana.

Family group at a water hole in Etosha National Park, Namibia.

An elephant cow nursing her young. Daphne Sheldrick's orphaned elephants are usually fed beneath a tarpaulin to simulate the mother's bulk.

When you act like a tough guy, it's hard to keep your dignity — as the baby elephant at right found out when he took a tumble while practising his charges on a flock of birds.

The African elephant, once found in North Africa on the shores of the Mediterranean, now ranges throughout the continent south of the Sahara and is found in almost all habitats from savannas to rain forests, swamps to deserts and seashores to high mountains. It shares these territories with most of Africa's other large wild animals and has an impact on habitat that affects its "neighbours" greatly. It is only in relatively recent times that its range has become fragmented, with populations being wiped out over large areas.

Little was known about the social orders of elephants in the wild until Dr. Iain Douglas-Hamilton made a series of definitive studies in the late 1960s and early '70s. His doctoral thesis in philosophy at Oxford University (1972) was on the ecology and behaviour of the African elephant. His study of elephant communities at Lake Manyara National Park in Tanzania led to other papers and the book *Among the Elephants* in 1975, which he co-authored with his wife, Oria.

So close did Douglas-Hamilton's relationship with his study subjects become that he was able to walk up to, touch, and be touched by some of the elephants in the herd. Few people have done that before and lived.

His findings destroyed forever the myth of fierce bull elephants leading the family herds. The social system among elephants is matriarchal. The matriarch that leads the herd is knowledgeable about trails, water holes, and good feeding areas. A network of females known as "aunties" and "nannies" guards the youngsters at all times, providing service and support to the mothers. The old bulls and adolescent males either live in their own herds or range independently until the females are in season.

A birth is a great occasion for the females of a herd — as might be expected after a gestation period lasting nearly two years. The delivering mother is usually attended during the birth by other females. The newborn calf is likely to weigh more than an average man (as much as 114 kilograms) but is helpless if surprised by a lion, hence the protective screen of "aunties."

The young elephants, once they are strong enough to leave the direct care of their mothers, play freely with other youngsters but are always under the eye of one of the females. More than one tourist, seeking a close-up photograph of young elephants apparently alone, has received a nasty surprise when the babysitters burst out of the bushes.

Daphne Sheldrick's young elephant charges mentioned earlier are not truly wild and yet not quite tame. They spend part of each day in the park interacting with other wild animals, but their handlers remain nearby. Nights are spent in their shed where the handlers sleep on beds rigged in the rafters. Daphne Sheldrick carefully monitors the youngsters' association with the handlers (whom she calls orphan attendants) and with herself, so that they will not pine when they are considered old and strong enough to be moved back to the wild. This happens once they are weaned and have recovered from their emotional traumas. Sheldrick insists that elephants show remarkably human signs of unhappiness when separated from loved ones.

The youngsters' reintroduction to the wild, usually at Tsavo, is cushioned by placing them in the care of "aunties" that willingly assume the roles of foster mothers or big sisters. Some of the young elephants will eventually be accepted into one of the wild herds, while others elect to retain some contact with humans. It is from this latter group that most of the aunties are chosen. They provide a perfect bridge between both worlds.

Perhaps the best known of these loving, maternal elephants is thirty-year-old Eleanor, an orphan raised during the Sheldricks' days at Tsavo and perhaps a prototype for the techniques now used so successfully.

"We have known Eleanor intimately since she was brought in at the age of two," said Sheldrick. "For many years she was the self-appointed matriarch of our Tsavo herd of mixed orphaned animals. Quite voluntarily she has opted to retain her bonds with people rather than join the wild elephants on a permanent basis and step down in rank, as have many of our other orphan elephants in the past. She does, however, mingle with the wild herds when the whim takes her."

Sheldrick believes elephants' development and life span parallel those of a human being and regards the youngsters in her care as being equivalent to human children of the same age — or perhaps a bit smarter.

Furthermore, she unabashedly describes elephant behaviour in human terms. She interprets actions and motivations in the light of human intelligence. Unscientific her methods may sometimes be, but her opinions cannot be disregarded. She has more hands-on experience with elephants than nearly all of the more objective scientists and has lived among these animals for more years than it might be polite to mention.

"They understand everything that is said to them and display all the traits apparent in human children, such as precociousness, mischievousness, selfishness and so on," she said.

"At one time my approach was considered very anthropomorphic and unscientific," she says with relish, "but I think even the scientists have changed their minds on that one, because we are animals too. When you know animals intimately, you realize that they feel and they think. They have memories and loves and loyalties and things like that just as we do.

"Elephants, in particular, have a very human type of intelligence. Other animals are equally intelligent, but on a different branch of life.

"People say the rhino is stupid, but anyone who thinks that is very ignorant because they are different from us. They say one should never be arrogant and relate the intelligence of animals in human terms, but with elephants you can."

Even as she was talking, one of the youngsters picked up a garden hose that was spurting water and put the end in its mouth. Two orphaned eland and a buffalo trotted up to see what was happening, but retreated to a safe distance a few minutes later when the elephants began to play with their human attendants in a mud wallow in the back yard.

From time to time, a pair of inquisitive warthogs wandered in from Nairobi National Park, observed the strange goings-on for a while and trotted off with self-important, stiff-legged strides. It was a scene of such remarkable peace and happiness that I felt a pang of longing for the myth of Eden or its equivalent that lies in the collective unconsciousness of the human race — of a time before the relationships between humans and the other beings with whom we share this planet became suspicious, exploitive contests.

The elephant's use of the hose, though it astonished me, was not too remarkable. Other young elephants have learned to turn on taps to get a drink, while older elephants have reached up with their trunks to dislodge the covers of household water tanks and get at the contents. The trunk is actually remarkably versatile. In one mood it can delicately pluck tender sprigs and in another stretch out to casually rip a large branch from a tree. It can be used to caress and to punish. It can suck up and squirt water and even be used as a snorkel in deep water. This purposeful use of the trunk is regarded by many people as yet another indication of the high intelligence of elephants.

In open range, unsegmented by highways, railway tracks and fences, a herd's foraging territory extends from about thirty square kilometres to many hundreds, depending on the availability of food and water. Usually they travel in single file, often along trails that have been used by herds for generations.

While in Africa, I heard numerous stories of elephants demonstrating qualities above the more primitive survival instincts. When an elephant is ill, other herd members have been seen to move in on either side of it to support it with their bodies. Elephants have been observed apparently grieving for dead herd-mates, grouped around those who are dying — even covering the body with branches and earth. They cooperate to a remarkably sophisticated level in defence, rescue operations, or simple mischief, such as teasing belligerent rhino interlopers. They display great interest in elephant bones they encounter during their travels and will often pull the tusks out of a recently dead elephant and smash them on rocks and trees.

Can we imagine Africa without its elephants? They are part of its landscape and their loss would be a tragic reminder of our greed and thoughtlessness. These two were photographed at Savuti, northwestern Botswana.

Douglas-Hamilton's pioneering elephant study and those of others who have extended his findings, have shown that elephants communicate at close range with a deep chest rumble and, at distances, with a subsonic sound, which carries over several kilometres. This means a herd can break down into smaller family groupings while feeding and yet remain in contact. It also explains the almost telepathic coordination that has been observed among elephant groups.

This new communication sound was discovered by chance — and not even by someone in Africa.[1] Dr. Kathy Payne, a research fellow of the New York Zoological Society who had earlier studied the songs of the humpback whale, felt a strange throbbing in the air when she was standing near a group of elephants in the Portland Zoo, Oregon. She compared the sensation to experiencing the lowest note of a big pipe organ.

Returning with special acoustic equipment, she recorded the sound, which lasted ten to fifteen seconds, and noted that a part of the elephant's forehead "fluttered" during the time the sound was emitted. She discovered that females would emit the sound when a calf screamed or use it to communicate with each other. Later, recordings were also made in Kenya's Amboseli National Park.

Elephants are often wary about crossing even isolated roads such as this one in Chobe National Park, Botswana. The group lingered in the scrub until assured that the photographer's van posed no threat. They then crossed quickly and hastened from sight.

The discovery of this long-distance form of communication among elephants demonstrates how much we have still to learn about this supposedly familiar animal. Who knows what other discoveries lie ahead.

The various studies of elephants in the wild have demonstrated the existence of clearly defined social structures. For example, even though all youngsters are nurtured in the family herds, at about the age of fourteen or fifteen, the young males are sent to join the bulls. There they learn their place in the social order, gain more survival skills, and develop the etiquette necessary for peaceful coexistence with the older bulls.

A young bull might not develop a serious interest in breeding, or acquire a successful courtship technique until he is as old as thirty.[2] When the urge comes upon them, the bulls will move closer to a family herd and wait for the females to come into season. As preliminary courtship, a bull may begin to associate with a particular cow until she is in heat. After they have mated, the association usually ends; and the bull moves on to other conquests and other herds.

Poachers who kill the bigger bulls and herd matriarchs seriously disrupt this social order. Their assault not only reduces the numbers but also slows the replacement rate. The immature bulls are not yet effective breeders; and when mature females are killed, the family herds lose leadership and much of their knowledge about food and water sources.

Dr. Joyce Poole, an elephant researcher in Kenya, flew over parts of Tsavo during the February, 1988, survey. Although she saw more than two thousand elephants, only one male was obviously bigger than the adult females[3]. From this she concluded that few of the males left in Tsavo were over twenty-five years old. During a visit in August the same year, her observations were confirmed.

Poole said that in the absence of the matriarchs, the social structures of the herds disintegrate. In their leaderless state, the families become weak and even more vulnerable to poachers. In these circumstances, a motherless calf under two years has no chance of survival, while two- to five-year-olds and five- to ten-year-olds have only 30 per cent and 40 per cent chances respectively. The young animals simply disappear — dying, or falling prey to predators.

"For every poached female found," says Poole bleakly, "another elephant can therefore be assumed dead, although its carcase is unlikely to be counted."

◁ Elephant group at Hwange National Park, Zimbabwe.

Besides drinking and bathing, there is mud to wallow in and dust bowls to complete the toilet. When the mud dries, it provides protection against sun and insects. Later, the mud is rubbed off, taking with it trapped parasites. Then it's time to go back to the water hole . . .

ELEPHANT "MANAGEMENT"

In spite of the growing sympathy for the plight of Africa's elephants, there is also a degree of criticism. It is pointed out that too many elephants can harm wildlife habitat, that they can destroy trees, denude the landscape, and, eventually, create deserts. Poaching can't be tolerated, of course, but wouldn't there be disastrous problems if areas became overpopulated with elephants?

That question deserves serious consideration. Because an elephant's diet contains a large amount of cellulose and relatively little protein, they feed constantly, day and night, taking short rests or naps when they can. If an elephant browses for an average of sixteen hours a day and lives for sixty years, about forty of those years will have been spent feeding.

A particular sore point in habitat management of parks is that elephants routinely push over trees to get at the foliage. This isn't too serious in an unlimited range, but when you're trying to deal with a finite number of hectares in a park, elephant actions can be seen as a direct threat to other species.

One response in the past has been "culling" — selective slaughter to preserve the balances imposed on the park by human judgement. Elephant populations are now so low that this technique is rarely used outside South Africa and Zimbabwe, two countries with apparently stable park populations.

33

Graham Child, past director of national parks and wildlife management at Harare, Zimbabwe, gives this example of a typical culling operation. It was carried out at the Chirisa Safari Area in the Sebungwe region of northwest Zimbabwe.[4]

During culling, a suitably sized group of elephants is located from the air, and the ground party, of two or three hunters and their assistants, are then guided to the group by radio. In such a tightly coordinated operation the pilot, who is also an experienced hunter, is informed of the wind direction by the men on the ground, whom he then guides to the group to be shot. Killing is quick and effective, and the shooting is usually over within one minute.

The killing is done so rapidly that the group does not disperse and the carcases remain conveniently close to each other. Each carcase is numbered and the cuts to remove panels of hide are marked out. While the skinning and butchering proceeds, useful scientific data on reproductive status, stomach contents, physical condition and age are collected.

This particular culling was part of Operation Windfall, organized when the elephant population rose to a level where trees and other plants were endangered. During Operation Windfall, 110 labourers were employed to skin and cut up the carcases, which were then transported to a processing yard. There the hides were flensed, washed, and salted, and the meat was cut into thin strips, brined, and sun-dried on wire mesh racks. Another 110 workers were employed on these activities and on preparing the products for market. Nothing was wasted.

In South Africa in recent years, sophisticated culling operations have used helicopters and refrigerated trucks so that meat can be rushed to central abattoirs and processed to such standards that it qualifies for export. The traditional use for game meat in South Africa, apart from some home consumption, has been to dry it and sell it as biltong. At Kruger National Park it is possible to buy canned buffalo stew and other game food products.

It should be remembered that commercial gain is not the primary motivation for properly organized culling programs. The benefits include not only scientific data and protection of the habit, but ultimately the conservation of the species being culled.

But the success of culling as an elephant management practice is mixed. Elephants have sometimes

Elephants in a sea of gold at Meru National Park, Kenya.

suffered from costly administrative errors of judgement. One of the factors influencing these has been the difficulty in obtaining accurate population counts.

While in Africa I was told of an early culling program in Uganda where so many elephant-human encounters were occurring that the game wardens of the day (the 1930s and '40s) assumed there had been an elephant population explosion. A "guesstimate" put the population twice as high as it actually was and the culling started. By the time it was realized that the reason so many elephants were being seen was because they were being compressed into ever smaller areas by the human population explosion, it was almost too late to save the herds.

The opposite happened in Kenya, where elephants were able to lose themselves in the vastness of such parks as Tsavo. Because fewer elephant-human encounters occurred, the population was estimated at about half the actual number.

These events had an echo as recently as 1988 when WWF representative in East and Central Africa, Dr. Hugh Lamprey, spoke out against suggestions that culling should be introduced to control elephant populations in Botswana and Zimbabwe. He described this approach as "oversimplified" and said his own findings were that pressures from loss of habitat and the growing human population had forced the elephants to concentrate in smaller areas, creating the impression of greater numbers.

During a visit to the Natal Parks Board area in South Africa, I was told to be careful how I spoke to a certain official because he was still smarting from the aftermath of an abortive culling operation in 1982-83. As it was explained to me, a computer study had indicated that various species (other than elephants) had become too numerous in one of the parks and were threatening the delicate balance that existed. A culling program was started to reduce the populations to manageable levels.

However, as the work progressed, the hunters began to feel a growing unease. After the first flurry of shooting, they were not encountering animals with the frequency they had been led to expect. Eventually, they became so alarmed they refused to shoot any more until the figures were checked.

When the check was made, horrified officials found that more than 80 per cent of the park's animals had been wiped out. The "overpopulation" was in fact an error in computer programming. Amid great embarrassment, the park was restocked from other areas.

So far as elephants are concerned, Daphne Sheldrick, for one, cites the much larger Tsavo National Park, where no artificial management of any kind is used, as evidence that such interference is pernicious. Faced by periodic droughts and a shortage of food, the elephant population in Tsavo declined naturally, she said. The first to go were the younger ones that couldn't reach the high browse, were not able to walk the longer distances to find food, or didn't have the knowledge of water and food sources required to survive. Large gaps were opened in the age chain, which sent the population into decline for several years. This in turn gave the vegetation time to recover. These cycles were ''part of the rhythm of life,'' she said.

''Elephants are nature's gardeners. Their job is to open up the thickets, to pull the trees down, to bring the browse to a lower level for the other animals. They also provide water in arid places like Tsavo by puddling the water holes, carrying off large quantities of earth on their bodies. They create water holes and seal the bottoms. They also tunnel into, or walk down dry river beds on their huge feet, bringing the water to the surface so it's available for other animals. They are actually crucial to the environment.''

Moreover, says Sheldrick, elephants plant many trees by carrying in their stomachs the seeds they have eaten and depositing them far and wide in their droppings.

Elephants are often condemned for their destructive feeding habits. Sometimes whole trees are pushed over in the remorseless quest for food. However, this opens new spaces for grazing animals. Elephants, with their digging, gouging and trampling, also create water holes in otherwise dry river beds. They also expose sources of salt which they and other animals consume.

Browsing amid trees at Aberdare National Park, central Kenya.

Some of the smallest of the world's big movers — dung beetles with elephant droppings. The dung contains seeds which germinate when the beetles drag their spoils underground.

Tsavo has passed through several ecological changes, in which the elephants have played a part, said Sheldrick. The park was dense scrubland when it was established in 1949; but a century earlier in 1840, when the German missionary, philologist and explorer, Johann Ludwig Krapf, passed through the area, it was open grassland in many places.

"After the elephants rooted out the *Commiphora* scrubland over large areas of Tsavo, grasslands became established and over one hundred springs and streams began to flow," Sheldrick said. "Now, with the demise of the elephants, the scrubland is returning. The growth of grass will be inhibited again, and the springs will cease as before. The dreaded trypanosomiasis-bearing tsetse fly will no doubt re-emerge." An ironic smile plays about her lips. "Now that might succeed in driving the domestic stock out of the park. Every other method seems to have failed."

Overleaf: Elephants are very social animals and one of the best opportunities for mingling comes during daily visits to water. The two elephants touching trunks in the centre of the photograph are engaging in a common expression of affection and recognition.

No elephant mother has to care for her youngster alone. Care of the young is a group responsibility, as any lion that approached this group in Etosha National Park, Namibia, would discover.

Elephants at a water hole in Etosha National Park.

During one of her years at Tsavo, Sheldrick saw a drought kill nine thousand elephants in three months; but even that, she said, painful as it was to witness, was nothing like the anguish caused among the elephants by poachers and cullers.

The drought-stricken elephants died of malnutrition, not starvation. Their stomachs were full, but their inefficient digestive systems were not able to derive sufficient nourishment from what they had eaten. They became weak and tired and stayed close to permanent sources of water. Listless, disinclined to move, the elephants spent much of their time sleeping.

"Once an elephant stops feeding," she said softly, "the end comes very quickly — within a day or two. They just die. But the end is very peaceful, because they are surrounded by their family and friends. Of course there is a great psychological torment just as it would be in human terms under the circumstances, because you can relate to everything that happens to elephants from a human point of view.

"I believe there are few people who understand elephants as I do; I have known them intimately as a mother, known their happiness and their grief. And I believe that if an elephant has to die, he would rather die quietly and peacefully, surrounded by his loving family and closest friends, near water and under the shade of a tree, to the song of birds."

To Daphne Sheldrick, the recently discovered long-range communication ability of elephants makes killings by poachers even crueler. Nor is the supposedly more humane culling of whole herds — so that survivors will not be left to grieve — less barbaric.

"When they start cropping in the Kruger National Park (South Africa), the elephants throughout the park are absolutely traumatized," she claims.

"Consider it in human terms. How would we feel if every single year people from Mars descended and mowed down a section of the population and we could remember it from last year and the year before and the year before . . . When they arrive the message is passed like an alarm. It's a terrible sort of thing and so the whole population is tense and traumatized and they have no sanctuary and no peace."

At this point she broke off the interview to search for a magazine article she had written in an attempt to describe culling and poaching from an elephant's point of view.

"Think of the experience of an individual elephant as her most feared and dreaded foes move in, en masse, to gun her and her family down," she had written.[5]

"Perhaps she might be lucky. She might not die that particular day, but she would hear the agonized cries and screams of her terrified people; their suffering transmitted to every other member of the community — all, in turn, so traumatized by the message borne on the wind that they run and run and run, until the young drop of exhaustion and heat and, since they can run no more, are left to die in unspeakable agony, alone and abandoned in the bush.

"Can people understand what it is to be fearful even resting beneath a tree for twelve hours of every day, fearful of approaching any source of water where the foe may be lurking, no matter how thirsty you are — never safe, never secure, never happy or at peace, in permanent mourning for lost loved ones, persecuted from all sides? And then, when the killers are gone, wondering when and where and at whom they will strike again.

Timeless and majestic, a lone bull strikes a dramatic pose beside another symbol of Africa, an acacia tree in Amboseli National Park, southern Kenya.

"Now is the time for all of us to shed tears of remorse, for, at the present rate of decline, the elephants in Kenya will be a tragic memory in another decade. Unless we change. Elephants' survival must be the responsibility of all thinking people. We are all custodians of the creatures over which we have dominion . . . .

"You can replant forests and even reclaim deserts in time." Her voice was soft, her eyes hard as she read her punchline. "But no one, when the last elephant has gone, can make another."

[1] "Finding Out About Elephants — Facts and Speculations," Peter Jackson, *Swissair Gazette,* September 1987, p.21.
[2] Dr. Joyce Poole, paper to East African Wildlife Society seminar, Kenya, September, 1988.
[3] Ibid.
[4] Quoted from a paper delivered by Graham Child to the 1982 World Congress of National Parks in Bali, Indonesia. Published by the Smithsonian Institution Press, Washington, D.C., 1984.
[5] "All of Us Should Shed Tears of Remorse," Daphne Sheldrick, *Weekly Review,* September 16, 1988, p.28.

RHINOS: The Animal Most in Peril

Africa has two of the world's five species of rhinoceros — the black rhinoceros and the white. In the mid-nineteenth century, European explorers and hunters reported seeing almost uncountable numbers of both varieties, with the black being the most common.

But in one incredible decade between 1969 and 1979, half of the world's rhinoceros population disappeared — scythed down in a merciless sleet of bullets and poisoned arrows.

The poachers were busy in Asia, but the brunt of the attack was borne by Africa's black rhinoceros. During that decade, *nine-tenths* of that species was swept from the Earth.

In 1962 there were only 100,000 black rhinoceros left in Africa. Between 1962 and 1987, poachers and other factors slashed this number to just under 3,800.

The black rhino once had an enormous range over most of southern Africa and extending as far north as Guinea and Liberia in the west and Ethiopia and Somalia in the east. By 1987, its range had been reduced to a few isolated pockets in fourteen countries.

"I never thought I would see the day when there were more white rhinos than black rhinos in Africa," a South African safari tour operator told us at Hluhluwe. But that day is here, with 4,650 white rhinos surviving in 1987.

In 1963, Kenya was said to have about ten thousand rhinos. Today the most optimistic figure is three hundred and fifty. In the whole of Africa, there are only about eight thousand rhinos left. In the last century, there were millions.

And the saddest story of all is that of the northern subspecies of the white rhinoceros. In 1987, there were only eighteen survivors, huddled in Garamba National Park. In recent years, the WWF has poured many thousands of dollars into Garamba in an effort to save the rhino population.

Think again about the slaughter of nine-tenths of a species within a single decade. Put it in human terms. If a superior invader from another planet killed off 90 per cent of the people in the United States, would their actions be considered justified because they were superior? But forget the invaders. What judgment will our grandchildren in the twenty-first century pronounce on the extinction of the rhinoceros? I think they will look upon their biologically depleted world and say of us, as we say about those who destroyed the passenger pigeons and buffalo, "How could they have been so blind?"

What are the arguments for rhinos? For a start, extinction would be the end of an animal that has been on the Earth in various forms for sixty million years. Furthermore, unlike other "natural" extinctions it would be a loss that didn't have to happen. It is not necessary to kill off the rhinos to preserve human life on Earth. It is not even necessary to kill them to take their horns. If the rhinos become extinct, it will be an immoral, engineered extinction, an everlasting shame that our generation must bear.

◁ White rhinos grazing in bush at the Umfolozi Game Reserve in Natal, South Africa. Once less than thirty remained. Now the African population has been bred back to nearly five thousand in a campaign led by the Natal Parks Board.

Lush green grass provides ideal feed for white rhinos at Umfolozi Game Reserve. Note the size of the horn on the rear rhino.

EXTINCTION BECKONS THE AFRICAN RHINOCEROS

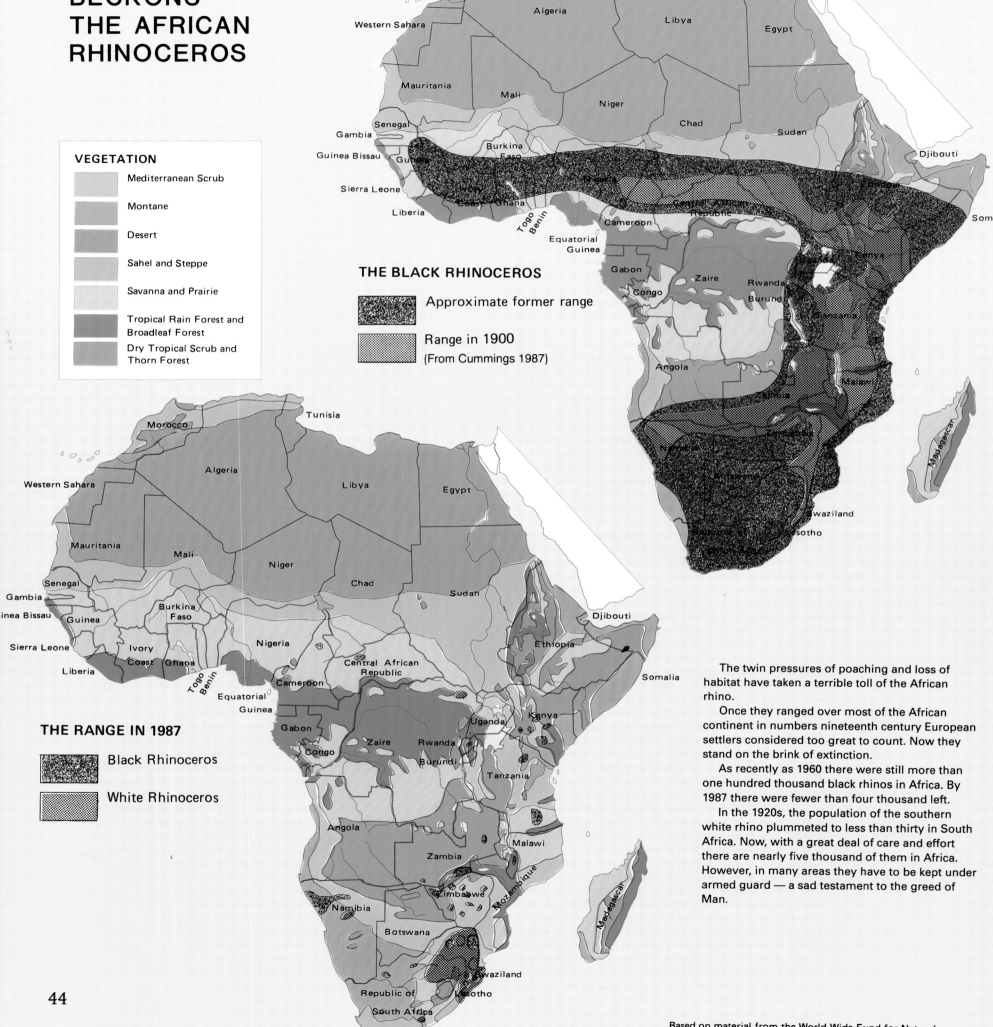

VEGETATION

- Mediterranean Scrub
- Montane
- Desert
- Sahel and Steppe
- Savanna and Prairie
- Tropical Rain Forest and Broadleaf Forest
- Dry Tropical Scrub and Thorn Forest

THE BLACK RHINOCEROS

- Approximate former range
- Range in 1900

(From Cummings 1987)

THE RANGE IN 1987

- Black Rhinoceros
- White Rhinoceros

The twin pressures of poaching and loss of habitat have taken a terrible toll of the African rhino.

Once they ranged over most of the African continent in numbers nineteenth century European settlers considered too great to count. Now they stand on the brink of extinction.

As recently as 1960 there were still more than one hundred thousand black rhinos in Africa. By 1987 there were fewer than four thousand left.

In the 1920s, the population of the southern white rhino plummeted to less than thirty in South Africa. Now, with a great deal of care and effort there are nearly five thousand of them in Africa. However, in many areas they have to be kept under armed guard — a sad testament to the greed of Man.

Based on material from the World Wide Fund for Nature's "Continental Strategy for the Conservation of Rhino in Africa" prepared by Dr. John Hanks, December 1987.

Using information from the African Elephant Rhino Specialist Group (AERSG), it is possible to obtain a detailed continental picture of black and white rhino distribution as of May, 1987. Rhinos and elephants are being killed so quickly that surveys are soon out of date. Nevertheless, the AERSG figures in the tables below are the best available and freeze a moment in time.

(The reliability of the rhino census at each of the locations is graded from 1 to 4. These should be interpreted as follows: 1 = total count; 2 = estimate based on survey within last two years; 3 = estimate based on survey carried out more than two years previously, a recent non-specific survey, or equivalent surveillance; 4 = informed guess. Under the heading "Recent Trends" the term "n/a" is used occasionally. This indicates "not applicable" — often because the population was established too recently for a trend to be indicated. In the "Locations" column, several abbreviations have been used. These are: NP = National Park; NR = Nature Reserve; GR = Game Reserve; RP = Recreation Park; FL = Forest Land; CA = Conservation Area.)

A black rhino, showing the prehensile lip, marking it as a browser rather than a grazer. Also visible are the three toes which put the rhino in the Perissodactyla order of mammals whose members have an odd number of toes.

WHITE RHINO POPULATION OF AFRICA, MAY 1987

Location	Area in sq. km.	Number of rhinos	Reliability of census	Trend in last 5 yrs.
Southern White				
(*C. s. simum*)				
BOTSWANA				
Moremi/Chobe areas	—	100-150?	4	?
KENYA				
Meru NP	870	6	1	Stable
Lewa Downs Ranch	20	1	1	n/a
Solio Ranch	62	40	1	Up
NAMIBIA				
Waterberg NP	400	28	2	Up
Private land	—	35	2	Down?
SOUTH AFRICA				
Hluhluwe/Umfolozi GR	900	1,660	2	Up
Ndumu GR	100	60	2	Up
Mkuzi GR	251	40	3	Up
Itala GR	297	50	3	Up
Weenen NR	29	14	1	n/a
Kruger NP	19,485	1,200	2	Up
Pilanesberg GR	500	222	2	Up
Queen Elizabeth Park	5	2	1	n/a
Midmar	28	3	1	n/a
Chelmsford	68	5	1	n/a
Spioenkop	45	5	1	n/a
Loskop	148	46	2	Stable
Bloemhof Dam NR	220	5	1	n/a
D'Nyala	—	4	1	n/a
Rolfontein NR	47	6	1	n/a
Thomas Baines	10	3	1	n/a
Kuruman	—	3	1	n/a
Vryburg	—	3	1	n/a
Willem Pretorius GR	120	16	1	n/a
Tussen die Riviere GR	220	9	1	n/a
Botsalano GR	—	39	2	Up
Tembe Elephant Reserve	181	4	1	n/a
Transvaal private land	—	525	2	?
Cape private land	—	15	2	?
Orange Free State pivate land	—	20	2	?
Natal private land	—	103	1	?
SWAZILAND				
Whole region	—	60-100	4	Down?
ZAMBIA				
Livingstone Game park	—	4	1	Down
ZIMBABWE				
Hwange/Matetsi	18,400	110	3	?
Matopos NP	432	28	1	Stable
Private ranches	—	26	1	Stable
Lake Kyle RP	90	30	3	Stable
Lake McIlwaine RP	61	8	1	Stable
Ngamo/Sikumi FL	—	4	1	n/a
Cecil Kop Reserve	—	2	1	n/a
Northern White				
(*C.s. cottoni*)				
ZAIRE				
Garamba NP	4,900	18	1	Stable
TOTAL WHITE RHINO POPULATION		**4,650**		

UNDERSTANDING RHINOS

While a modern rhino may look like a tank on legs, straight from the age of the dinosaurs, it is not a reptile and not a living fossil. Four genera of fossil rhinos did occur in the early Miocene epoch, about nineteen to twenty-three million years ago, but they were very different from those on Earth today.

One of these, the hornless *Baluchitherium grangeri*, found in Europe and North America, stood six metres high, was nine metres long, and weighed twenty-five tonnes.

The modern rhinoceros actually belongs to the same order of mammals as the horse, Perissodactyla, whose members have an odd number of toes. The horse has one toe and the rhino has three.

A mature male white rhinoceros, *Ceratotherium simum*, can weigh more than three thousand kilograms, while the average black rhino bull, *Diceros bicornis*, is only half that size.

The names, white and black, have nothing to do with the colours of the animals. Both are grey. "White" is a corruption of the colloquial name given to them by the early Dutch hunters, *witte renoster,* or, in Afrikaans, *witerenoster.* It means literally "wide mouth," or "wide nose," and refers to the square shape of the mouth, a feature adapted to its feeding habits. The white, or square-lipped, rhino is a grazing animal, whereas the black rhino, with its prehensile upper lip, is a browser, feeding on bushes and shrubs. In any event, the apparent colour of a rhino depends on the hue of the mud and dust in which it has been rolling.

There are other differences between the species. For example, the black rhino has a shorter head, longer neck, and smaller, more rounded ears. Their silhouettes are also different. The white rhino has a well-developed shoulder hump, unlike the black rhino.

Both species have poor eyesight, acute hearing, and an impressively keen sense of smell. Rhinos favour semi-arid environments, but they visit water holes every four to six days and often bathe in pools and mud holes. Here, they have been known to have brushes with elephants — often caused when the highly territorial rhino has been possessive about the local amenities.

This aggressiveness has earned rhinos a bad public image and may have even harmed efforts to raise funds for their preservation. It is easier to get funds for a warm, friendly animal than one regarded as bad-tempered and anti-social.

Popular lore labels the larger white rhino as relatively docile but the black as "a fight waiting to happen." A safari company owner in South Africa agreed grudgingly with this description but asserted persuasively that captivity reversed these roles. Behind bars, he said, the white became cantankerous and the black more docile.

Others say the troublemaker image is unfounded in fact. The rhino's eyesight is so bad that it automatically adopts an aggressive attitude until a strange sound or smell can be identified as friend or foe. It could then just as easily retreat as charge, depending on the circumstances.

When we arrived at South Africa's Natal Parks, lodge staff were still talking about a British woman who had been killed by a rhino a week earlier. It was all over in a few seconds. The woman, who was preparing to take over a baboon study project, was being escorted along a hiking trail by the person she was about to replace. Suddenly, a female white rhino burst out of the bushes with a calf at heel and gored the woman in the back as she was turning to move away. She died instantly, and the rhino returned to the bushes, leaving her shaken escort unharmed.

Rhinos are not even very tolerant of other rhinos living in the same area. Because they establish communal dunging places in their territories, a newcomer is promptly noticed and challenged.

For this reason, before Daphne Sheldrick returns a young rhino to the wild from her "orphanage" at Nairobi Park, she adds samples of its dung to the community pile for at least two months. By the time the young rhino arrives in person, it is more likely to be accepted into the neighbourhood.

As formidable as a tank on legs, a young black rhino surveys his surroundings at Ngorongoro Crater, Tanzania.

BLACK RHINO POPULATION OF AFRICA, MAY 1987

Location	Area in sq. km.	Number of rhinos	Reliability of census	Trend in last 5 yrs.
ANGOLA	No reliable information available.			
BOTSWANA				
Moremi and Chobe	—	10?	4?	n/a
CAMEROON/CHAD				
Whole region	—	30?	4	Down
CENTRAL AFRICAN REPUBLIC				
Whole region	—	10?	4	Down
KENYA				
Amboseli NP & region	800	10	1	Stable
Nairobi NP	117	32+	2	Stable
Aberdares NP	700	60	4	?
Maasai Mara GR	1,500	19	1	Down
Meru NP	870	5+	3	Down
Tsavo NP	20,200	150+	4	Down
Nakuru NP	140	2	1	n/a
Marsabit NR	140	5?	4	Down
Tana River	168	6	3	Down
Ngeng Valley	—	18	2	Down
North Horr	—	3	3	Down
Nguruman Escarpment	—	5	3	Down
Laikipia Ranch	350	47	1	Stable
Lewa Downs Ranch	20	11	1	n/a
Ol Jogi Ranch	—	7	1	n/a
Solio Ranch	62	91	1	Up
Mount Kenya NP	700	50	4	?
MALAWI				
Kasungu NP	2,316	20	3	Stable
Mwabvi GR	340	5?	4	?
MOZAMBIQUE	No reliable information available. Dramatic decline in black rhino during last ten years due to civil unrest.			
NAMIBIA				
Etosha NP	22,270	350+	3	Stable
Damaraland	13,000	85-100	2	Up
Kaokoland	3,500	5-8	2	Stable
RWANDA				
Akagera NP	2,500	15	4	Stable?

Location	Area in sq. km.	Number of rhinos	Reliability of census	Trend in last 5 yrs.
SOUTH AFRICA				
Hluhluwe/Umfolozi GR	900	220	2	Down
Ndumu GR	100	42	1	Stable
Mkuzi GR	251	70	3	Stable
Itala GR	297	35	3	n/a
Eastern Shores GR	800	10	1	n/a
Weenen NR	29	6	1	n/a
Kruger NP	19,485	140	2	Up
Augrabies NP	650	5	1	n/a
Addo Elephant NP	77	17	1	Stable
Andries Vosloo NR	64	4	1	n/a
Pilanesberg GR	500	27	2	Up
Transvaal private land	—	1	1	n/a
SUDAN				
Badindeguru GR	5,000	3	1	Down
TANZANIA				
Selous GR	55,000	200?	3	Down
Lake Manyara NP	320	5?	4	Down
Ngorongoro CA	8,288	20-30	3	Down
Ruaha NP/Rungwa GR	27,216	10?	4	Down
Serengeti NP/- Maswa GR	14,763	10	4	Down
Rubondo NP	457	20-30	4	Stable?
ZAMBIA				
Kafue NP	22,400	20?	4	Down
Mweru-Wantipa NP	3,134	5?	4	?
Luangwa South NP/- Monzi	9,050	15?	3	?
Kapiri-Kafuma	—	35?	3	Stable?
Chindini Hills	—	6+	3	Down
Lukusuzi NP	2,720	5?	4	Down
Lumimba	4,500	10	4	Down
Luano/ W. Petauke	13,000	10?	4	Down
ZIMBABWE				
Lower Zambezi Vly.	11,000	750	3	Down
Sebungwe Region	5,000	650	3	Stable/Up
Hwange/Matetsi	18,400	260	3	Stable/Up
Gonarezhou NP	3,900	75	3	Down
Matopos NP	432	5	1	n/a
Private ranches	—	14	1	n/a
TOTAL BLACK RHINO POPULATION		**3,794**		

THE ROAD TO EXTINCTION

Human beings and rhinos have been together for a long, long time. Cave drawings twenty thousand years old show rhinos among the other animals. Despite their size and ferocity, rhinos are relatively easy animals to kill. Early man was able to bring them down with large-scale hunts and the Bantu tribesmen of more recent times managed well with *assegais* (spears) and pitfalls lined at the bottom with sharp-pointed stakes.

Archaeological evidence suggests that various African people have hunted the rhino systematically for the last two thousand years. Rhino horn was fashioned into clubs, the skin into shields, and the meat fed the hunters' families.

However, the slaughter began on a serious scale when Europeans arrived in Africa with their guns. Between 1830 and 1890, horn and hide hunters seriously depleted the herds, at first seeking trophies and then fuelling the ornamental and medicinal trades. No detailed counts were possible in the pre-aircraft era, but numerous writings chronicle the diminishing numbers. The first Europeans in Africa had seen an almost uncountable number of rhinos, but as the end of the nineteenth century approached, there were urgent calls to stop, or at least control, the shooting.

Rhinos were not the only wildlife in peril — some species, such as the quagga and blue antelope[1], vanished from the continent during this period. The rhino that came closest to joining them was the southern white. By 1895, it was estimated that no more than fifty remained in South Africa, once a stronghold of the species. Although South Africa established its first game reserves the same year, the decline continued until, by 1922, there were between twenty and thirty southern white rhinos left — all in Zululand.

Through strict controls and careful conservation, and in spite of several times of peril, the numbers were gradually built up to the point where, by 1962, white rhinos could be moved elsewhere in South Africa and even to East Africa, which is outside the normal range of the subspecies. Others went to zoos and wildlife parks throughout the world, creating further cushions against extinction. Kenya has a small herd of these reintroduced rhinos, which is kept under armed guard, and across the world, in the San Diego Wild Animal Park, another herd is flourishing.

However, praiseworthy as the efforts of the park staff and conservationists were, the white rhinos also benefited from sheer luck and the tsetse fly, one of the scourges of Africa. This pest spreads nagana, an often fatal cattle disease also known as the sleeping sickness.

The Umfolozi and Hluhluwe reserves in Natal sheltered the white rhino survivors — and the tsetse fly. Today the Natal Parks Board maintains that if the fly had not been present in the reserves, making them unsuited to cattle, farmers would have claimed the land and the rhinos would have lost their sanctuaries.

The pressure to eradicate nagana began to grow as soon as Zululand was opened to European settlement in 1905. One of the control measures advocated was to slaughter the herds of wild grazing animals, which were regarded as reservoirs of nagana. This policy also had the advantage of removing competition for the grazing land. Great sweeps were conducted during the next few decades and according to the Natal Parks Board as many as ninety-six thousand animals were killed in buffer zones around the reserves.

During the period 1930-1950, Umfolozi lost and regained its status as a reserve several times. Between 1932 and 1952 it was administered by the Division of Veterinary Services.

By 1952, when the fly was finally eradicated by

aerial spraying, the reserves were firmly established; and the southern white rhino, along with many other wild species, had a sanctuary. Today, the preservation of the southern white rhino is still considered one of the greatest conservation successes of modern times.

In 1987, the now amalgamated Hluhluwe-Umfolozi Game Reserve (they are linked by a narrow land corridor) had a white rhino population of 1,660 and Kruger National Park had 1,200 (see table page 45). Both achievements show what can be done by conservationists with solid financial backing and determined anti-poaching measures.

To a certain extent, this has overshadowed the efforts the Natal Parks Board is making to repeat the success with the black rhino, which in the 1930s had been reduced to between 100 and 150 in Hluhluwe, Umfolozi and the neighbouring Mkuzi Game Reserve. By 1987, the population in these three areas alone totalled 290 and the next largest concentration was 140 at Kruger National Park. As with the white rhino, the Natal Parks Board began translocations in 1962 and by 1987, some 157 had been shipped to other areas.

Unfortunately, few African countries have the same resources. For them, the struggle against the modern waves of poaching has been desperate. The troubles which began in Kenya in the early 1970s subsequently swept westward through Uganda to the Central Africa Republic and southward through Tanzania and Zambia to the Lower Zambezi Valley in Zimbabwe.

By 1987 there were only two black rhino populations of over 400 remaining in the wild — both in Zimbabwe. There were 750 in the Lower Zambezi, a population that had declined during the previous five years, and 650 in the Sebungwe region, where the population was thought to be either stable or increasing slightly (see table page 46). The AERSG survey credits Zimbabwe with 1,754 black rhino — 46 per cent of Africa's total. Zimbabwe also has some pockets of white rhino, as do Botswana and Namibia, while in northeastern Zaire, the northern white rhino sub-species is making its last stand.

World-renowned elephant and rhino expert Dr. John Hanks, in a 1987 study prepared for the World Wide Fund for Nature[2], identified the Lower Zambezi populations as the most threatened. Most of them are in the twelve thousand square kilometres of national parks and wildlife estates that include Mana Pools National Park and the Chewore and Sapi Safari Areas, which collectively comprise a World Heritage Site.[3]

There are times when even the best of parents and children don't see eye to eye. Or maybe it's just that bad rhino eyesight again.

Highly efficient and well-armed gangs of poachers are infiltrating the reserves, crossing the Zambezi River from Zambia, some reportedly posing as fishermen during the day.

"Unless urgent action is taken," said Hanks, "the rhino will continue to decline rapidly. From July 1984 to July 1987, 288 black rhino were killed in this region."

The situation became so serious that, in response to a request from the Zimbabwe Department of National Parks and Wildlife Management, the World Wide Fund for Nature agreed to meet the cost of keeping a helicopter in the area to help control poaching along the Zambezi River.

"This is a holding action," warns Hugh Lamprey, the WWF's senior representative in Central and East Africa. "It's been extremely costly — US$250,000 — to keep that aircraft flying for six months.

"The reason they had it there was because it was a desperate situation. The poachers coming across the Zambezi from Zambia were killing the rhinos at a rate of two a week and the only way to control it was by having a helicopter patrolling all the time. When the helicopter stopped, or had to go in for servicing, the poachers got to know immediately, so the government guessed it was an inside job and information was being sent back."

Nevertheless, department staff reported significant declines in poaching during the times the helicopter was operating. It normally carries an officer from the department and two scouts, whom it deploys in the field as close to reported poachers as possible. With the helicopter, an anti-poaching unit can be on the tracks of a poaching gang in about an hour. Before the helicopter, these initial contacts often took more than twenty-four hours.

Anti-poaching units are also deployed in areas known to be frequented by poachers and are collected by helicopter at the end of their patrols if they are far removed from their base camp.

Hanks also reported that the majority of poachers resisted arrest. This involved department staff in acutely dangerous shoot-outs. Between 1985 and 1987, twenty-one poachers were captured and twenty-nine killed by these anti-poaching units.[4] Prison sentences ranged from six to eleven years.

In contrast, in some other parts of Africa, the punishments have amounted to a figurative slap on the

Rubbing pole used by rhinos to scrape off dried mud and remove parasites.

wrist. Meat poachers, who take species other than rhino as food for their families, are regarded sympathetically by magistrates and, to a certain extent, by groups such as the WWF. However, when the courts extend their sympathy to commercial poachers, conservationists are irate because they know the poachers will soon be back in business. (In Kenya, Daphne Sheldrick told me her husband caught one poacher six times.)

The money involved in poaching means that the stench of political corruption hovers around the fight for the rhinos. The African Elephant and Rhino Specialist Group says corruption is still widespread in most government wildlife agencies. As an example, it cites a report from a senior member of the Kenya Department of Wildlife Conservation and Management, which discloses that members of that very department have shot more than a third of the rhinos poached in Kenya during the last ten years. In addition, government officials have made it easier to move horn between African countries.

△ Typical white rhino habitat at Umfolozi.　　　　　　　　　　　　▽ Mud-caked rhino grazing.

THE HIGHLY MARKETABLE RHINO

Nowhere did I see the plight of the rhino summed up more succinctly than on a collection box in the lobby of the New Stanley Hotel in Nairobi. The box was actually a sculpted rhinoceros. Around its neck hung a sign which said simply "My Horn Is My Dilemma."

Rhino horn is composed of a tight mass of fibres continuously built up by a special tissue covering a bump on the nasal bones. It is not attached to the bone, but is an extension of the skin, and it is possible to remove the horn without killing the animal, although poachers have neither the time nor the inclination to worry about such niceties.

Just how people came to attach special properties to the horn is difficult to say, but rhinos are shrouded in myth and magic. In the speculative Middle Ages, Arab traders with a sharp eye for a profit often sold rhino horn as "unicorn" horn. Perhaps this marketing device was the beginning of the magical properties ascribed to rhino horn, and the ghost of that belief still lingers.

Another popular belief in medieval times was that if anyone poured poison into a cup made of rhino horn, the poison would effervesce and become harmless. In those times of assassination and intrigue, there was a ready market for an anti-poison device. The French court was using rhino horn cups as late as the last half of the eighteenth century, and Elizabeth I of England reportedly kept a rhino horn in her bedroom at Windsor.

As strange as this claim sounds today, it could contain a grain of truth. The poisons used in those days tended to be strongly alkaloid and could well have fizzed when they contacted the largely keratin and gelatin rhino horn.

Today, as in the past, the major use for rhino horn is in various medicines reputed to relieve fevers, headaches, toothache, flu-like symptoms, and even insanity. There is no medical proof of its efficacy, but minute quantities of rhino horn are still used in many traditional Asian remedies and people are still buying them. Asian horn, which tends to be smaller than the African variety, is considered more potent because its energies are "concentrated." Accordingly, it attracts higher prices.

Almost no part of the rhino escapes the attention of the apothecaries — horn, hide, organs, and even urine and feces are all ascribed medicinal properties. Indeed, the rhino is regarded as a walking pharmacy.

The other major use of rhino horn is in North Yemen, where it is carved into dagger handles. The daggers are regarded as status symbols, or marks of manhood, and sell for thousands of dollars. Even the rhino horn shavings and "off-cuts" are collected and sold for other decorative or medicinal uses.

Once only the wealthiest of the Yemenis could afford a rhino horn jambia, as the daggers are known. Now, workers returning from Middle Eastern oil fields have the money and want to make a statement about their new status.

Rhino horn has other ornamental uses besides dagger handles. It polishes to an attractive amber and is used for buttons and other fasteners, combs, pins, handles, bracelets, the butt plates and grips of weapons, and the tips of walking sticks and riding crops.

The illegal trade in rhino products is currently worth between US$3 million and $6 million a year. In 1987, for example, rhino horn was still fetching US$750-$1,500 a kilogram in Asia.[5]

It is little consolation that returns appear to be declining, because the numbers of rhinos are falling faster than the prices can rise. Observers in Africa and elsewhere believe the market demand is such that the poachers will continue to hunt until the last rhino has gone.

The sturdy feet of rhinos (and elephants) have been put to a variety of grotesque uses by man, such as stands, door stops, footstools and umbrella holders.

White, or square-lipped, rhino grazing at Meru National Park, Kenya. The
white is bigger than its black cousin.

THE ROAD BACK

The World Wide Fund for Nature — not the only conservation organization in the fight, but one of the most respected — believes there is still room for hope, albeit at a price. The price has to be paid in money and in resolve. The type of resolve required has been demonstrated in Zimbabwe, where the 1975 Parks and Wildlife Act has been beefed up in respect to poaching rhino and other protected species.

The penalty for a first offense of unlawfully hunting or killing a rhinoceros or any other specially protected animal, and the possession of rhino horn, ivory, or trophy from any other specially protected animal, is now a minimum fine of Z$15,000 (in 1987 this was about US$24,900) and/or minimum imprisonment for five years.

For a second or subsequent conviction, the minimum fine rises to Z$35,000 (about US$58,100 in 1987) and the minimum prison term to seven years. In a country where the best of wages was unlikely to be more than a few thousand dollars a year, these amounts are crushing penalties, designed to strip poachers of their profits.

This legislation also addresses another political reality of Africa — civil disorder. The breakdown of law and order in Angola, Mozambique, southern Sudan, and Uganda has at various times in the past decade made it impossible to enforce wildlife legislation, or to protect designated wildlife areas. With the ready availability of high-powered weapons, populations of both elephants and rhinos have been depleted severely, or even eliminated.

Black rhino and avian attendant at Ngorongoro Crater, Tanzania.

◁ White rhino stands in solitary splendor. Rhinos often defend their territory fiercely.

And the Act makes a further, important point: "Far too many national parks and game reserves in Africa are seen as irrelevant and inaccessible to local communities, who derive little or no benefit from them. Thus there is no incentive for the local communities to discourage poaching activities."

A way must be found to increase the awareness of the value of sharing the continent with diverse animal life. But whatever is done throughout Africa to save the rhino should not be attempted piecemeal by government agencies and conservation groups working in isolation. This point is recognized in the Continental Strategy prepared by Dr. Hanks for the World Wide Fund for Nature.

"A continuation of uncoordinated and largely underfinanced projects will have little or no effect, and the decline will continue unabated," Hanks argues. "If the WWF is to become involved in a major rhino campaign, an essential prerequisite is to define obtainable goals for rhino conservation which would thus form an integral part of a Continental Rhino Strategy."

He believes that operational directives in the form of an action plan must be associated with the strategy. It should have phased developments, clearly defined priorities, identification of essential components which require simultaneous support, and most importantly, an allocation of funds for each element of the plan.

Hanks states bluntly that the WWF has neither the manpower nor the resources to implement a comprehensive and effective action plan on its own. Furthermore, to underfund or ignore essential components of the plan which require simultaneous support will almost certainly result in additional examples of failed projects and wasted resources.

Successful implementation of the plan will require "a hitherto unique level of coordination and cooperation between the fundraisers and conservation agencies at both the government and NGO (Non-Governmental Organization) level."

However, the work is not being left to government and conservation agencies alone. One of the most significant developments with the African rhino of both species in recent years is the influence of private ranches. In fact, after the white rhinos at Hluhluwe-Umfolozi and Kruger, the next largest population in Africa is not found in other parks but on private land. There are 525 white rhinos on private land in South

Africa's Transvaal alone. In 1987, Kenya had 521 white rhinos, 156 of which (nearly 30 per cent) were being raised on private ranches. Usually the range is well defined, the census very accurate, and the rhino population stable or rising. The ranches also have efficient anti-poaching patrols and supervision.

The pockets of black rhinos on private ranches are generally small, but in 1987 there were 91 on Solio Ranch in Kenya.

As with elephants, some conservationists have suggested abandoning the effort to preserve large wild populations of rhinos in favour of maintaining smaller sanctuaries. Hanks disagrees. While he admits the sanctuary proposal is attractive, given the high costs of present conservation, he believes Zimbabwe's government would almost certainly interpret such a policy shift by the WWF as a vote of no confidence in the ability of its Department of National Parks and Wildlife Management to conserve the Lower Zambezi Valley area. Furthermore, it could be interpreted as a message to the rest of the world that the WWF believes the battle to protect large, designated wildlife areas in Africa has been lost (outside South Africa where wildlife populations and reserves are still secure).

But saving the rhinos is a goal that will not come cheaply. Hanks has calculated the costs of rhino survival in the wild, and the minimum annual expenditure for effective protected area management programs in the Lower Zambezi Valley alone is US$2.4 million. Helicopter protection for black rhino throughout the whole area would take another US$320,000 — a total annual expenditure for the Lower Zambezi Valley of US$2.72 million, or a staggering US$13.6 million during the next five years from his base date of 1987.

When Hanks prepared his estimates, the funds available for conservation in the valley came from a variety of sources. The Zimbabwe government supplied almost 20 per cent and the rest came from international aid and wildlife organizations and the Zimbabwe National Conservation Trust. However, there was a shortfall that year of US$820,000.

Given the shortfall, the uncertain ability of the Zimbabwe government to contribute a larger percentage, and the lack of assurance that non-governmental organizations will continue their support at the same level, it may well be that future efforts will centre on preserving the World Heritage Site in the valley.

The banks of the White Umfolozi River in Natal, South Africa, display the scars of floodwaters, but the serenity is still enjoyed by buffaloes (right) and a solitary white rhino (left).

However, "if we cannot, or are not prepared to raise the funds [for anything larger]," Hanks reminds us grimly, "then the wild populations have no future."

Hanks's coordinated assault on poaching and cooperation in preserving the endangered rhino should not be left to the aid organizations alone. Instead it should extend to millions of concerned men, women, and children throughout the world who are prepared to lend their voices, money, equipment, lobbying skills, and time to saving a unique species from extinction.

The benefits would not be confined to Africa's rhinos but would ripple outward to the rest of its animal and plant species.

Ultimately it would make our planet a more secure place for life in all its forms.

[1] *Equus quagga*, a zebra-like animal which once existed in vast herds in Africa, became extinct in 1872 or 1883 (reports differ). The head and upper parts of the body were brown and irregularly banded with dark-brown stripes. The legs and tail were nearly white and without stripes. The bluebuck antelope was wiped out by about 1800.

[2] "The WWF's Continental Strategy for the Conservation of Rhino in Africa," by Dr. John Hanks, WWF International, December, 1987.

[3] The International Convention concerning the Protection of the World Cultural and Natural Heritage (UNESCO, 1972) provides for the designation of areas of "outstanding universal value" as World Heritage Sites. The sites must be of international significance and the designation is designed to protect the natural features; provide information for world-wide public enlightenment; and to provide for research and environmental monitoring.

[4] The shoot-outs are continuing. In August, 1989, we learned that the death toll since January that year was twenty-two rhinos and nine poachers.

[5] The figures cited in this paragraph come from the "WWF Continental Strategy for the Conservation of Rhino in Africa," prepared by Dr. John Hanks in December, 1987. The per kilogram price of rhino horn was quoted from a report by E. and C. Bradley Martin, 1987.

CHAPTER THREE
At Home with the Mountain Gorillas

There we were, bumping along the main street of Ruhengeri in Rwanda, looking for somewhere to eat. Our driver who, in the previous few days, had brought us safely through the Akagera National Park and then up the steep and winding road through the mountains to Ruhengeri wasn't doing very well with his suggestions. At last we spied a small hotel and, in a mixture of hunger and desperation, pulled into the car park.

As we got out of our van, I noticed that we had parked alongside a late-model pick-up. Painted in black across its doors were the words "African Wildlife Foundation." Just the group we had hoped to meet! But our good luck didn't end there. In the hotel dining room we found Craig Sholley, director of the Mountain Gorilla Project, who agreed to an interview that night.

The next day we were due to hike up into the Parc National des Volcans (Volcanoes National Park) in hopes of seeing the mountain gorilla, *Gorilla gorilla beringei*, championed by conservationist Dian Fossey. Her life and untimely death were recorded in the book and motion picture, *Gorillas in the Mist*, and Farley Mowat's book, *Virunga, the Passion of Dian Fossey*.

Sholley, a fair-haired, affable American, listened to our concerns about elephants and rhinos but put his special charge at the top of his list of Africa's most endangered species.

"At maximum we have five hundred animals in the wild," he stressed (including Bwindi, the impenetrable forest in Uganda). "That means it's probably the most critically endangered large mammal in the world. Five hundred animals is an extremely fragile population. Ten thousand animals is an extremely fragile population, so I don't believe we'll ever take the mountain gorilla off the endangered list. I believe we can save it. I believe we can take it into the twenty-first century with us, but I think it will remain endangered simply because of the low numbers."

Five hundred. It's the number of pupils in a small public elementary school. And it's all the mountain gorillas there are in the world.

The territory of the mountain gorilla straddles the borders between Rwanda, Uganda, and Zaire. The Parc National des Volcans is situated in the Virunga massif of northwest Rwanda and is contiguous to Virunga National Park in Zaire and the Gorilla Game Reserve in Uganda which share the mountain gorilla population.

Four groups of gorillas in the Parc National des Volcans have been accustomed to humans; and once a day, up to six visitors are allowed to approach each group and spend an hour with them. These visits are strictly controlled, and the parties must be led by park guides. Visitors are even given a crash course in gorilla etiquette: don't point, don't carry sticks, avoid direct eye contact, and move slowly and unaggressively. If the setting permits, the visitors will often sit down near the gorillas and observe them quietly.

As gorillas are susceptible to some human ailments, tourists suffering from contagious diseases such as respiratory and intestinal infections are not allowed to join the visiting groups. The guides can also exclude anyone they consider unfit to handle the terrain. Not only is the hiking steep and often through forests of nettles and bamboo, much of the park is over three thousand metres above sea level. At this altitude, the air is thinner than most Westerners are used to, which in combination with the frequent rain, mist, and cold temperatures, can make an "easy" hike of several hours an unexpectedly exhausting experience.

Of course, the weather is not always bad. Some groups have enjoyed great weather and encountered the gorillas a short distance from the starting point of their hikes. Sixty- and seventy-year olds have made the climb with relative ease. However, our visit was made in October when temperatures are cooler and rains more likely.

We were warned at the outset by our guides that the gorillas were further away than usual, so we were not surprised when it took just over three hours to make contact and more than seven hours for the full excursion. During the first hour, my lightweight "city" poncho was flayed to ribbons by the undergrowth; and the misty, but steady, rain soaked through every centimetre of my unprotected clothing.

The guides and porters refrained from comments on our deficiencies and instead did everything they could to make the experience as pleasant as possible. In addition to carrying our cameras and gear, at one stage a guide took a practical green jungle cap from his pocket and jammed it on my unprotected head. "Here," he said. "You ranger now!" Another gave me a heavier poncho to wear.

One of the rarest mammals in the world, the mountain gorilla, *Gorilla gorilla beringei,* made famous by conservationist Dian Fossey.

To my embarrassment, they were also prepared to push and pull me up and down the steeper slopes that had been made slick by rain. "Hey! How many kilos do you have?" they joked in fractured and heavily French-accented English. I told them and triggered cries of astonishment, many smiles, and much raising of eyebrows.

As the rain continued to fall, water began to pond on the tracks. My slick-soled army surplus boots were completely useless in the clay. I slipped often and fell at increasingly frequent intervals. At first this was merely annoying and somewhat embarrassing, because I love hiking and have always felt at home in the bush. On our way back, it got downright depressing, as the falls became more frequent and I rose from each one more tired than before.

As I slipped and slithered along, I couldn't help but admire the sure-footedness of the guides and porters, but I also managed to excuse my own poor perform-ance. "They are used to the altitude — after all they do this every day and probably have all the proper gear." Then, on one particularly steep slope, I found my eyes only a few centimetres away from the feet of the guide in front of me. He was wearing blue supermarket-style plastic slip-on shoes . . .

How my respect increased for these gentle, tireless men who smelled so strongly of wood smoke!

On the outward journey, the three-hour mark passed with our guides still casting about for signs of the gorillas. I began to believe that we would never find them, in spite of Craig Sholley's assurance that "if you do the hiking you will see the gorillas." The night before he had told me the successful contact rate was "almost 100 per cent."

That "almost" had assumed large proportions by the time the guides slowed and set off in different directions through a section of bamboo forest, whistling to each other like birds.

"Close now," said a porter who had remained with us. He slid one of our cases of camera gear from beneath his poncho, and Hans busied himself setting up equipment.

Off to the left I heard a strange popping sound, followed soon after by crashing in the undergrowth. One of the guides came back and motioned me forward.

Master of his domain, a silverback in the Virungas.

In the gloom I could just make out the black bulk of a gorilla, hunched down among the bamboo trunks, stripping stems and stuffing shoots in his mouth. He put up with our scrutiny for a while, then turned his back on us and shambled away. As he did so, I saw a broad, silver-grey band extending across the small of his back. He was the silverback, the ''leader of the tribe,'' as the guides called him. He was never very far away from us as we spied on the rest of his family. The females and juveniles were much smaller than him, but it was still a strange and exhilarating experience to be guests in what Craig Sholley called ''the living room'' of wild animals of great and dangerous strength.

The gorillas moved warily away, stripping and munching shoots as they went. Some remained hidden by the undergrowth while others continued to feed, glancing at us frequently as though to make sure we weren't getting too close. Behind them patrolled the burly silverback, his distinctive band of colouring flickering in the gloom as he moved about.

Eventually, the group browsed slowly from sight, pursued by the park guides and Hans with his cameras. I put my own camera away and remained behind for a moment to experience the sensation of being alone in the jungle. To be honest, I was also so tired from the thin air and sliding about in the mud that I needed to rest. Soon I was in almost complete silence, my back to the fading sounds of primate progress.

This group of gorillas in Rwanda had been accustomed to contact with humans, but seemed on edge the day we visited them. They kept wary eyes on us as they munched their way slowly through a bamboo grove. Bamboo shoots are but one item in a varied vegetable diet.

That was when I heard a crashing in the under-growth ahead of me. I realized it must be a gorilla that had lingered behind the others and was hastening to rejoin the group. And coming straight for me! The park rules hadn't covered this case. Should I shout out, stay where I was, or get out of the way in a hurry? I elected to stay put, but by then the crashing sounds were very close. Suddenly, the gorilla burst from the undergrowth no more than a couple of metres away, hunched over with its head down, moving fast, knuckles raking the ground as it concentrated on the pursuit of its fellows. Quite obviously, it was unaware that I was there.

In that instant I thought the gorilla was going to bowl me over, but at the last moment it looked up and saw me. Direct eye contact. A social gaffe.

For the proverbial split second nothing happened, then the gorilla screeched, cartwheeled into a ninety-degree turn to the right, and raced off into the jungle. And then I knew the awful truth: I've got a face that can stop a charging gorilla!

This private joke between a member of another species and me was just one of the gifts of the gorillas. I sensed something awesome, perhaps even miraculous, in seeing the echoes of humanity in these marvellous animals and struggling to understand the world from their perspective.

"You are one-on-one with the animals out there," Craig Sholley had said. "You're not in a vehicle. You're not behind glass. You are face to face with them." And face to face also meant, to me, intelligence to intelligence, even spirit to spirit.

Mountain gorillas at lunch. One of them displays the distinctive patch of a silverback and was the leader of the group we encountered.

UNDERSTANDING GORILLAS

The classification of gorilla species and subspecies has provided academic fodder for many learned battles; but today, only three subspecies are recognized — *Gorilla gorilla gorilla*, the western lowland or coast gorilla; *Gorilla gorilla graueri*, the eastern lowland gorilla; and *Gorilla gorilla beringei*, from the Virunga volcanoes.

Nearly all of the gorillas seen in zoos are lowland gorillas, and their constrained life leads them into one of man's seven deadly sins, gluttony, with its resulting obesity. Gorillas in captivity have sometimes weighed more than three hundred kilograms.

According to one comparative study of wild gorillas (C. P. Groves 1970), *gorilla* is likely to stand 166.6 centimetres tall and weigh 140 kilograms. The corresponding figures for *graueri* were 175 centimetres and 165 kilograms and, for *beringei*, 172.5 centimetres and 155 kilograms. Later studies (D. Cousins 1972) suggest that *beringei*, although heavy, was probably the shortest of the three.

A typical *beringei*, or mountain gorilla, group consists of a mature adult male, or silverback, and a harem of females with young. Unless there is another mature silverback present — a rarity — the leader will probably be twice the bulk of the next largest animal in the group.

Gorillas are not territorial. They do have a range, but they do not defend it. Groups that encounter each other during feeding often ignore each other. Different groups may sometimes nest together at night, but there will be little inter-group contact, except for a few females who may temporarily change allegiances.

The gorilla diet consists primarily of herbs, vines, shrubs, trees, grass, sedge, ferns, and epiphytes — plants which grow on others and depend on them for support, but not nutrition. The various studies that have been made in the mountains of Zaire, Uganda, and Rwanda offer the not-surprising conclusion that the percentages of food types eaten by various groups depends on what is available. At Visoke in the Virungas, for example, gorillas are said to favour plant stems, pith, and leaves, whereas the diet of other groups might be weighted more to fruit or bark.

From my own readings about the mountain gorilla, it is clear that even now there is still much to learn.

Dian Fossey once wrote in her journal that she had completed 485 hours of observation — more than pioneer gorilla researcher George Schaller — but was not satisfied with what she had learned. Instead she wondered what the next 485 hours would bring and hoped that it would be twice as much information.

Schaller, an American zoologist, held a special place in Fossey's thoughts. It was his book, *The Year of the Gorilla*, detailing his work in what was then the Belgian Congo that sparked her own interest in the mountain gorillas. His observations and conclusions laid the foundation upon which later researchers have built.

CREATING THE GORILLAS' SPACE

Craig Sholley, a biologist, became fascinated by the gorillas after spending thirteen months working with Dian Fossey in the late 1970s. He returned to the United States to continue his studies and eventually became a curator with the Baltimore Zoological Society, but Africa was in his blood and he leaped at the chance to return as director of the Mountain Gorilla Project.

The project is jointly financed by the African Wildlife Foundation, the Fauna and Flora Preservation Society, the Peoples Trust for Endangered Species, and the World Wide Fund for Nature.

"We are basically a consulting body that is responsible for the management of the park and works in collaboration with the Rwanda government," said Sholley. "We have basic responsibilities that range from policy decisions, tourist management, and tourist control, to conservation education programs that filter throughout the region and sensitize people in the area to what the park and gorillas are all about. We also coordinate all the anti-poaching patrols in the park."

Direct poaching of the gorillas, whose skulls and hands were once used to make ashtrays for tourists, has ceased to be a problem. However, snares set by meat poachers after other animals will always endanger gorillas using the same trails.

Dian Fossey became extremely protective of the gorillas and led a vigorous international campaign to save a population that had clearly been dwindling steadily as their habitat was chipped away by the encroaching human neighbours. Her writings show

Enjoying the easy life, a burly lowland gorilla at San Diego Zoo. Often gorillas in captivity tend to obesity, far outweighing their kin in the wild.

that she was constantly seizing and destroying snares set in the park and chasing poachers off "her" mountain. She appeared to have little confidence in the ability of the government agencies of the day to protect the gorillas and was always on the alert for trappers who snared young, live gorillas for private collectors.

Sholley told me that up to about five years ago (1983) there was still a demand from collectors, but he thought this too had abated.

At the same time, local people have become more tolerant of the gorillas and no longer regard them as a threat to their crops. This change in attitude is attributed to the efforts of Fossey and later workers to convince the people that there is value in preserving the gorilla population. However, according to Sholley, present-day methods differ tremendously from those of the pioneering Fossey era.

"I think you need to look at the world of conservation at large to understand what has happened here in Rwanda," he said. "Back in the late 1960s it may have been appropriate to approach conservation the way Dian did, with gun in hand and yelling and shouting and screaming and believing that you had to do it all yourself.

"But, over a period of time it became apparent that we were outsiders living in someone else's country and that in order to accomplish anything in that kind of situation you've got to approach things collaboratively and cooperatively. I think that's the major difference between the Dian Fossey era and the present era."

Each member of the Mountain Gorilla Project staff works with a Rwandan counterpart and the group operates in conjunction with the Office Rwandais du Tourisme et des Parcs Nationaux (ORTPN). While corruption is a severe problem throughout Africa, Sholley says he has encountered less in Rwanda than elsewhere. The main difficulty is with bureaucracy.

"We're able to work fairly well within the confines of Rwandan bureaucracy," he said, "but African bureaucracy is a slow, tedious process. In order to get anything done, you move slowly. That's just a reality in Africa and if you can't accept that you don't do very well."

In Rwanda the pressure for agricultural land is so great that the foothills are terraced to the peaks for pastures and crops. In the mountainous higher reaches, such as the point where we began our hike to see the gorillas, the crop is often the pyrethrum daisy used in insecticides. Large areas of the Parc National des Volcans were shaved off for pyrethrum plantations between 1958 and 1978 in pursuit of overseas earnings. Now that the daisy's properties can be duplicated artificially, the demand for this crop is falling. However, the land has been lost to the gorillas who are the new revenue earners.

The boundary between the Parc National des Volcans is the point where cultivation stops. This means that in the past, people living on the perimeter occasionally encountered gorillas in their fields and stoned them to frighten them away. They believed the gorillas were leaving the forests to feed on their crops. Dietary studies have since shown this is not so, although gorillas do like the tender shoots that can be found in areas of secondary forest growth on previously cultivated land. In any event, gorillas are nervous about open spaces.

Human-gorilla encounters are more often caused by the humans invading the gorillas' territory. Often gorillas have been disturbed by people who entered the forest to graze cattle, gather firewood, or collect honey.

Smugglers too have had an impact in the past. In 1973, researcher A.F.G. Groom wrote of seeing groups of ten to twenty smugglers passing by every half-hour along the route over the Sabinio-Mgahinga saddle between Uganda and Rwanda. There was almost as much traffic on the Mgahinga-Muhavura route as well.

One of the most striking features in Rwanda — mountain foothills terraced almost to their peaks to provide flat land for farming.

This human progress eventually created a strip of meadow twenty-eight metres across, which Groom said would form an effective barrier to gorilla migrations.

The Parc National des Volcans has special security problems. Because it abuts international borders, poachers can enter it from Rwanda, Zaire, or Uganda and retreat over the borders if pursued. Roger Wilson, a field officer with the Mountain Gorilla Project, outlined this situation in a 1984 progress report on the group's activities.[1]

"Furthermore, the park has a boundary more than sixty kilometres long, but it is less than two kilometres deep in some places, and there are some 42,000 people living within 2,000 metres [two kilometres] of its periphery. This means that the small proportion among these people who are poachers still adds up to a respectable figure. They can easily reach and penetrate deep into the park, while the dense vegetation and broken terrain makes the job of catching them difficult."

Sholley believes the gorillas were "fairly much a nonentity" to the local people before the coming of Dian Fossey.

"For the most part, the majority of Rwandans — I would say 90 per cent — had no idea what the gorillas were all about before Dian Fossey," he said. The change of attitude that she triggered remains in his mind as one of her greatest achievements.

Although the gorillas have been studied closely since the eighteen years of painstaking work by Fossey, researchers are continuing to learn from them. One of the great hopes is that new pockets of population will be found in some of the remoter areas of forest in the three countries bordering the park. In the meantime, the researchers are content with a steady rise in numbers in the gorilla groups under study and signs that poaching is at last under control.

"The 1981 census indicated 239 mountain gorillas in the Virungas," said Sholley. "The 1986 census indicated 280 animals, so there is a positive reproductive trend there. I certainly hope it will continue. The holding capacity of the park is lots more than 280, but I can't tell you exactly what it is. We've got some prime gorilla habitat out there on a variety of the volcanic peaks that are not being used at this point."

Although Sholley's main concern has been the mountain gorillas, he is also concerned for the western lowland gorillas that are believed to number more than fifteen thousand and are the type we are most likely to see in a zoo. In his eyes nearly every primate is an endangered species — in some cases severely endangered.

"So long as we continue to destroy forests, the likelihood of other primate species going extinct before our eyes is very, very high," he warns.

Rwandan countryside.

RWANDA'S FUTURE

If the mountain gorilla population seems destined to remain small, the human population does not. Rwanda is a poor and tiny country. In fact at 26,338 square kilometres, it's not much larger than the Etosha National Park in Namibia (South West Africa) and is about half the size of the Selous Game Reserve in Tanzania. However, Rwanda has 6.6 million people, which, at an average of 258 people per square kilometre, is one of the highest population densities in Africa. Around the Parc National des Volcans the density rises to 356 per square kilometre and is increasing by almost 4 per cent a year.

Once, we stopped our van in the middle of nowhere to admire the Akagera River from a lofty viewpoint. Its muddy waters flow into Lake Victoria and so contribute to the source of the Nile sought by explorers Burton and Speakes. Suddenly, I noticed a young Rwandan boy watching me from a few feet away. Where he came from, or who he was, I have no idea, but I need no more convincing that Rwanda has one of the highest human population densities on Earth. You can't get away from its people.

Rwanda's countryside is lush and vividly green, with banana plantations everywhere in the lower regions. The hills and mountainsides are striped by cultivated terraces. Every now and then the predominant emerald colouring is offset by splashes of red-orange. These are pyramids of bricks made from local clay, stacked so that fires can be lit beneath them to complete the curing process.

At times Hans put down his camera long enough to exclaim, "This is beautiful. It reminds me of parts of Europe . . . Look at those mountains — it's just like Switzerland," or "See those terraces? We could be in China." Anyone contemplating a visit to Rwanda should take plenty of film.

In spite of its population pressures, Rwanda has maintained 11.6 per cent of its land as protected areas — one of the few countries in the world to exceed 10 per cent. This concern for nature has not gone unrecognized internationally, but neither have the problems.

The International Union for Conservation of Nature and Natural Resources (IUCN), in a 1986 review of protected areas in the Afrotropical Realm, warns that there should be no further areas excised from the existing reserve system. It lists the Volcanoes National Park in particular as "already reduced to the point where it is questionable if it is viable." It praises efforts to educate people in conservation matters, but urges an extension of the program.

KARISIMBI   4507m

BISOKE   3711m

KARISOKE RESEARCH CENTRE ▲

The Akagera River winds its way through a Rwandan valley en route to
Lake Victoria and a place in history as part of the fabled source of the Nile.

The wild and lofty Virunga mountains, one of the last strongholds of the
mountain gorilla.

SABYINYO 3674m

GAHINGA 3474m

MUHABURA 4127m

Lush green valleys with misty mountains beyond make Rwanda a photographer's delight.

Fields of tea, one of Rwanda's most important crops.

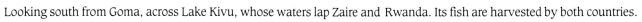

Looking south from Goma, across Lake Kivu, whose waters lap Zaire and Rwanda. Its fish are harvested by both countries.

However, under the heading "Need For International Assistance," the IUCN report says: "The Rwandan Government is to be congratulated on its conservation efforts, especially the protection and management of the Volcanoes National Park. International assistance should be continued to aid protection and management of Volcanoes National Park, one of the last strongholds of the endangered mountain gorilla."

The salvation of the gorillas has been that they are not only paying for their own conservation through tourism but are also producing revenue for the country as a whole. Tourism is now Rwanda's third biggest earner of foreign exchange and is continuing to grow.

"If it were not for gorilla tourism as it began ten years ago," said Sholley, "I think we would have many fewer gorillas than at present. I think there's also a strong likelihood that very little of the park would be left."

Sholley said he enjoyed working with the Rwandan people and numbered many among his friends. While anxious not to sound condescending, he said that one of their most endearing qualities was an innocence now rarely found in the West.

My own experience with the people was that they were ever-present and ever-delightful. Many of them were just as poor materially as in other parts of Africa where the poverty distressed me, but they invariably

emerged from their mud houses clean and smiling. Many of the rural houses didn't have chimneys — the smoke being left to escape through the eaves, making them look as though they were on fire. Some had windows covered with wooden shutters rather than glass. All, in the absence of electricity, were very dark inside.

In contrast, the women were usually clad in bright colours. The men wore a variety of clothing styles ranging from slacks and blindingly white shirts to sport coats and suits. The suits were worn in the most unlikely places — even by men doing manual work on the roads.

During dinner on our first night at Akagera Lodge, we met a tour bus driver who told us earnestly: "I don't just like my President, I love him. He tells us not to have so many children while he has got nine, but that's okay. He is a good man." This pride was one of the most noticeable differences between the Rwandans and the poor of, say, Nairobi. The spirit of the Rwandans was invigorating.

Everywhere we drove, there were scores of people walking along the road, the women carrying loads on their heads, the men driving cattle or toting plastic jerrycans of water. Our driver used the van's horn constantly to clear the way ahead. The people moved aside quickly and often smiled or waved as we went by.

En route to Akagera Lodge, we picked up the hotel manager and his wife at a small village where they had been shopping. Several kilometres down the road we noticed another combi van racing after us. As it got closer, the driver began sounding its horn fiercely. We stopped at the roadside and the hotel manager got out to talk to the group of five men in the van. I saw one of the men give him some money and understood enough French to know that he had forgotten to take his change at one of the shops in the village. The men had chased after us for nearly ten kilometres to make sure that he got it.

"That is the Rwandan way," said our driver, his face creasing in a broad smile.

Rwanda is a small country with big problems, but after my short stay there I feel confident in its future. No matter how big its problems may be, I am sure its heart is bigger.

[1]"The Mountain Gorilla Project: Progress Report No. 6," Roger Wilson, *Oryx,* Vol. 18, 1984, pp. 223-229.

CHAPTER FOUR
The Enigma of Conservation

Embattled and harried Africa's wildlife may be, but it is still among the most diverse and spectacular on Earth. In common usage the term ''wildlife'' is sometimes taken to mean the larger, better-known animals, but in the purest sense it includes not only all animal life, but the multitude of plant species on which they depend.

Among Africa's animals, five rule the public imagination as the glamour animals — the lion, elephant, rhinoceros, buffalo, and leopard. All have earned their status through the respect with which we have learned to treat them. All have been the targets of egocentric, big-game trophy hunting. All have clashed with farmers and pastoralists. Three of the five — elephants, rhinos, and leopards — are now listed as either endangered or threatened species.[1] Loss of habitat and the money that can be obtained for their ivory, horn and skins have put them there.

Lions are not regarded as endangered, but they have survived some shaky times and their future is far from secure. Only buffaloes are in no immediate danger, now that the tsetse fly and nagana are contained.

The Big Five get the best press coverage, mobilizing support for conservation, but their publicity conceals the plight of scores of equally imperilled but less famous animals. The less-glamorous animals and the plants deserve attention too, because their part is just as important as that of the Big Five even if they don't produce tourist revenue.

Wildlife is really inseparable from the habitat and the plant life that sustains it. Plants are likely to be overlooked when discussing wildlife conservation: they are background; animals are foreground. Bamboo is something gorillas munch. Trees are something elephants knock over. Grass is something the big cats slink through.

But take the plants out of the equation and the grazing and browsing animals will die. Take away the browsers and grazers, and the predators will follow. Take the predators away, and the browsers and grazers will proliferate, eating the plants out by their roots.

Poachers don't bother the plants and poaching isn't a serious problem for many African species of animals; but the second great concern of this book — the increasing loss of wild habitat due to human encroachment — is a major problem for all species. In its own way it is more deadly than bullets, because it affects everything, including man.

Wildebeest graze at Amboseli National Park before one of Africa's most spectacular backdrops — Mount Kilimanjaro.

OUR DELICATE ECOSYSTEM

Our planet's 1.4 million species[2] are tied together in a complex and little-understood web hopefully labelled "ecology." Ecology is derived from a Greek term that means the study of the home. "Home" in this sense is an uncomfortably broad term for the science that studies the relationships of all living things to their surroundings and each other.

It is terrifyingly easy to upset the delicate balance established by nature in fragile environments; and it is surprising, if not alarming, to observe the speed at which the grasses bow out and the deserts roll in to replace them.

Unfortunately, weaving a new thread into an ecological system all too often produces a reminder of our human fallibility and the complexity of the relationships between living things. While I was in Africa, Hugh Lamprey and other conservationists walked me through variations of a hypothesis that went something like this. Let us suppose that a study of a struggling community's problems indicates that the answer is as elementary as a better water supply. Engineers are called in to sink a well and create a new water hole. End of problem? No, it may be barely the beginning.

Among animals and humans alike, the news soon spreads — there is water here. More people move into the district, bringing with them their livestock. Local farmers increase the size of their herds because now they have more water. Improved water supply means improved crop yields and grazing. Competition between wild and domestic animals increases. The area's trees quickly fall, to be used as fuel, tools, weapons, fences, and structures. Soon the fragile grass around the water source is trampled to death. The water hole, intended as an oasis, is surrounded by hard-packed, bare earth and becomes the centre of an expanding mini-desert.

Today, the aid organizations have learned to be cautious. Engineers, ecologists, and others in different disciplines have learned that to succeed in Africa they need to work together. Water supplies are not the only concerns. Such apparently benign gifts as improved health measures, better education, more advanced agricultural techniques and crops, modern roads and transport can contain hidden perils for communities with so little and as close to nature as those in Africa.

Thomson's gazelles normally obtain sufficient moisture from soft food, but in dry weather they need water every day. Desert conditions are being created through human intervention, such as overgrazing by domestic animals.

Maasai family group.

Change is coming to Africa so swiftly that the world this Maasai girl will inherit will be vastly different from the one her parents have known.

Abandoned Maasai kraal — once the humans and their livestock move out, the wild animals return.

It is important to realize that in Africa a farmer who responds to a better water supply by increasing the size of his herds might not be doing so in order to become richer. That is a Western idea. The African is more likely doing it to survive. Given the poor grazing, the smallest number of cattle a family of seven could probably live on, according to Hugh Lamprey, is about forty. The family is at risk at all times from potential disasters. One hard blow from rustlers or disease could leave them destitute. In Africa that doesn't just mean losing your money and a few possessions. It means starving and can mean dying.

But even a subsistence lifestyle leaves its mark on the environment. The impact of merely one nomadic family can be great in a year. In northern Kenya, each time a small Turkana family of up to ten people moves to a new area, they need to cut at least forty trees to build new huts and bomas (fences) for their stock.[3] Assuming they move once a month, they could easily fell five hundred trees a year — and this in an area where vegetation replacement is slow.

These aren't the only problems. Africa is catching up to the rest of the world slowly and could be doomed to replay some of the scenarios the West is still struggling to escape. According to Dr. Richard Leakey,[4] chairman of the East African Wildlife Society and director of the National Museums of Kenya, certain parts of Africa will move into industrial development during the next decade on a scale that, while small, will still be large enough to increase the danger to the environment.

"The superpowers and industrial powers, at the moment, are dumping," he says. "By this I mean putting in plants that are not necessarily appropriate in our current understanding of the environmental sensitivities.

"I think Third World countries are going to take short-cuts, if they can, to industrialize as quickly as possible. We are going to see a serious pollution threat affecting Africa — acid rain, degradation of lakes and water systems, the heavy loss of oxygen in some of the lakes as wetlands are drained — these are all very serious issues with a big impact on wildlife as well."

Mount Kilimanjaro, in Tanzania, seen from Amboseli National Park, Kenya.

Reticulated giraffe, showing the distinctive sectionalized markings that inspired its name.

Wetlands are one of the world's most productive ecosystems. Their natural wealth provided the foundation for almost all early civilizations. Now, as the wetland wildlife habitats are swallowed up, in Africa and elsewhere, the species they shelter are becoming extinct. Half a million life forms may have vanished forever by the turn of the century.

"The death of any species diminishes us all, both for moral reasons and because nature is a storehouse of substances potentially valuable to humanity," said WWF director general Charles de Haes of Belgium. "All our food and about half our medicines originally came from the wild. Large-scale extinctions threaten our very future by tearing the web of life and impoverishing the biological diversity on which we depend. Yet by the middle of the next century, half of all living species — half the diversity produced by three billion years of evolution — may be lost."

While some species will be hastened on their way by wilful acts of man, many others will become accidental victims. Sometimes we just don't think enough before we act.

When an individual goes hunting with a rifle, two of the most important rules are to identify the target before firing and to make sure that a bullet continuing beyond the target area will not harm anything else. However, a person who practises these commonsense rules often ignores them when using pesticides. The immediate target might be insects that are endangering crops or predators that are raiding herds. But what about animals further along the food chain and outside the target area?

Let us suppose that a farmer uses poison to kill insects devouring his or her crops. Before they die, many of these insects will be eaten by birds, in whose systems the poison will eventually reach harmful concentrations. The birds in turn become prey to other animals which ingest the poison in its concentrated form and suffer as well. The further along this carnivorous chain the animal is, the higher the level of intake. This is one reason why many birds of prey are facing extinction.

Inevitably, some of the insect-eating birds will die from the poison too. In their absence, the insects are likely to increase. The farmer may then shake his head at the resistance of the insects and increase the pesti-

Lush tropical forest near Victoria Falls. Elephants are said to distribute the seeds of the palms in their dung.

cide dosage, ultimately doing even more harm to the birds, which, ironically, are on his side.

In Namibia (South West Africa), the intended targets of poison range from malaria-carrying mosquitoes, tsetse flies, and locusts to jackals, wild dogs, and leopards. However, for every jackal killed, up to a hundred non-target animals may die, according to Dr. John Ledger, director of the Endangered Wildlife Trust, writing in the magazine *African Wildlife* (Volume 40, No.3) in 1986.

The editor prefaced Ledger's article with a note which drew attention to the conflict between livestock farmers and "problem animals" in the arid south-western part of the southern African subcontinent. "Our concern," said the note, "is for the thousands — nay, millions — of innocent, often useful creatures which are the victims in this never-ending war."

Ledger quoted statistics compiled by Chris Brown, an ornithologist with the Directorate of Nature Conservation and Recreation Resorts, who conducted a survey in 1984 to determine the amount of poison being used in Namibia. About 40 per cent of the 6,527 farmers polled responded to Brown's survey, which

established that five kinds of poison were being used. These were: strychnine (80 per cent); 1080 (ten-eighty), the trade name for sodium mono-fluoroacetate (10 per cent); arsenic; cyanide; and organophosphate insecticides.

According to Ledger, the only poison that could be obtained legally to kill problem animals was strychnine. The survey showed, however, that much more poison was used by the farmers than the amount dispensed officially — a discrepancy that the farmers admitted.

Every year, about thirty-two kilograms of strychnine were distributed on Namibian farms, according to the survey — enough to kill eight hundred thousand people. Some farmers were loading baits (usually small blocks of meat) with ten, twenty, or even fifty times the amount of strychnine considered necessary.

Ledger said in his article that some farmers scattered up to three hundred baits a month as they drove around their properties — more than three thousand baits every year. He maintained these would remain poisonous for up to ten years, even when completely dried out, and represented a constant danger to non-target animals.

The blackbacked jackal (left) and the African wild dog have been frequent targets of poisoning programs. The jackal, besides scavenging from kills made by larger animals, feeds on hares, rodents, reptiles, birds, insects

and even fruit. The wild dog, known as Africa's wolf, hunts in highly organized packs and can take quite large prey.

Not only are we killing animals unnecessarily, we are doing it at an accelerating rate. The U.S. National Science Foundation included a sombre warning in a report which was endorsed by its policy-making National Science Board on August 18, 1989.

"The rate of extinction over the next few decades is likely to rise at least 1,000 times the normal rate of extinction and will ultimately result in the loss of a quarter or more of the species on Earth."

The report blamed the trend on man-made destruction and asked developing countries to join the industrialized nations in research aimed at identifying the world's animals, plants, and fungi and seeking better understanding of their role in the environment.

The International Union for the Conservation of Nature and Natural Resources (IUCN) publishes the Red Data Book, the authoritative source of information on the world's threatened vertebrates. At the beginning of 1986, the Conservation Monitoring Centre in Cambridge, England (now the World Conservation Monitoring Centre, jointly managed by the IUCN, WWF, and United Nations Environment Program), declared that extinction imminently threatened 593 bird species, 406 mammals, 242 fish, 209 reptiles and 867 of the best-known insects, such as butterflies.

But many more non-animal life forms are in trouble. The IUCN estimates that at least twenty-five thousand plant species are endangered. Assessments that include invertebrate animals and lower plants, such as mosses, liverworts, fungi, lichens, and seaweeds, predict that between half a million and a million species will become extinct by the end of the century. What will this mean to us?

While some may argue that the loss of an obscure mollusc or plant may not play a great part in the overall scheme of things, biologist Paul Ehrlich, an outspoken advocate of the world's conservation cause, likens the network of plant and animal species on Earth to the rivets of a spaceship. One or two rivets can be lost here and there without causing too many problems, but by the mid-to-late 1990s we could be dropping as many as ten thousand a year — one every hour. The more "rivets" lost, the greater the chances for explosion or disintegration of our frail Spaceship Earth.

In its 1988 review, the World Wide Fund for Nature lists a few of the advantages gained from species diversity. For a start, the review maintains that biological diversity made both the agricultural and industrial revolutions possible and continues to provide raw materials for industry, chemicals for medicines, and genetic strains that produce high-yielding crops.

The WWF says that regular gene infusions from wild plants, used to increase productivity and fight disease, now add US$1 billion to the value of crops in the United States alone. In 1970 a leaf fungus swept across cornfields from the Great Lakes to the Gulf of Mexico, killing a sixth of the crop and costing farmers and consumers US$2 billion. Wholesale disaster was averted by using new disease-resistant strains originating in Mexico.

The review lists other previously hidden treasures of nature:

● Paraguayan Indians know of a plant that provides a calorie-free substance three hundred times sweeter than sugar.

At times, butterflies form a moving carpet underfoot. Even small life forms such as these are endangered by loss of habitat.

The southern cape of Africa is covered by a profusion of wildflowers, many of which are found nowhere else on earth.

• A caffeine-free coffee has been found in the remnants of forests in the Comoros Islands.

• A wild and nearly extinct relative of corn was found by researchers in the mountains of southern Mexico in 1978. The few plants they gathered have since been crossbred with commercial corn, producing a disease-resistant hybrid that springs up each year like grass.

What are natural bonuses such as these worth? For a start, the WWF estimates that if the disease resistance of the wild corn relative can be introduced to just 1 per cent of the U.S. crop, it would save US$250 million a year. Breakthroughs like these are expected to generate new agricultural products worth up to US$100 billion a year by the end of the century — if we don't destroy the wild genetic material before it can be used.

The WWF sees plants continuing to play a major role in modern-day medicine also. As proof, it cites the generally overlooked fact that about 40 per cent of all drugs prescribed in the United States owe much, or all, their potency to chemicals from the wild.

There are hidden treasures here too. For example:

• An insignificant-looking plant from Madagascar, the rosy periwinkle, is credited with boosting remission rate for childhood leukemia from 20 per cent in 1960 to 80 per cent today. While the plant survives, the forests where it once grew have been destroyed.

• Drugs from curare, made from an Amazonian liana, are used in surgery as muscle relaxants.

• Quinine from a Peruvian tree cures malaria.

• Digitoxin and digoxin from the Grecian foxglove fight heart disease.

• Chemicals from the Indian snakeroot plant relieve hypertension and high blood pressure.

The WWF maintains that at least fourteen hundred tropical forest plants have the potential to be used against cancer. For example, an algae found in Hawaii shows promise in combatting leukemia and the U.S. National Cancer Institute hopes to screen ten thousand substances a year in its search for new cancer cures.

But, according to the WWF review, only a fraction of 1 per cent of the world's species have been examined intensively for potential value in meeting human needs. Who knows how many treasures have been lost already and how many more might go before the end of the century?

"Cures for cancer and unknown foods await discovery. But as they wait, they are being destroyed. It is as if we were burning a vast library of irreplaceable knowledge — before having done more than glance at a few pages in its more accessible volumes," says the review.

The rate of loss is far greater than that at which new species evolve. The disappearance of a single plant species can, through chain reactions, trigger the extinction of up to thirty insect and animal species. Tragically, these plants are being lost at a time when we need them the most.

The problem is exacerbated by another factor — many of the Earth's genetic "eggs" are in the one basket. Tropical rain forests cover only 7 per cent of the Earth's surface yet probably contain over half the known species. This remarkable diversity has developed only in the narrow equatorial belt where the climate has been stable for millions of years.

The olduvai plant, esteemed in Maasai medicine, also gave its name to the Tanzanian gorge whose archaeological records have contributed much to knowledge about the origin of man.

Native peoples occupied the forests for millennia without destroying them, using the plants not only for food, shelter, tools, and weapons, but also for medicine. For example, WWF statistics show that traditional healers in Asia use more than sixty-five hundred plants and Indonesian forest people use more than four thousand species for food and medicine.

However, the WWF estimates that since the 1940s, about half the world's rain forests have been destroyed. Unless present trends change, all rain forests outside the most protected areas will be lost in thirty to forty years.

This means that as the tropical rain forests in Africa, Asia, and Central and South America give way to development projects, half of the world's species are being placed directly at risk. If the land clearing is for agriculture, the gains to farmers are not likely to be great in the long term because rain forests usually develop on poorer soil. Indeed, there is a strong case for arguing that nature was putting the land to its best use already.

That biologically rich target of human destruction, the world's wetlands, are also suffering from the effects of reclamation projects. While it is recognized that not all developments are bad for the environment (some even sponsor conservation programs), the overriding rule should always be "handle with care."

Collectively, the wetlands make up about 6 per cent of the Earth's surface, but, as with the rain forests, they are of great value to the environment. So far, only forty-three nations have signed the Ramsar Convention,[5] the world's only international treaty

aimed at protecting the most vital wetland habitats.

The WWF reports that more than half the world's wetlands have been destroyed since the industrial revolution — most in recent years. Of some two hundred major polder-type schemes developed in the past twenty years to drain wetlands world-wide, only nine have been seriously examined for their environmental consequences. Many of the projects were funded by aid agencies, including the World Bank.

WWF director general Charles de Haes pointed out in a 1988 report that just over a century ago, pioneers began draining the vast southern Florida swamps. Now only a tenth of the original 2.5 million wading birds remains.

About half of the world's tropical forest has already been cut down, perhaps half of its wetlands already destroyed. In the last thirty years alone 160 million hectares of mountain ranges in tropical developing countries have been degraded. And "these are not isolated catastrophes," said de Haes.

Putting this in perspective, 160 million hectares represents an area greater than France, Italy, the United Kingdom, Austria, Switzerland, Belgium, the Netherlands, Luxembourg, and both Germanies combined.

The lesson from this is simple — forests precede human beings; deserts follow.

Where there's water there's life, whether it be (clockwise from top left) a lazy crocodile basking at Mzima Springs, Kenya; elephants in the swamps of the Moremi Wildlife Reserve, Botswana; hippos at Moremi; or other examples of Moremi's abundant waterside life. The Moremi Wildlife Reserve (bottom, left) is part of the inland delta of the Okavango River which originates in western Angola.

THE NEW DESERTS

Even small variations in climate have caused immense changes in the nature of the land and altered the distribution of fauna and flora.

For example, researchers believe that the northern areas of Africa were arid as far back as the Cretaceous period (63 million to 135 million years ago). By the time of the geologically recent Pleistocene epoch, as glaciers advanced and retreated globally (10,000 to 1.75 million years ago), the Sahara was apparently less arid. Fluctuations in the size of the Antarctic ice cap during these glacial and interglacial periods are thought to have had considerable impact on the African Sahel zone, the buffer between savanna and desert.

Today, the cycles continue. The Sahel areas are growing again and the deserts are advancing at a rate that is alarming ecologists. Climatic changes — particularly droughts — still share some of the blame, but much of the new desert has been created by human error.

In 1985, a meeting of the IUCN in Gland, Switzerland, sounded a global warning about what was happening in the Sahel. It cited an IUCN report which said that rainfall had been decreasing steadily in Africa and any rehabilitation strategy for the area should accept drought as a permanent factor.[6]

Decreased rainfall is a factor of nature over which human beings have little direct control. But the IUCN report also documented a decline in natural productivity of arable land and rangeland because of human pressure on vegetation. Serious deforestation had created a fuel wood shortage and had inevitably led to desertification.

This is a problem with echoes throughout the world. Deserts are advancing at a rate of more than six million hectares a year (an area about the size of the Irish Republic) as drier areas are stripped of their trees.

Huge areas of African forests are cleared every year, opening the way to floods, famine, soil erosion, and desert.[7] A case in point is Ethiopia, which has lost 90 per cent of its forests within this century and has seen its human population racked by disease and starvation.

When the trees are removed from the fragile African environment, the elements combine to strip the already meagre topsoil from the land — as much as one hundred tonnes per hectare each year, according to the

Amboseli National Park has faced many threats in the past, but the most insidious one today is the constant struggle against encroaching deserts.

The slash and burn land-clearing techniques of many Africans may yield crops for a season, but can be harmful in the long term.

Surely there can be few sights more graceful than the stately progress of giraffes.

WWF. Crop yields decline. Regular water sources dry up and when the rains come they run off the denuded slopes more quickly, increasing erosion, swelling rivers, and bringing floods which devastate huge areas. More than a quarter of Africa's land area is now desert and the percentage is increasing every year.

The change from grazing land to desert is also fairly easy to bring about. As the human population of a district increases, so do the herds of the predominantly pastoral community. These herds are kept together for protection from predators and poachers, so they tend to eat everything that is available, including replacement seedlings. Perennial grasses are eaten out, or at best become seasonal fodder. Paths form, compacting the soil and reducing water penetration.

Browsing wildlife competes with the domestic animals for fodder, and the predators that accompany

them must also be driven off or killed. In southern Africa, European settler-farmers have reacted similarly, but have added wide-scale poisoning to their arsenal.

For many native tribal groups, the traditional method of clearing scrubland of pests and preparing it for pastoral use is the slash and burn system. This method provides land for grazing or cropping, but simultaneously destroys wildlife habitats and increases the risk of desertification. Several generations ago, the tribal groups would move away after a few seasons and leave the land to recover for up to twenty years. In modern times, the population pressure and demand for food is such that the land is fortunate to get a five-year respite and often gets none at all.

All through Africa the human population suffers from loss of habitat too. Population pressures force people to attempt farming less desirable land. Better areas are given over to revenue-producing export crops that are needed to reduce debts and support armies.

Domestic cattle blend into the landscape outside Amboseli National Park in Kenya.

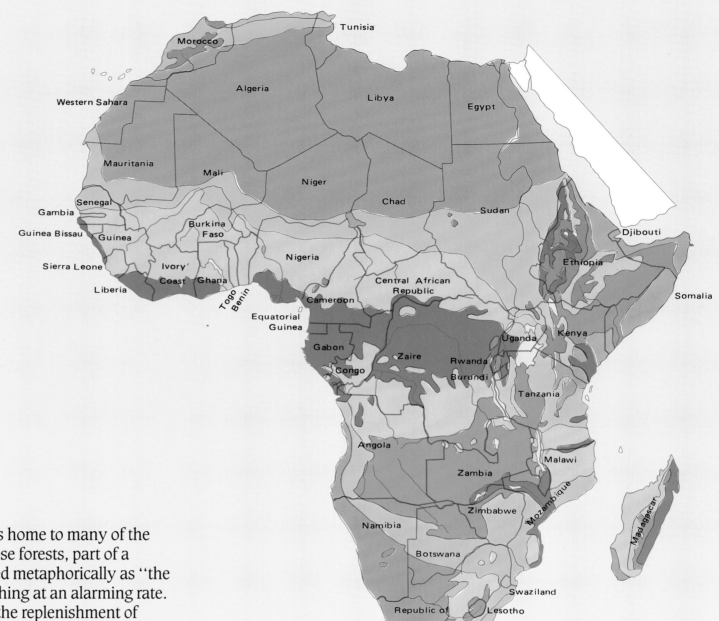

VEGETATION

- Mediterranean Scrub
- Montane
- Desert
- Sahel and Steppe
- Savanna and Prairie
- Tropical Rain Forest and Broadleaf Forest
- Dry Tropical Scrub and Thorn Forest

AFRICA'S LANDS

Africa began this century as home to many of the world's great forests. Now those forests, part of a system that has been described metaphorically as "the lungs of the Earth," are vanishing at an alarming rate. Without their contribution to the replenishment of oxygen, the very air we breathe is changing. Rain forest, woodland, thorn forests, and temperate brush now cover 18 per cent of Africa's land surface. The great lowland and alpine grasslands cover 42 per cent, while semi-arid scrub and desert make up the rest.[8]

True rain forest is limited to the Congo Basin and the Cameroons, with an area of deciduous rain forest north of the Dahomey Gap from Sierra Leone through to the Ivory Coast. These areas of rain forest are enclosed by the Atlantic Ocean to the west and the great sweep of the Guinea savanna on the other three sides. The Guinea savanna, which has more than one hundred centimetres of rain a year and covers much of southern Africa, gives way in turn to the Sudan savanna where the annual rainfall is only fifty centimetres.

Still further north and eastward, the Sahel savanna, with its twenty-five to fifty centimetres rainfall, provides the final barrier to the true desert lands, including the 4,800-kilometre-long and 1,600-kilometre-wide Sahara.

Baboons moving peacefully among other species at Lake Manyara National Park, Tanzania.

Madagascar's ring-tailed lemur is yet another forest dweller struggling to retain a place in today's world. They can survive falls of fifteen metres unhurt, but may yet find contact with man too much to endure.

Generally, the greatest species diversity among Africa's large mammals occurs in those regions of the continent which sustain the high-standing crop biomasses of moderately long-lived herbivores and their predators. The variety of herbivores extends from browsers through mixed feeders to grazers, depending on whether they are feeding on the scrub of the low-elevation savannas or the grass-dominated upland savannas of East Africa.

Water-independent species, the oryx and gazelle, for example, favour desert environments. Semi-arid regions, like Tsavo in Kenya, are home to elephants and other mixed feeders, browsers such as the black rhino, gerenuk, lesser kudu, and smaller numbers of grazing species that occupy patches of grass in the dense scrub. Grazing species are found in much greater numbers to the south, in the open grasslands of the Serengeti in Tanzania, particularly the white-bearded wildebeest, Thomson's gazelle, and the topi.

Once the animals ranged largely unhindered over the areas to which they were suited. Now, increasingly, they are being confined to islands of wildlife parks and reserves amid seas of humanity.

Particularly hard-hit is the island of Madagascar, off Africa's southeast coast. If present trends continue, by the year 2000 it will lose up to 30 per cent of its remaining rain forest. About four-fifths of its plants,

90 per cent of its reptiles and many of its mammals are types found nowhere else in the world.

Dr. Richard Leakey, speaking as chairman of the East African Wildlife Society and director of the National Museums of Kenya, denounced what he saw as ''the total lack of concern on the part of many of the big conservation lobbies for endangered plant communities, isolated patches of forest and wetlands that are going under in the face of agriculture and hydro-electric schemes.'' Nothing is being done about them, he told me.

''The glamour animals are getting all of the attention and I think it's just as serious to think of the germ plasma, the depletion of the whole genetic resource base. I'm deeply, deeply concerned about that.''

TREASURES, TROPHIES AND PESTS

As in all wars, propaganda has been used frequently in human conflict with the animals of Africa. One of the deadliest weapons has been the euphemism. For example, anyone whose conscience is troubled by killing animals can go into the business of vermin eradication and sleep much easier at night.

In the early days of European settlement, the lions, leopards, cheetahs, and other cats were all regarded as vermin because they had difficulty distinguishing between domestic livestock and their usual prey. Similarly, the clean-up squads of hyaenas, jackals and wild dogs were considered cowardly pests.

The elephants also suffered from their unfortunate habit of regarding crops as a delightful salad laid out for the benefit of passing pachyderms, but humans persisted in making farms and settlements in areas the animals had used for untold generations.

Later, the cats became acceptable as trophies, or for their skins, which became luxury furs for the well-to-do who somehow never quite managed to look as good in them as the animals did. Once the tide of public opinion turned against natural furs in fashion, the leopards, in particular, gained a reprieve. But they still have to battle against loss of habitat and efforts to relocate them have not always been successful.

This baobab tree growing near Victoria Falls is believed to be the largest in Africa. According to legend, the famed missionary and explorer, Dr. David Livingstone, rested in its shade.

Perhaps it's fitting to give top billing in this section to "The King." *Panthera leo*; the African lion, is a truly impressive killing machine, fast, agile and armed with immensely powerful jaws and shoulders. The big-maned males with their regal air have been favoured with the honorific, "King of the Beasts," and until relatively recent times young Maasai warriors hunted them with spears as a test of manhood.

As with all of the cats, there is an element of grace in their idle movements and even at some of the killing times. They also share with other cats an ability to relax which makes them a photographer's delight.

Although lions usually amble about at five kilometres per hour they often cover fifty kilometres in a night and can reach a top speed of around forty-eight kilometres per hour in short bursts. They have been known to leap as high as 3.7 metres vertically and 10.8 metres in a horizontal bound. A mature male stands just under a metre tall at the shoulders, has an overall length of 2.8 metres, and weighs up to 204 kilograms. The female stands some 15 centimetres shorter at the shoulder and is 22.7-34 kilograms lighter on average.

The lion's eyes are yellowish and, unlike most cats, have round pupils. The body is a uniform sandy buff, fading to a paler cream on the belly (lionesses we saw in Rwanda were the colour of sun-bleached grass). The ears have black tips and are often the only thing to give the lion away when it is crouching in long grass, or stalking its favoured prey — zebra, antelope, and waterbuck.

The lion's forelegs are so powerful they can usually break a zebra's neck with one blow. Another common method of making a kill is for the lion to grip the prey's nose with its claws and pull the head back and around, throwing the victim to the ground. The neck bite that follows usually produces death by strangulation.

Lions have a strong sense of territory and roar frequently to announce their proprietorial rights. They generally associate in prides which can number as few as three or four members, or as many as thirty.

Although they are heavy animals, they sometimes climb trees, using their powerful forelegs to haul themselves into the lower branches. At Lake Manyara National Park in Tanzania, the lions spend a large part of each day resting in branches several metres off the ground. Animal behaviourists consider this habit might be adaptive.

◁ Enjoying life at the top of the food chain, this lion takes his ease. Lions are essentially family animals, living in groups, or prides, that can number as many as 30 animals, most of which will be females, sub-adults, or young.

Lions spend large parts of each day resting. But even in this they may be "working." Their resting places are often near water holes, and although lions rarely kill when they are well fed, their presence denies other animals access to water. By the time the lions are ready to hunt again, their prey may be weakened or less cautious than usual.

With their supple, muscular build, keen sight and exceptional hearing, leopards are consummate hunters. They are capable of pulling down the larger antelopes, but have also been known to take domestic dogs and livestock.

Sudden death in one of its most beautiful forms. Leopards are active by day and night, but when hunted they become secretive and nocturnal.

The leopard, *Panthera pardus*, is the other feline member of the Big Five. Leopards are found in a variety of habitats from jungle to grasslands and semi-desert to snow-covered highlands. Not surprisingly, they travel well, being proficient climbers and swimmers. Leopards usually lead solitary lives except for brief interludes during mating seasons. To farmers, they are somewhat of a mixed blessing — hunting many of the animals considered pests, but displaying a fondness for dog meat. Leopards have even been known to enter bungalows to carry off dogs. They also take baboons, monkeys, pigs, deer, domestic livestock, antelopes, porcupines, and various other species of small game.

Leopards often drag their kill into trees, out of the reach of jackals and hyaenas, even if it exceeds their own weight. They average 2.1 metres from tip of nose to tip of tail and are usually a dark yellow, their back and flanks mottled by black rosettes. However, the melanistic, or completely black, leopard known as the panther is quite common, particularly in regions that

Above: Buffalo herd at Amboseli National Park, Kenya. Below: Raw power lurks behind the fixed stare of the bovine member of Africa's elite Big Five.

experience heavy rain. In extreme cases, the black colouring can extend to gums, tongue, and palate, while the eyes are blue.

The final member of the Big Five, the buffalo, *Syncerus caffer*, is a one-tonne-plus tower of mean muscle; a real presence on the African landscape. Anyone who has ever been fixed by the stare of a buffalo will quickly sense the raw power and potential for violence that lurks behind that gaze. It's easy to imagine how the buffalo has earned a reputation as one of the most unpredictable and dangerous big game animals to hunt. We saw them when we were driving at night. We parked amidst them to take photographs during the day. Not once was I tempted to get out of the van!

With a single buffalo capable of chomping through eight tonnes of grass a year and raising the spectre of nagana, farmers haven't wanted them around. The buffaloes were victims of early shooting drives in some countries, but are now left in peace.

The hunter becomes the hunted — a cheetah pauses in flight from a camera-wielding party of tourists in the Serengeti.

Cheetah with kill at Amboseli National Park, Kenya.

Cheetahs are not numbered among the Big Five, but I include them here because they are being harried by another species of human — the tourist. Diurnal hunters capable of spectacular bursts of speed of ninety kilometres per hour or more, cheetahs have the potential of providing some of the most spectacular photographs tourists are likely to get in Africa. The drivers of the ubiquitous combi vans in the game reserves know this and, in the desire to please their clients, often put animals at risk.

A cheetah expends an enormous amount of energy in its fierce dashes and can be left exhausted after two or three fruitless chases. If camera-happy tourists continue to spook the prey, the cheetah will go hungry that day. If one van driver finds a cheetah eating after a successful hunt, the animal is soon likely to be ringed by vanloads of happily snapping tourists and may abandon its meal.

Park wardens have reported finding cheetahs that have starved to death amidst plenty, and they have

The spotted hyaena is perhaps best known for its bloodcurdling "laugh" after success in the hunt, but is capable of seventeen different sounds. It is an efficient hunter. Note the powerful muzzle.

The topi is reputed to be the fastest of the African antelopes, but the young is easy prey to the even faster cheetah. ▽

blamed the tourists. However, there have also been reports of some cats using the vans as game locators and thus developing a kind of symbiotic relationship with tourists in much the same way as dolphins and gulls follow fishing boats.

My own limited experience confirms concerns about the effect of tourism on the cheetahs. At Amboseli National Park in Kenya, the driver of another combi flagged us down and told us there was a cheetah feeding up ahead, a few metres off the road. We closed in cautiously and took some photographs. As we shot, other vans arrived. Soon the cheetah was ringed by an audience commenting loudly on its feeding habits, clattering, banging, and revving motors. After a few minutes of this, the cheetah abandoned its meal. I can't say whether the cheetah left because it had eaten enough or because it was scared away, but this experience lends weight to claims that the animals are being harried by tourists.

Lions, leopards, cheetahs, and other predators live near and prey upon the immense variety of herbivores on Africa's savannas. Not only are there different species of herbivores, but there are divisions within the species which blur into confusion for the casual observer. For example, most people would have little difficulty listing giraffe, zebra, and antelope as animals they would be likely to encounter in Africa, but they would be largely unaware of the variations that exist within each species, some of them now listed as endangered.

Many herbivores are the targets of meat hunters as well as their natural predators and all are suffering increasingly as habitat is lost. This problem of loss of habitat is sometimes given a lower priority than other concerns that are considered more immediate, but it is ultimately the most serious threat to all life in Africa.

Giraffes browse like hedge-cutting gardeners through high-standing foliage. Generally, they prefer to feed in the early morning and late afternoon, seeking shade from the midday sun. Most of their diet is leaves, buds, shoots and fruit, with a preference for acacia trees. Occasionally, grass, plants and watermelon, maize or other crops find their way down that long neck too.

Just about the only time a giraffe doesn't look graceful is when it's taking a drink. Fortunately, when its food is lush and soft, a giraffe needs to drink only once a week.

Grevy's zebra, the largest of Africa's equines. Distinguishing characteristics include a long, narrow head and long, broad ears, rounded at the tips. Its numerous black stripes are narrow and almost vertical on the body. There are white areas on the rump and belly.

The giraffe, *Giraffa camelopardus*, which shows regional differences in colouring, can grow to a height of 5.5 metres and must surely rank as one of the most striking animals on Earth. Its beautiful, flowing motion and extraordinary long neck and legs give an impression of ethereal grace — unless you happen to see one splay-legged at a water hole. However, giraffes can survive in areas where there is little or no water, apparently drawing sufficient moisture for their needs from the leaves they consume.

This is perhaps just as well, because giraffes require a sophisticated arterial system to prevent blood rushing to the head when they bend over to drink. The blood then has to pump its way back up that long neck.

Another animal that, while not a member of the Big Five, certainly represents a substantial presence in Africa is the hippopotamus, *Hippopotamus amphibius*. Although most photographs show them in water, hippos don't stay there. At night they leave the water and graze strips extending up to ten kilometres inland from their home lake or river.

In Akagera National Park, Rwanda, Hans and I found a hippo dying in a mud hole a long way from water. At first, we thought the shiny, grey shape was a rock, but as we got closer we saw that it was an animal. It was so emaciated we didn't recognize it as a hippo at first. Bones stood out under its skin and there was an open wound about the size of a saucer on its left flank. Flies were active amid the gore, and we assumed the hippo was dead until it moved feebly. I found myself wishing for a gun. Park laws or no, I would have ended that hippo's suffering in that instant if I had the chance.

Later, in the same park, we were able to observe a family group of hippos grazing amid bushes a few yards from water. The contrast between the dying animal and its healthy kindred couldn't have been more marked. The grazing hippos were fat and sleek, giving credence to the claim that the hippo is a relative of the pig.

The hippo ranks as one of the world's largest land mammals and is fast enough at full gallop to overtake a running man. Possibly the largest ever recorded was a bull in Kenya which weighed 2,664 kilograms and was over 4.5 metres long, but the average weight is about a thousand kilograms less.

Contrary to popular belief, hippos often range far from water in nocturnal grazing forays. This one, shown here close to death in Akagera National Park, Rwanda, didn't make it back.

[1]"Endangered and Threatened Wildlife and Plants," published by U.S. Fish and Wildlife Service and U.S. Department of the Interior, 50 CFR 17.11 and 17.12, April 10, 1987.

[2]No one knows exactly how many species share the planet with us. According to the World Wide Fund for Nature, 1.4 million have been identified so far. "Until recently," says the WWF, "at least three times as many — five million — were thought to exist, but new studies suggest 30 million as a more realistic minimum."

[3]"African Wildlife Resources," Malcolm Coe, in *Conservation Biology, an evolutionary- ecological perspective,* edited by Michael E. Soulé and Bruce A. Wilcox, 1980, pp. 273-302.

[4]A few months after we returned from Africa we learned that internationally renowned paleontologist Dr. Richard E. Leakey had been appointed director of Kenya's Wildlife Department. At the time of our interviews Dr. Leakey was chairman of the East African Wildlife Society and director of the National Museums of Kenya.

[5]The Ramsar Convention takes its name from the city of Ramsar, Iran, where it was drawn up in 1971.

[6]"Desertification in the Sahel — Diagnosis and Proposals for IUCN's Response." Issued by IUCN, Avenue du Mont-Blanc, CH-1196 Gland, Switzerland.

[7]The total area of the African Continent is 28,672,000 square kilometres. Forests comprise 18 per cent of this total.

[8]"African Wildlife Resources," Malcolm Coe.

Hippos at Mzima Springs, a delightful oasis on the western boundary of
Tsavo National Park, Kenya. Note the fish eagle perched in the trees.

Although hippos have no sweat glands, they exude a pink, sticky secretion from their skin glands which was once thought to be blood. In fact, the substance dries to form a protective lacquer over the skin when the animal is on land and may also have some antiseptic properties.

Hippos are often shot by poachers for their meat. A combination of hunting and loss of habitat has made this intriguing animal, once common over most of Africa, an increasingly rare sight outside game parks.

Another outstanding feature of Africa is its birdlife. There are fifteen hundred species to lure bird-watchers to regions which range from dense, tropical forests, through wooded and grassy steppes to arid areas of scrub and semi-desert. There are literally millions of birds in the eastern mountains and inland waterways alone.

No matter where we travelled, or how barren the countryside appeared, there was always a bird perched

atop a scraggly tree or hopping about among some rocks. It was easy to become diverted from original photographic targets by yet another flash of colour or unusual call.

In spite of this richness, at certain times of the year some of the most numerous bird species in Africa are ''visitors'' from Europe and Asia. Each year, about five billion of them arrive as refugees from colder winter climes. The European varieties use the Mediterranean as a final staging point before flying up to twenty-four hundred kilometres across the deserts or around the coastlines of North Africa. Warblers, chats, wagtails,

Surrounded by flocks of birds, a hippopotamus herd sports at Lake Manyara National Park, Tanzania. Although it is relatively small and the lake makes up two-thirds of its 32,500 hectares, the park has possibly the greatest density of wildlife in the world. Its highly varied habitats include mountains, the Gregory Rift Wall, spectacular gorges, swamps, grasslands, forests and even hot springs.

hawks, waders, and numerous types of waterfowl help make up the total of one hundred and fifty migrating species.

About a third of the birds don't survive the journey. Some are swept away in storms, and many fall prey to hawks and other raptors, which line the migration routes. Thousands of birds arrive in Africa so weakened that they cannot compete with ''locals'' for food and soon starve. But those that do make it are another element in the mystery and mystique of Africa.

Truly, Africa abounds in wonders and miracles. No single book could do the wildlife of Africa justice, let alone a chapter. Each species plays a part in the intricacy of life and the loss of any will be felt. Some are endangered; others, while reduced in numbers, seem to be coping; but all have suffered the effects of the swarming of man throughout the continent.

In the past, Africa has been perceived as a rough, raw, environment filled with primitive vigour. However, while these qualities are still present, they mask an underlying fragility, evidenced by the reactions to forest loss, over-grazing and the agricultural methods used by its farmers.

This fragility, now so terribly evident in Africa the strong, Africa the invincible, extends a chilling warning to us all.

Wildebeest and zebra herds mingle in the early morning at Amboseli National Park, Kenya. In the background is Mount Kilimanjaro. Although the countryside looks dry, seasonal rains bring an almost overnight change and relief for wildlife.

From Antelope to Zebra

Out on the African savanna there is an enormous diversity of herbivores. Nothing is quite as simple as it seems at first glance. Not only are there species and subspecies, but there are regional differences in size, colouring, and habits to take into account.

For example, African antelopes, or buck, as the larger types are often called, belong to four distinct sub-groups of the zoological family, Bovidae, some of them further divided into two or more types. The four sub-groups are:

• The ox-like type, or Bovinae, which has two divisions. The first includes buffaloes and the second the "twisthorned antelopes" (Strepsicerotines) which include the eland and other large bush, woodland, swamp and forest forms such as kudu, nyala, sitatunga and bushbuck.

• The duikers (Cephalophines) — small, primitive bovids, with short, straight horns and tufted tails and a tuft of hair on the forehead. They live in thickets, bush and forests and sometimes scavenge around human settlements. They are divided into two main groups — forest duikers and bush duikers. Forest duikers have squat features, a hunched back and short legs. Both

sexes have horns. Bush duikers, which live on more open ground, have straighter backs and long legs and generally only the males have horns.

• The "horse antelopes," which come in three distinct types. There are the true Hippotragines, such as the sabre, or rapier-horned sable, roan and oryx. Next come the plains dwelling Alcelaphines, sometimes called "deer antelopes" with their sloping withers, long face and short horns — often oddly shaped — kongoni and other hartebeestes, topi, tsessebe, wildebeest and blesbok. Then there are the marsh-dwelling Reduncines, medium-sized and deerlike in build — waterbuck, lechwe, kob, puku and reedbuck.

• Finally, there are the antelopes proper, in two varieties. The first are the Neotragines, including the pigmy types such as royal antelopes and dikdiks. Slightly larger types include the klipspringers, which favour rocky habitats, and plains and bush species such as the oribi, steinbok and grysbok. The second are

Grant's gazelles in scrub at Tsavo National Park, Kenya. They are found in varied habitats. Because their liquid needs are met by food, they are not dependent on open water.

the true Antilopines, among them gazelles, impala, springbok and gerenuk.

But, numerous as they are, the antelopes are only part of the savanna scene. Many other species share the territory with them. Some are hunters and others are the hunted, but all share the common perils of life in a shrinking habitat. No matter what their place in the animal kingdom, they are subservient to humans and their needs. Even the king of beasts has become at best a vassal lord.

In the following pages is a representation of the startling variety of animals found in Africa. Some are well known, while others are rarely seen by tourists. A book several times the size of this one would be needed to show all the variations, but our sampling is an intriguing introduction to some of Africa's other animals.

The tiny blue duiker may stand only 30 centimetres high (one foot) at the shoulder and weight between four and ten kilograms. While some do have a bluish sheen, others are greyish brown, or brownish black. The blue duiker is found throughout southern Africa. ▷

The impala, a lightly built and graceful animal, stands a metre or less at the shoulders, but is capable of leaping to three times that height, or covering more than nine metres in a single bound. These were at Akagera National Park, Rwanda.

Greater kudu male. One of the larger antelopes, the kudu is slender and elegant. Males can tip the scales at around 318 kilograms.

Greater kudu female. Considerably smaller than the male, weighing perhaps around 200 kilograms, the female has no horns.

Immature male nyala. When fully developed he will have the dark brown shaggy hair, curved horns and orange stockings typical of his species. The development of the underside is more pronounced than in other antelopes.

Top: A mature male.
Bottom: Mature female.

Sable antelope herd at Hwange National Park, Zimbabwe. Noted for their long, curved horns (sometimes exceeding 1.5 metres) and dark colouring, sable antelopes can weigh as much as 250 kilograms. The giant sable, found in Angola (particularly Kangandala National Park) and sometimes considered a separate species, has a darker face and even longer and more massive horns. Both types prefer wooded areas rather than open plains.

The South African gemsbok is a large antelope standing 120 centimetres tall at the shoulder and weighing about 200 kilograms. They are gregarious by nature and are able to withstand long periods of drought in their frequently dry habitat by varying their diet of grasses to include fruit, especially melons and wild cucumbers, as well as the bulbs of succulents.

Fringe-eared oryx. Similar to the beisa oryx, but with heavier horns. The colouring is usually a richer brown than that of the beisa, with distinctive tufts of long, black hairs on the ears.

East African beisa oryx. Although mingling placidly with zebra here, they are very pugnacious and have been known to kill lions, lowering the head between the forelegs to bring those long horns into play.

South African oryx antelope, or gemsbok, at Etosha National Park, Namibia. The powerful, straight horns of a burly male are the longest of any oryx, often reaching more than a metre in length.

The parched ground of the Etosha Pan in northern Namibia awaits the first rainfall of the rainy season, which is only minutes away. The heavy cloud cover has trapped the heat enough to create a mirage in the distance, but soon there will be plenty of real water around as the pan becomes a short-lived lake.

Oryx and giraffes can both go without water for long periods, but neither will pass up a drink when the opportunity arises.

Topi. These antelopes probably have the greatest population of any African species and are often found mingled with herds of hartebeest, zebra, or wildebeest. Several regional variations exist and are distinguished by colouring and the size and development of the horns.

The Arabian oryx was snatched from the brink of extinction by the San Diego Zoological Society and is now being released back into its natural habitat. However, it is still an extremely rare sight and is under strict protection. The Arabian oryx, separated from its fellows by continental drift, developed as a separate subspecies. Its adaptations include widespread hooves for easier travel on sand and an almost white hide to reflect the sun's rays. This photograph was taken at the San Diego Zoo.

Bongo. Weighing in at around 230 kilograms, they are the largest of the forest antelopes. They are also one of the most brightly coloured — a vivid chestnut red with white stripes and a spinal crest.

Roan antelope. Third only to the eland and kudu in size, the roan is primarily a grazer. Regional variations range in colour from grey to a rich, earthy brown. With some resemblance to a horse in proportions, the roan is aggressive, learning to fight from a young age.

Cape eland in Nairobi National Park. Massive, but relatively docile, eland have sometimes been semi-domesticated for their excellent milk and meat. Bigger specimens can weigh in around 900 kilograms and the species has a general ox-like appearance with a distinct dewlap. However, in spite of their bulk, eland are nimble enough to leap more than two metres into the air.

Red hartebeest at Etosha National Park. Once found in enormous herds, they are now having to be reintroduced in many areas from herds bred in sanctuaries.

Kongoni at Tsavo National Park. They are members of the hartebeest family, which is distinguished by high shoulders and backs which slope down to the rump. Besides the several varieties of hartebeest, the grouping includes topi and wildebeest.

Topi with young at Akagera National Park.

Tell-tale rump ring marking identifies the common waterbuck.

Male common waterbuck. Usually has a dark brown, shaggy coat. The horns are long, heavily ringed and tilted forward in a gradual crescent.

Above left: Female common waterbuck.

Defassa waterbuck, showing white rump patch rather than the ring of the common waterbuck. Colouring varies from grey-brown to almost orange-brown.

Female gerenuk. The most obvious difference from the male is the absence of horns. They are replaced by a dark patch on the crown.

Male gerenuk.

The gerenuk is a browser, but dwells in dry, or even desert areas (these are in Tsavo National Park, Kenya). It is sometimes called the giraffe gazelle because of its relatively long neck (gerenuk means ''giraffe-necked'' in Somali). The eyes are also very large.

Grant's gazelle at Meru National Park, Kenya. There are many regional variations of this large and heavily built gazelle, which is most commonly found in open plains or bush country.

123

Springbok (springbuck) in Etosha National Park, Namibia. The symbol of the South African rugby football team, it is the only gazelle found south of the Zambesi. It once used to swarm in huge herds that swept all before them in seasonal migrations. They are famous for their "pronking," a series of spectacular, stiff-legged leaps soaring more than three metres into the air.

Thomson's gazelle, Serengeti National Park, Tanzania. Small and graceful, coloured a deep, sandy fawn, with a black lateral band and white underparts, they are among the most familiar and affectionately regarded wildlife in East Africa.

Impala herd, Nairobi National Park, Kenya. A medium-sized, graceful animal, active by day and night, they browse on leaves and bushes, but also feed on short grass and fruit. Unlike many browsers, they are highly dependent on water. Harem herds, as many as fifty strong, are led by a single adult male.

Red lechwe buck at Moremi Wildlife Reserve, Botswana.

Red lechwe at the Moremi Wildlife Reserve, Botswana. These medium-sized antelopes live in swamps and wetlands. They are unable to run very fast on firm ground but, as good swimmers, take refuge in the shallows. Lechwe are divided into three main variations, the black, red and Kafue lechwes, while the Nile lechwe is listed separately. Lechwe once existed in enormous numbers, migrating in the wake of receding floods, but are now in serious decline.

Reticulated giraffe.

Maasai giraffe.

Baringo giraffe.

Southern giraffe.

Kenyan giraffe.

Nubian giraffe.

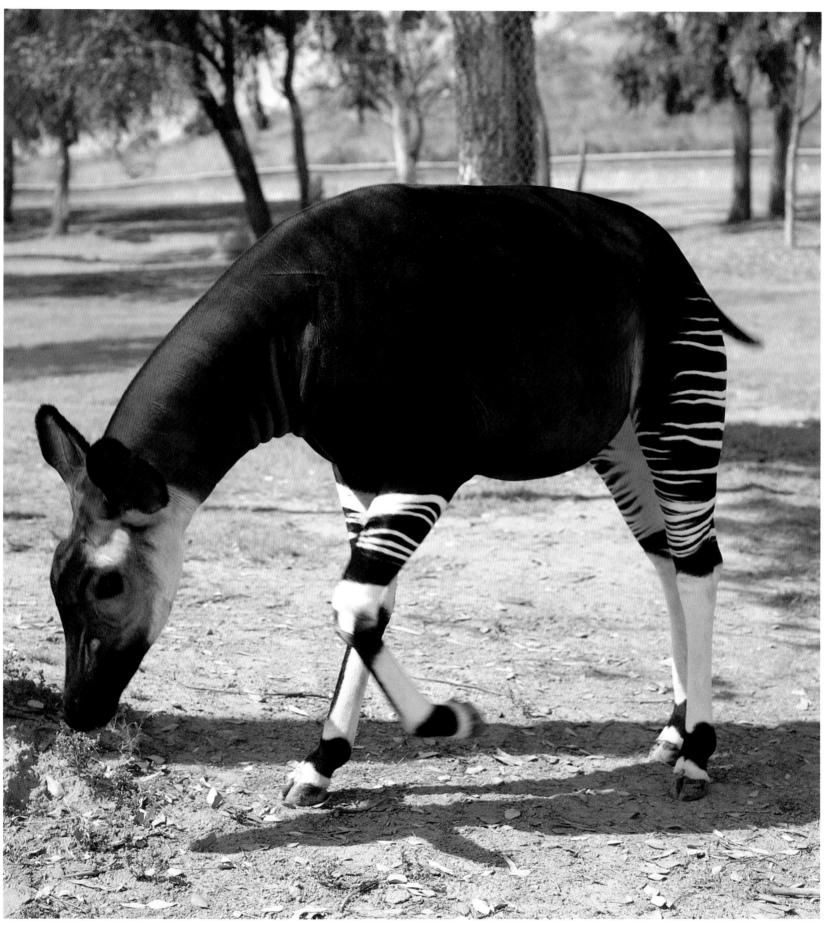

The okapi is a relative of the giraffe, but has a shorter neck. It is a forest dweller.

Giraffe bull at Moremi Wildlife Reserve, Botswana. Note the dark, almost chocolate brown colouring.

◁ Group of Southern giraffes at Kruger National Park, South Africa.

Brindled gnu (or wildebeest) at Hluhluwe Game Reserve, Natal, South Africa. This ungainly looking animal has been described as having the forequarters of an ox, the hindquarters of an antelope and the tail of a horse. For the record, it is an antelope.

Herd of white-bearded gnu at Lake Manyara National Park, Tanzania. The white-bearded gnu is the northern cousin of the brindled gnu which has a black beard.

Brindled gnu bull at Etosha National Park, Namibia.

Wildebeest herd in the Serengeti during the February calving season. The placenta can be seen trailing from a cow that has just given birth. The young animal, partially concealed by its mother, will face a torrid first few weeks.

Hyaenas on the prowl for wayward wildebeest calves. Although the hyaena has a reputation as a scavenger, it is also a formidable hunter in its own right, taking a good percentage of the 300,000-400,000 calves born each season.

Protecting the young becomes a major concern for wildebeest herds as lions and other predators surround them during the short calving season. The key to the species' survival within the ring of fangs and claws is safety in numbers. With all the calves being born around the same time, there are far too many for the hunters to eat.

Once separated from their mothers, wildebeest calves become easy prey to the numerous predators stalking the herds.

Here is one that didn't make it. When experienced hunters separate a young wildebeest from its mother, the result is inevitable.

Vultures gorging on the remains of a wildebeest carcase in the Serengeti.

Lions are capable of eating a third of their bodyweight at a sitting. This one's belly is so distended that standing up is just too much bother.

Lions usually hunt as a group, often by driving their prey downwind to where one of their number lies in ambush. Generally, most of the killing is done by females, such as this one, seen resting after eating and helping drive off hyaenas and other opportunists.

Overleaf: Grevy's zebra in Samburu National Reserve, Central Kenya.

A young male lion lazing about after a meal. Because of the group tactics used, each lion may be required to kill as few as twenty times a year.

Trio of Chapman's zebra. △

Herd of Grant's zebra in Serengeti. ▽

Thomson's gazelles, or "Tommies" as they are affectionately known, are the most common gazelle in East Africa. Although they are relatively small (about 65 centimetres high at the shoulder, weighing 20-30 kilograms) their herds sometimes number in the thousands. However, this availability makes them prey to not only the cheetah, but lions, jackals, leopards, wild dogs, and in some areas the spotted hyaena.

The relationship between hunter and hunted is essentially one of life and death. On the open plains of the Serengeti the hunters include the feline sprinter, the cheetah. It stalks close to its prey (in this case Thomson's gazelles) and runs them down with bursts of speed sometimes exceeding 100 kilometres per hour. However, the cheetah is not as ferocious as other cats and has been tamed and used for hunting.

Aardwolf. Although it is sometimes mistaken for a small striped hyaena, the aardwolf does not have the latter's powerful jaws and would probably be incapable of killing anything larger than a rodent. Its usual diet is insects.

Blending in well with its environment, a black-backed jackal is a creature of the open savanna and light woodlands.

◁ Spotted hyaena near the rim of Ngorongoro Crater, Tanzania. Aware of the photographer, it stood its ground for several seconds, but bolted at the sound of the camera shutter.

Oblivious to the hordes of animals on the horizon, this wild dog has eyes only for Egyptian geese.

Wild dogs, because of their efficient pack hunting tactics, make formidable predators. They strike with such savagery that the feasting on the prey, perhaps a waterbuck, often begins while the animal is still alive. Although the wild dog resembles the domestic variety, its feet have four toes instead of the five of true dogs.

Quite apart from their ferocity in packs, the African wild dog brings to the business of hunting a relentlessness that frequently sees the prey give up in exhaustion.

◁ Serengeti lions basking in the sun — one of their favourite pastimes. Lions usually hunt at night, but are the most diurnal of the cats. They are very sociable and are rarely seen alone.

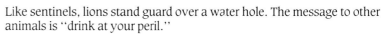
Like sentinels, lions stand guard over a water hole. The message to other animals is "drink at your peril."

Older buffalo bulls often become loners or form their own groups. These three have just enjoyed a mud bath in a salt lake in Ngorongoro Crater, Tanzania. Crystals of dried salt can be seen on their hides.

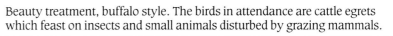
Beauty treatment, buffalo style. The birds in attendance are cattle egrets which feast on insects and small animals disturbed by grazing mammals.

Top: Buffaloes are considered among the most unpredictable and dangerous of big game animals. The red-eyed stare of this group at Tsavo Park, Kenya, reinforces that reputation.
Bottom left: Two bulls engage in a stare-down, while a third (centre) appears to act as a referee.
Bottom right: Showdown over, the subordinate bull approaches the dominant male cautiously, still unsure of its reception.

As massive as they are, lone bulls often fall prey to lions when they are away from the protection of the herd.

This loner paid the ultimate price.

The big predators and scavengers have eaten their fill and gone, giving this banded mongoose and other smaller animals a chance for a hurried meal.

152

The narrow line between life and death in Africa may seem cruel, but even in the transition, animals such as these buffaloes have roles to play.

Eventually, every part of the buffalo will be used. Even the blood and bones will fertilize the ground.

Honeymooning lion couple. Females come into heat every three months for four to eight days. Lions are polygamous, usually living in family groups, or prides, of up to thirty individuals. They are at the top of their food chain and have no natural enemies except man and occasionally packs of wild dogs.

Lioness with cubs. The mortality rate among the lively and inquisitive youngsters is high, particularly for males. The young weigh less than half a kilogram at birth, but grow vigorously, being weaned at about ten weeks. Although they become increasingly independent, they remain with their mother until eighteen months old. Adult status is usually reached after three years.

At one moment a lioness can be enjoying the heat of the day benignly, paying no attention to the flies buzzing around her nose . . .

. . . At the next she is a killing machine, engrossed in stalking zebras on the other side of these trees.

The giant forest hog, a huge and heavily built pig, may weigh as much as 230 kilograms. However, in spite of its size, it seldom ventures into open country.

While it would be unlikely to win prizes in a beauty contest, the warthog's senses of smell and hearing are very acute. It is omnivorous and highly adaptable within its hostile environment.

The warthog is a favoured prey of lions and leopards and has learned to be wary of ambushes at water holes. Before drinking it checks out the neighbourhood carefully.

Baboons enjoying the last rays of a setting sun aloft in a big fever tree. The fever thorn, or *Acacia xanthophloea,* has beautiful, smooth, yellow-green bark and delicate green leaflets. It is usually found in damper areas — and so are mosquitos. When travellers resting in its shade were bitten and contracted malaria, the trees were unfairly maligned as the source of the fever.

Baboons are careful approaching water holes, often not drinking until midday, when large predators are likely to have fed or moved on.

Baboon male on guard at a water hole while females and young drink.

True baboons live in savanna and dry, semi-desert country, but they are among the most versatile of Africa's animals. While they still sleep in trees, most of their time is spent on the ground where they move about in large groups for protection from predators such as leopards and lions. These groups are guarded by sentries and once the alarm is given the baboons will mount a combined defence against marauders. They are well able to defend themselves with their powerful jaws and canine teeth, sometimes killing incautious leopards.

Early afternoon at lake Manyara National Park. Baboons are relatively late risers and have two feeding binges — one in the morning and the other in the late afternoon. The heat of the day is passed by resting in the shade.

Young baboons are full of mischief. They are also temperamental, one moment peacefully grooming each other and the next engaged in noisy fights which sometimes have to be broken up by adult group members.

Vervet monkey, one of many forest dwellers that face an uncertain future as their habitat diminishes.

The blue monkey is at home in the forest too, but is also found in wooded savanna areas and has a range that varies from sea level to mountain country up to 10,000 feet high.

Crocodile drifting with the current in the Ewaso Ngiro River, northern Kenya.

In Africa, a watchful eye can make the difference between catching lunch, or becoming lunch.

Nile monitor, or water leguaan. Despite its name, it is common as far south as South Africa's waterways, although at one time it was hunted almost to extinction for its hide, which was popular for shoes and other leather goods.

Giant African snail.

The Ewaso Ngiro River, like many in Africa, is stained brown by silt eroded from its banks.

Serrated hinged terrapin.

Leopard or mountain tortoise.

Bushy-tailed mongoose.

Common African python. The biggest snake in Africa, it is capable of killing animals as large as impala, monkeys and wild pigs. Adults average between 3.5 and 4.5 metres, but specimens up to 6 metres in length and weighing more than 60 kilograms have been found.

The ostrich needs no introduction, but few people in other parts of the
world know just how remarkable this bird is.

CHAPTER SIX
The Birds

Cliches and superlatives are hard to avoid in Africa, but it is almost impossible to escape them when trying to describe the birdlife.

It doesn't matter whether the birds are native to Africa, or refugees from winters in other parts of the world (see Chapter 4). It doesn't matter what their habitat, or even if they are flyers, or ground dwellers. Africa's birds are brilliant, living jewels.

The birds of the open country offer a staggering variety of plumage, colours and behaviour patterns. In the Great Lakes of the Rift Valley, more than two hundred species can be seen in a single day by a dedicated birdwatcher.

The rain forests are rich in birdlife too, but many remain unseen, living their lives in the tree canopy thirty metres above the ground.

Other African avians spend their lives on the ground. The best known is the ostrich, *Struthio camelus,* which has suffered much at the hands of man, but is still widespread. In South Africa, ostrich farms maintained for plumes and leather provide an additional assurance of survival, and this approach is regarded by some conservationists as an indication of the way things must go for other African wildlife.

Often ostriches have been portrayed as objects of humour, but it doesn't pay to mess about with them. They can weigh more than 130 kilograms, are capable of gazelle-like bursts of speed, and pack a mean kick. The male has distinctive black and white plumage, while the female is a drabber brown-grey. The sturdy legs of both vary in colour from a flesh pink in the Sahara to a bright blue in Somalia. Like camels, they are at home in arid areas and temperatures as high as 56 degrees Celsius appear to cause them no distress. Normally they eat succulent plants, berries and seeds, but they have been known to devour small animals and poke about among vegetable refuse.

Another ground dweller is the secretary bird — so called because of its crown plumes which look like quill pens tucked behind the ears of a Victorian clerk. *Sagittarius serpentarius* is a very deceptive bird. It seems inoffensive enough mincing its way fussily through short grass on its long legs until you remember that it is looking for snakes which it will kill by kicking

and stamping. Those impressively taloned feet bring quick death to small prey and can give humans a nasty injury.

One of the most graceful flying birds is the marabou, *Leptoptilos crumeniferus,* although it looks ungainly and rather ugly on the ground. This huge African stork can have a wingspan of about 3.3 metres and feeds on carrion, but will vary its diet with frogs, snakes, insects and rodents. It is often found in arid country jostling with vultures for meals, but is not at all shy, occasionally nesting in village areas where it can check out the refuse heaps.

The head and neck are naked, to avoid fouling its feathers when eating. Another distinctive feature is a 45-centimetre-long inflatable pink throat pouch which is most conspicuous in the breeding season. As unlikely as it sounds, the downy parts of its plumage were once used to trim women's hats and clothing.

Great ground hornbill — its cry is a series of lion-like grunts.

Yellowbilled hornbill.

Redbilled hornbill.

Hornbill nest.

Grey hornbill.

Hornbills are medium-to-large birds characterized by their prominent, curved bills. Their nests are usually built in tree trunks and the females are walled up behind a barrier of mud and animal droppings during incubation. A narrow slit is left in the wall, through which their mate passes food.

For spectacular flying — or rather, tumbling — it's hard to match part of the courtship ritual of the African fish eagle, *Haliaeetus vocifer.* Pairs lock claws in mid-air and plummet dizzily toward the ground, pulling up at the last moment. This is the smallest of eight species in the sea eagle genus, standing about 75 centimetres tall, but it's a pirate, often chasing and harassing other birds — even members of its own species — to steal fish they have caught.

The fish eagle is usually found perching atop waterside trees from which it makes almost nonchalant dives to make one-legged snatches at fish swimming near the surface. When there are few fish around, it might prey on young mammals, small birds, or even eat carrion.

However, if there is one bird which symbolizes Africa to most non-Africans, it is the flamingo, even though they are also found in Asia. Great hordes of them swarm around Africa's saline lakes in flocks that have been estimated at a million or more in the past. Flurries of flamingoes as far as the eye can see have, in other parts of the world, inspired the creation of wooden or plastic imitations as pervasive garden ornaments.

The greater flamingo, *Phoenicopterus ruber,* and the lesser flamingo, *Phoeniconaias minor,* exist side by side, but not in competition. The greater flamingo filters small organisms such as arthropods, worms and molluscs from the muddy ooze in the lakes, whereas the lesser flamingo uses an intricate filter system to feed on microscopic cells of blue-green algae from the clear water above the mud. Although they are able to screen out the salt from the water, both types will drink fresh water wherever possible.

Another bird that no one who has been on a game drive can have failed to see is the noisy and gregarious helmeted guinea fowl, *Numida meleagris,* which always seems to be scurrying out of the way of motor vehicles at the roadside. However, their speckled plumage make them hard to spot amid trees and scrub. They have a distinctive red, bony ''helmet,'' except in Kenya, where the crested guinea fowl, *Guttera pucherani,* sports a tuft of crisp, curly black feathers.

The redbilled oxpecker, *Buphagus erythrorhynchus,* is another African eccentric. Possibly a relative of the starling, it spends most of its time clinging to antelopes, giraffes, cattle, rhinos and hippos, feasting on the ticks, flies and other parasites it finds there. The host animals tolerate this personal valet service unless the oxpecker gets too enthusiastic, or starts to probe around a wound the animal may have received. Oxpeckers usually roost among reeds at night, although some, perhaps anticipating an early start the next day, sleep on their hosts.

This relationship between birds and other animals exists elsewhere. Wagtails and egrets feed at the feet of cattle, bee-eaters ride goats, and Egyptian plovers are said to pick the teeth of crocodiles.

The bee-eaters, of which there are seventeen varieties, are some of the flashiest dressers in Africa. Besides their brilliant plumage they are, as the name suggests, also known for their ability to catch and devour bees and wasps, some of them venomous. Rarely do they succumb to the poisons.

But even as we admire them, there comes the sobering thought that ours might be one of the last generations to have that privilege. If we term them ''jewels'' and ''riches'' and consider them to be an important part of our heritage, shouldn't we treat the birds as though we value their continued presence? The next few pages will demonstrate how richly the African continent has been blessed.

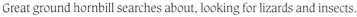

Great ground hornbill searches about, looking for lizards and insects.

Woollynecked stork.

Secretary bird heading for cover. Note the quill feathers behind its ears.

Kori bustard. Large ground dwellers sometimes standing more than one hundred centimetres tall, they favour open plains country, open dry bush and semi-desert areas. During display, the kori bustard can inflate its neck like a balloon.

Below: While the neck colouring is constant, the rednecked spurfowl's body colouring varies considerably throughout its range. It is known for its loud, shrill cries from cover in early morning and at dusk.

Blackbellied bustard. Smaller than the kori bustard, it is now in decline in many areas.

The yellownecked spurfowl is perhaps the most common of the francolins in its range — East Africa, northeastern Uganda, Kenya and northern Tanzania. It favours open bush country and the edges of forests.

Marabou stork, whose feathers once adorned women's hats.

Saddlebilled stork. Next to the marabou, it is the largest stork in Africa.

Bottom left: The helmeted guineafowl, about the size of a chicken, is a common sight through most of East and Central Africa. Its name comes from the distinctive red, bony spike on its head.

Slightly smaller than its helmeted cousin, the crested guineafowl sports a topknot of long, curly black feathers. The face and neck are a bare blue and red respectively. It frequents rain forests, riverine forests, thickets and dense scrub.

Birdlife at Moremi Wildlife Reserve, Botswana. Among the species shown are the whitefaced duck, pelican, yellowbilled stork and great white heron.

Yellowbilled stork and herons at a man-made water hole in Meru National Park, Kenya.

Grey heron, whitenecked cormorant, sacred ibis and redbilled duck communing at Lake Nakuru National Park, Kenya.

Sacred ibis — a resident of the Ethiopian region, but common throughout East Africa.

African spoonbill. It feeds on small fish and aquatic invertebrates.

Whitenecked cormorant at Lake Nakuru National Park, Kenya.

Pelicans and Egyptian geese at Lake Manyara National Park, Tanzania.

Blackheaded heron.

African darter, a most efficient fisherman.

Longtailed cormorant.

Two over-achievers — hamerkop, a builder of gigantic nests, and nearby a Goliath heron. Goliath is Africa's largest heron, sometimes more than 150 centimetres tall.

Inset: Egret in breeding plumage, a feature of which is a slight pink
shading on the breast and back.

A colony of cattle egrets in the wetlands of Meru National Park, Kenya.

Yellowbilled storks and Egyptian geese, Lake Manyara National Park, Tanzania.

Hadada ibis, common throughout most of Africa.

Crowned crane in Serengeti National Park, Tanzania.

Blue crane at Etosha National Park, Namibia.

The European (or white) stork and Abdim's stork will always gather around large herds of zebra in search of small creatures, such as insects, frogs and lizards, that are disturbed by the hooves of the grazing animals.

Crowned plover.

Blacksmith plover.

Wattled plover.

Hottentot teal (on left). Blackwinged stilt (on right).

Slaty egret.

Yellowbilled egret.

Little egret.

Avocet.

African jacana.

Black korhaan.

Yellowbilled duck (on left). Whitefaced duck (on right). African skimmer.

Egyptian goose.

Knobbilled duck.

Spurwinged goose.

Chestnut weaver.

Blackcollared barbet.

Pintailed whydah.

D'Arnaud's barbet.

Spottedbacked weaver.

Yellow weaver.

Whitethroated bee-eater.

Burchell's starling.

Yellowbreasted starling.

Bluebreasted kingfisher.

Pied kingfisher.

Whitefronted bee-eater.

Lilacbreasted roller.

Abyssinian roller.

Silver bird.

Little bee-eater.

Whitebrowed sparrow.

Palewinged starling.

Weaver birds belong to one of the largest avian families in Africa. The males are regarded as nature's architects for their nest-building achievements, but they have to be good. The male brings his prospective mate to the nest he has prepared for her, but if she doesn't like it she usually tears it apart.

185

Martial eagle, a massive hunter common in East and Central Africa. Its favourite prey include monkeys, hyrax, small antelopes and game birds.

African fish eagle.

Tawny eagle. Smaller than the martial eagle, it frequently associates with vultures and other carrion eaters around lion kills. However, it also hunts on its own behalf.

Inset: A grey meerkat, or suricate, stands sentry for his fellows. This small mongoose is preyed upon by the tawny eagle.

Verraux's eagle, a rare sight seen most frequently in Ethiopia and Kenya. It nests on rocky crags and inland cliffs.

Brown snake eagle. Hunts from lofty perches rather than in flight. It is capable of killing snakes up to three metres in length, including cobras, adders and mambas, and enjoys an occasional side dish of monitors and lizards.

Blackshouldered kite. Another hunter of rodents, it is able to hover in flight and is frequently seen looking for prey at dusk.

Augur buzzard. Possibly East Africa's most common bird of prey, it is a favourite of farmers because it feeds almost exclusively on rodents.

Long-crested eagle. Favours wooded country and also feeds almost entirely on rodents and other agricultural pests.

Pale chanting goshawk, known for its prolonged, fluting cry.

189

Some of the birds of Lake Bogoria National Reserve.

◁ A pair of African fish eagles perch high above Lake Bogoria in Kenya. The eagles prey on flamingoes, which are otherwise safe from predators in their marshy habitats.

Flamingoes, a challenger to the ostrich for the title of Africa's best known bird.

The Greater kestrel, another efficient bird of prey.

An African fish eagle swoops in for the kill.

A kite demonstrates its hunting prowess.

CHAPTER SEVEN
Poachers and Politics

One moment the honorary warden had been driving quietly through a Kenyan national park in search of wildlife to photograph. Then he rounded the bend in the road and saw a scene that filled him with horror — a man with a high-powered rifle, standing at the roadside taking deliberate aim at an elephant.

"I stopped my car and said to him, 'Please don't,' but he just turned the gun on me and said 'Would you like to go home tonight, or would you like to die?'"

The warden looked up the barrel of the rifle, wondering if this would be his last day on Earth. The man pointing the gun at him was wearing a military-style uniform — "He might have been a prison guard, possibly a corporal, but I couldn't be sure. There was a government car parked on the side of the road and no one else was in sight . . .

"What could I do? I went home."

The warden was telling his story over dinner in the relaxed atmosphere of one of the better Nairobi restaurants, but at that moment he was clearly reliving his time at the wrong end of a gun. As he stared down at his plate, lost in thought, we — Hans, an official from the Kenyan Wildlife Department, and I — respected his silence. We all stopped eating, waiting for him to continue. Nearly a minute passed before he shrugged and looked up with a wry smile. "Life is cheap in Africa," he said, and speared some vegetables with his fork. The dinner continued.

He was right — and he was lucky. Others who have encountered poachers in the African bush have suffered the same fate as the animals they tried to protect.

A sad case in point was that of internationally renowned conservationist George Adamson, who was slain on August 20, 1989, near his bush camp in Kenya. His death occurred nine years after the murder of his wife, Joy, who wrote the story of Elsa the lioness in the books, *Born Free* and *Living Free*.

Adamson, who was expecting guests, sent three of his assistants to an airstrip to pick them up. About two kilometres from the camp, the men were ambushed and robbed by three poachers who forced them to stop by shooting out the tires of their vehicle.

When the eighty-three-year-old Adamson heard the shots he came to investigate with three other assistants. Earlier, he had gone on record as saying he would be prepared to shoot poachers. When he saw what had happened to his assistants, he tried to run the poachers down, but they opened fire with automatic weapons. Adamson and two of the assistants died. The third lived to tell what happened.

THE POACHERS

A single poacher, such as the man in the uniform encountered by the honorary warden, is probably an exception. Chances are he was just an unscrupulous individual who saw a chance to make some extra money and took it. There have always been opportunistic meat poachers and snatchers of passing ivory or rhino horn.

The poachers causing the great concern today, however, are highly organized and heavily armed bands of up to twenty men who strike quickly and vanish into the bush before they can be caught. They are armed with FN-G3 and Kalashnikov AK-47 automatic rifles — a form of foreign aid Africa can do without — and usually outgun the rangers opposing them. The gangs have even fired on parties of tourists in game reserves.

A glimpse into how they operate comes from this eye-witness account given by a tour operator, who was out for an early-evening game drive in the eastern part of Tsavo National Park on July 22, 1988, with his two assistants and two tourist clients.[1]

As their van rounded a bend on what is known as the river route, they saw a group of at least twelve men dressed in jungle fatigues crossing the road ahead of them. The operator stopped his van and had ten or fifteen seconds to study the group unobserved. At first he thought they were rangers or an anti-poaching patrol, then he realized the fatigues were much darker than those used by Kenyan forces and had a white sash running from shoulder to waist. The first three men had AK-47 rifles slung across their shoulders.

When the men noticed his van, he backed off quickly; but they made no move against the tour party. Those who were armed lowered their weapons in what seemed like a half-hearted attempt to conceal them, but the group as a whole continued calmly on its way.

In spite of this low-key response, the tour operator was convinced he had seen a group of poachers, the first three armed with automatic rifles to shoot the elephants and the rest there to help carry the tusks.

The next day he returned to search the area. On the river side of the road near where he had seen the men, he found an elephant carcase. Just over the brow of a nearby hill lay another six — all were freshly killed with their tusks hacked out.

The origins of the bandits vary. Many in eastern and central Africa are Somalis — tough, bush-wise, desert people who moved south after their country's costly and unsuccessful military campaign to wrest the Ogaden from Ethiopia in 1977-78. They have cut a swathe through eastern and central Africa as far south as Zimbabwe and west to Botswana and Namibia, leaving a trail of animal carcases behind them.

Some of the Somalis are former soldiers, others are bandits who are finding a use for the surfeit of guns after the fighting. First they turned their weapons on the animals in their own country. Then, when that source of revenue became depleted, they moved south in search of new herds to plunder. They are a large part of the reason why northeastern Kenya is under precarious government control at the best of times.

A similar pattern developed in Uganda when Idi Amin's regime was overthrown. Once the fighting stopped, the guns were turned on the animals and the elephant herds in particular were decimated. When we were in Nairobi trying to arrange a flight into Uganda, we were asked several times: "What do you expect to see? It is all gone." We were told that we could be taken as far as an airport, but after that there were no guarantees either about our safety or whether it was still possible to drive to parks that were once ranked among the most beautiful in Africa.

I was told that some of the poachers active elsewhere in Africa were rebels of various causes, guerilla fighters killing elephants and rhinos to raise money to buy weapons. Still others are local people, even government officials, working for middlemen who are often well-to-do business people or curio shop owners. All of them, in my mind, are no better than the amoral human flotsam involved in drug trafficking and dealing.

I am no sentimentalist about the "harmony of nature" presumed to exist between animals and prehistoric humans. During the last one hundred thousand years when tool-using human beings are believed to have been active in Africa, at least twenty-six genera disappeared — a rate twenty times that of the nineteen large mammal genera lost during the first 1.5 million years of the Pleistocene.[2]

Likewise, arguments that early human beings did not possess the weapons sufficient to fell a large mammal are hard to take seriously in Africa today, when a poacher can kill an elephant with bow and arrow. While hunters armed with high-powered rifles and poachers with their AK-47 automatics take a terrible toll of elephants and rhinos, an elephant hit by a poisoned arrow may take longer to die but ends up just as dead.

Even poisoned arrows are not necessary for a skilled hunter. The traditional method used by pygmies in Cameroon is to stalk and hamstring elephants with an axe or machete. The attack is usually made by one hunter and an apprentice. Once the hunter has crippled the elephant, he attacks its underbelly with a large spear, then retires and waits for the animal to die.

Snares have been used to take game animals as long as anyone can remember, but the modern use of steel wire makes them a particularly unpleasant killer. Smaller animals have been found with forelegs stripped to the bone by their desperate attempts to escape the traps. Elephants too, have been caught and killed by well-anchored wire snares. Today, in some African parks, hundreds of these snares are confiscated each year, arousing fears that many more go undetected.

The line between hunting and poaching is a thin one. Poaching is the illegal killing of an animal, motivated by the need for food or by the profit expected from selling the meat, skin, bones, tusks, or any other portion. I feel sympathetic to poachers who are simply trying to feed their families (as are many Africans) even though I recognize the illegality of their efforts. Trophy hunting is legal in some parts of Africa, but I personally find such a practice barbaric. It is partly justified by the substantial fees trophy hunters pay for their pleasure. Hunters also have a vested interest in ensuring that sufficient animals survive to support a trophy trade.

CORRUPTION AND VIOLENCE

While most of this information relates to Kenya, I don't want to imply that Kenya is worse than other parts of Africa. It's just that I spent more time there than in any other African country and was able to gather information relatively freely. However, the problems in Kenya are similar to those faced elsewhere and indicate the difficulties in dealing with poaching in countries that are still struggling to meet the basic needs of their human populations.

When George Muhoho took over as Kenya's minister of Tourism and Wildlife in 1988, he removed several high-ranking officials who were found to be working with poachers. He pledged that the purge would continue until all suspects were removed. But later the same year, conservationists accused him of being slow to act on a list of poaching suspects named by staff of his own ministry. The list was said to have contained the names of fourteen traders and three ministry officials involved in the killing of elephants in Tsavo National Park.[3]

Muhoho defended himself by saying the problem the ministry faced in bringing the suspects to court was in gathering sufficient evidence to ensure their conviction. Kenya's director of Wildlife Conservation and Management at the time, Dr. Perez Olindo,[3] supported him by saying, "The one thing we have absolutely no control over is human greed, and you cannot condemn people without proof."

These statements, no matter how reasonable they seem, were nevertheless galling to conservationists who thought the list should have provoked more action.

Olindo, highly respected in international conservation circles and the recipient of the 1988 J. Paul Getty Wildlife Conservation Prize, knows at first hand what it is like to deal with corruption. During an earlier stint in government employ, he removed several subordinates accused of being connected with poaching. However, they had higher-placed protectors who got Olindo removed from office. When he returned as director, the men were back at their desks and he had to start over.

The awarding of the Getty Prize (seen by some as the equivalent of a Nobel Prize for conservation) to Olindo was received with mixed feelings by conservationists in Kenya.

"He deserves it," said one, "but it's rather unfortunate that the award was made this year amid the concerns about elephants in Tsavo. He hasn't really had time to do much yet, and the award will give the impression that things are improving. That isn't so. Next year would have been better."

Olindo is regarded internationally as one of the pioneers of CITES (the Convention on International Trade in Endangered Species of Wild Fauna and Flora) and, at the time the award was made, was serving as chairman of the CITES African Elephant Working Group, a special committee created in 1987 to halt the trade in illegal ivory. As further evidence of the esteem in which he is held, the award was made not by fellow Africans but by an international jury of conservationists.

Meanwhile, the war between poachers and wildlife rangers continues with pitched gun battles and deaths on both sides. And, as mentioned earlier, tourists have sometimes been caught up in the violence.

Shortly before we arrived in Africa in October, 1988, a woman photographer was hacked to death in the Maasai Mara Game Reserve in southern Kenya, presumably by poachers. During the next two months a series of bloody events made newspaper headlines.

• Three rangers were killed in an ambush at Kenya's Kora National Park.

• Early in September, poachers fired on a bus in Kenya's Meru National Park, leaving a tourist critically wounded.

• Poachers slipped by armed guards to kill five white rhino in a sanctuary at Meru.

Kenyan president, Daniel arap Moi, declared in September that poachers were anti-Kenyan and should be shot on sight. I even heard suggestions from others that the poachers represented a deliberate attempt to harm Kenya by destabilizing its tourist industry.

After the Kora ambush the anti-poaching unit requested and received the aid of other police and military services in tracking down the culprits.

This prompted the unit's most vocal critics to argue that it should be strong enough to fight its own battles. They said it was weak and ineffective and should be disbanded and replaced with a commando-style military unit with highly trained independent officers.

Military training would seem to be a must, considering the scale of some of the anti-poaching operations. The biggest encounter I heard about occurred in 1980 when an ambush set by rangers left twenty-two poachers dead in the Maasai Mara National Reserve near Kenya's border with Tanzania.

Given the huge areas that the rangers have to patrol, the chances are high that the first indication of poachers in their vicinity will be the circling of scavenger birds above elephant or rhino carcases. This is a problem felt throughout Africa. Small, mobile bands of poachers, be they "locals," the tough Somalis, or other bandits, can strike quickly and get away just as fast. Trying to track them down without air support is like looking for the proverbial needle in a haystack.

This situation means that park rangers live with frustration. As several conservationists in Kenya observed: "What's the use of saying you will shoot them on sight if you never see them?" And while shooting poachers on sight is a very effective way of stopping them from re-offending, it also stops them being questioned and so closes off potential sources of information about the rest of the organization.

Kenyan authorities are reluctant to speak about the size of the anti-poaching unit or how it is armed or equipped on the grounds that such information would give the enemy yet another advantage. However, it is public knowledge that the main anti-poaching training institute at Naivasha graduates sixty men every six months with military-style training supplied by instructors drawn from the police, General Service Unit (GSU), and army.

Out-gunned and out-manoeuvred the graduates might often be, but no one can deny they are in the fight. As wildlife director of the day, Dr. Perez Olindo said: "You read recently that in the Kora area our men were ambushed and three were killed. How can someone claim that we are only paying lip service when our people are dying in the cause?"

Some conservationists interviewed would like to see a greater military involvement in anti-poaching patrols. The dream of many was to use fixed-wing aircraft to detect poachers and helicopters to fly in members of the anti-poaching unit to intercept them.

However, besides their military allegiance, soldiers have tribal affiliations which assume great importance in Africa. They were reflected in comments made by people who saw difficulties if the army was asked to play a greater role in controlling poachers.

This white rhino was being kept under 24-hour armed guard at Meru National Park in Kenya, but poachers killed it in a raid in 1988.

Among the high-ranking soldiers in Kenya are several Somalis, at least one of whom has publicly expressed opposition to killing his countrymen. Critics claim that this has affected the morale of anti-poaching forces in the field. Park staff and conservationists have accused them of dropping their weapons and running at the sight of well-armed Somali poachers.

"What do you think when you hear of an encounter where seven GSU are wounded and one killed and the shifta [bandits] have managed to get the dead man's gun and ammunition?" said one critic. "This means the owners of the battlefield at the end of the day were the Somalis."

But, asked who he would choose to oppose the bandits, he said: "Other Somalis — people who know how to fight, track, and survive in the wild."

This aroused memories of an anti-poaching tactic adopted by Bill Woodley, one of the former colonial era administrators now serving as an adviser to the Kenyan government. During the time when he was warden of the western part of Tsavo National Park he fought fire with fire by employing ex-Mau Mau terrorists as rangers. At one stage he received a call from a high-ranking official who asked: "Do you know what you are doing, old chap? These men have not only just got out of jail, they went in very reluctantly; and here you are giving them guns."

The results soon spoke for themselves when the ex-Mau Mau became some of the best rangers Tsavo has ever had. This doesn't mean that anti-poaching forces must be ex-terrorists in order to be successful. It simply demonstrates that men with bush skills, working under experienced commanders, are more effective in this kind of conflict than "city soldiers."

In the past the anti-poaching unit has been reluctant to call for assistance from other services for fear that it will be seen as an admission that the situation is getting out of control. But what use is pride if there are no elephants or rhinos left? If the poachers are "anti-Kenyan," surely all Kenyans are justified in working together to oppose them?

"We don't need an army unit," said one conservationist. "Our present rangers are capable of handling the situation if they are given the right leadership."

Another who feels the present forces can do the job — if given the right motivation — is Dr. Richard Leakey. Speaking to me several months before his appointment as director of the Wildlife Department, he said the key to the problem was a recognition that Kenya's economic wellbeing was linked to the preservation of its wildlife.

"If wildlife is seen in economic terms and the consequences of [the poachers'] looting is seen in terms of Kenya's ability to meet its schedule of repayment of debts, in terms of its ability to generate hard currency to pay for oil which is propelling our electricity, then I think tough action will be taken.

"The security forces in this country are perfectly capable of stopping people uprooting coffee trees and are perfectly capable of stopping people from taking money from the central bank. It is simply that thus far wildlife has been perceived as an emotional, cuddly concept, never seen in economic terms. People are still incredulous that if you lose the elephants, or even half the remaining elephants, the tourist industry could dry up. Nobody has done the sums of that and demonstrated that it's real.

"If the authorities were convinced of the economic consequences of allowing the present deplorable situation to continue, action would be taken. Kenya has got the personnel to stop it, but there's a political price for stopping things like that. People are going to get hurt. People are going to get taken to court. Some big names are going to turn up on the list of those who were involved.

"There is a price to pay for every action and you have to evaluate the cost in terms of the price. This has not been adequately done, in my judgement, but the time has come when we must act. I think we are well into a situation where it is almost too late to do it and this is why I have been raising my voice and encouraging others to do so."

In dealing with governmental corruption, Leakey suggests that the rest of the world maintain a perspective, not of haughty moral superiority, but rather of historical understanding: "I think what is going on in much of Africa is what was going on in Europe three or four hundred years ago," he said. "It was going on in America one hundred and fifty years ago when the robber barons were getting rich by counterfeit methods in many cases. A lot of the great wealth that is now given out in philanthropy was initially generated by some very hard-nosed, not necessarily friendly, people.

"The corruption, the exploitation of opportunity that you see in Africa is a parallel with Europe moving out of the Middle Ages into the Industrial Revolution, where, suddenly, great opportunities to exploit came about . . . You can't speed it up. Basically you have to go through it. There are too many human pressures to find any way around it. What one has to do so far as wildlife is concerned . . . is to minimize the long-term damage — and that's not easy."

(Soon after his appointment as director of Kenya's Wildlife Department in 1989, Leakey was reported as saying: "The staff of the new department will have counter-guerilla training. For the first time in years, the poachers are going to find somebody opposing them. They are now going to have a real fight.")

THE INTERNATIONAL IVORY TRADE

A festering sore for conservationists until recently was Kenya's near-neighbour, Burundi, a small country between the southern tip of Lake Victoria and the northeastern shores of Lake Tanganyika. Burundi has no elephants, yet in 1986 managed to export twenty-three thousand elephant tusks. When Burundi finally signed the Convention on International Trade in Endangered Species (CITES) agreement in 1988, conservationists noted sternly that it still had eighteen thousand tusks in store — a figure which they thought might be underestimated.

The international politicking that surrounds the illegal ivory and rhino horn trades is of great concern to conservationists like Hugh Lamprey, the World Wide Fund for nature's representative in East and Central Africa. Lamprey is a genteel, grey-haired, and soft-spoken man who conveys the air of a cautious diplomat very much aware that he walks a tightrope between being an honoured guest and a bloody nuisance.

He describes Burundi as a clearing house for ivory poached in Tanzania and Zambia from the early 1970s. Ivory from Tanzania came overland to Kigoma and Ujiji, port towns on the eastern shores of Lake Tanganyika. Tusks from Zambia went to Mpulungu at the southern end of Lake Tanganyika. Rhino horn travelled by a similar route. From these port towns, the ivory and rhino horn came up the lake in small boats to Bujumbura, the capital of Burundi. There it became "legal" under Burundi law and a large amount of it accumulated with dealers — along with ivory smuggled from CITES signatories, such as Kenya and Zaire.

Lamprey said the principal dealers were Lebanese or Omanis who arranged for the ivory to be flown out by Sabena Airlines to Belgium. From there, it was dispersed to various world markets. When pressure from conservation organizations persuaded Sabena not to carry the suspect cargoes, the dealers, good businessmen all, simply made the same trade profitable for Ethiopian Airlines, which has destinations in the Middle East.

"We don't know to what extent they are still doing it," said Lamprey, "because it is very secret. Nearly all the ivory that is travelling illegally is, like firearms, in containers labelled as something else. The last container that was found coming out of Tanzania along the coast had 'Beeswax' written on the outside."

The coast route, using Mombasa or other east coast ports, is a traditional one for illegal ivory and rhino horn, which was taken by dhow to the Middle East and Asia. In the days of the slave traders, captives were used with ghastly cost efficiency. They were forced to

It is beautiful countryside indeed, but this region of the Mara River in Kenya is typical of areas where gun battles have taken place between rangers and poachers.

carry thousands of tonnes of ivory from the interior to the coast, before joining it themselves as cargo. Today, the ivory and rhino horn are likely to go to Dubai, an autonomous state of the United Arab Emirates, which has become a major staging point.

In May 1989, Tanzania seized a single consignment of seventy tonnes of ivory said to be worth about US$15 million and representing eight thousand dead elephants. It was a victory worth celebrating for the anti-poaching forces; but Costa Malay, Tanzania's director of wildlife services, was well aware that the battle was far from over.

He accused a single Hong Kong ivory trader of earning as much as US$1 million a week — a sum Malay considered impossible to earn from legal operations. The trader literally had more resources than the whole country of Tanzania. "For countries like ourselves it is difficult to fight him," mourns Malay. "He has enormous money. He is good at greasing palms and gets away with it."

Tanzania and Kenya have renewed their calls for a total ban on trade in ivory and on July 18, 1989, Kenya underlined the depth of its conviction by stacking up twelve tonnes of ivory seized from poachers and burning it. The bonfire was touched off at Nairobi National Park by President Moi.

Until relatively recently, most of the laws controlling the export of ivory from African countries were easy to circumvent. The January-February 1980 issue of the IUCN Bulletin, for example, reported that false documents were "absurdly simple to acquire." In the early 1980s, CITES sought to overcome this by forming a Technical Expert Committee to tighten controls and ensure that the procedures required under the agreement for trade in ivory were followed in a uniform way.

Hugh Lamprey described CITES's efforts as "the best we can do towards regularizing the legal side of the trade." (Ivory obtained from culled or dead elephants.) In spite of this, he estimated that half to two-thirds of the world's trading in ivory is still illegal.

In July 1988, CITES was criticized sharply by Monitor, a consortium of conservation, environmental and animal welfare organizations, for leaving too many loopholes for the slippery middlemen to wriggle through.

Monitor's executive vice-president, Craig Van Note, told a U.S. government subcommittee that it was clear the CITES attempts to control the ivory trade were not working.[4] The proof, he said, lay not only in the continued high level of trafficking in ivory . . . but most tragically in the sharp, relentless decline in virtually every elephant population in Africa.

Almost all the ivory produced in Africa in recent years had been poached, he said in the statement to the subcommittee. Legal sources were strictly limited to animals that died of natural causes or were culled in reserve population maintenance programs, or confiscations from poachers. Few elephants now lived long enough to die of old age, and only a small percentage of the ivory from natural mortality was ever found.

"The estimated eighty thousand to one hundred thousand elephants that die each year to supply the ivory trade are almost all shot or poisoned by organized gangs of poachers," he said. "The tusks are moved easily across borders and overseas.

"The fact that some of this flood of ivory gets legitimized by governments, or by CITES, doesn't make it any less poached. Once we understand the myth of 'legal' ivory and recognize the unpleasant reality that monitoring and control of the ivory trade is a failure, then we must come to the conclusion that a total international trade ban on ivory may be the only solution to the problem of elephant conservation."

Van Note said one of the largest trades of ivory in all of Africa — and flowing outside Africa to Asia — was totally unmonitored.

"Tens of thousands of tusks annually — perhaps two hundred thousand or more over the last decade — have been smuggled out of central and southern Africa without a trace. This is the South African connection."

(I obtained my copy of the Monitor information in South Africa. My source assured me vigorous attempts were being made to stop the trade, but the dealers there are as slippery as everywhere else.)

Sources for the South African ivory listed in the statement by Monitor were Angola, Zaire, Zambia, Tanzania, Zimbabwe, Mozambique, and Botswana. Monitor and others believe a massive smuggling ring has been operating in South Africa for years, with the complicity of high-placed government and military officials. None of this ivory shows up on customs books in Africa and very little at destinations in the Middle East, India, and the Far East.

"The South African military has cynically aided the virtual annihilation of the once great elephant herds of Angola," Van Note said. "Jonas Savimba and his UNITA rebel forces in Angola, largely supplied by South Africa, have ruthlessly liquidated perhaps one hundred thousand elephants to help finance the twelve-year-old conflict."

Monitor told the U.S. government subcommittee that most of the tusks had been carried out on South African air transports or trucks, although some had moved through Zaire and Burundi. For example, four-wheel-drive trucks used to supply the rebels made the return journey laden with tropical hardwood and tusks. The contraband was housed in a staging post at Runtu in the Caprivi Strip from where tractor-trailers took it across Namibia to South Africa.

Van Note claimed the Angolan ivory trafficking operation was being managed at the time by two former Portuguese colonists from Angola who had close ties to the South African military.

Monitor mentioned two other major sources of illegal ivory which it said were encouraged by South Africans.

The first is Zambia where, in recent years, more than ten thousand elephants have been poached annually in the vast Luangwa Valley. Monitor alleged that corruption at the highest levels of the government and complicity with South Africa had "brought down a wall of silence" which helped in moving the ivory south. Much of the ivory is believed to have been transported in sealed railway boxcars on a South African government railroad. A small amount went north to Burundi.

The second source is Mozambique where the South African-supported Renamo rebels killed tens of thousands of elephants to help finance an insurrection in which more than one hundred thousand civilians also died in a single decade. Again, said Monitor, the booty went to South Africa and Burundi.

Other heavy flows of ivory have been coming to South Africa from Zaire, Botswana, and Tanzania, with the preferred method of transport being the military and civilian aircraft flying north to deliver arms, medicine, food, machinery and supplies throughout central and southern Africa.

"The first rule of pilots on these flights is to never fly empty," Van Note said.

"On their return flights to South Africa, from as far as northern Zaire, they load up on contraband and other valuable cargo. Not only ivory is on board, but also gold, diamonds, cobalt, and coffee. The secretive trade route operated by the South Africans has brought more than one hundred tonnes of ivory annually into South Africa."

Most of the ivory is eventually shipped or flown to Taiwan — a non-CITES nation — and to India and China.

"An investigation of South African exports for the years 1982 and 1983 showed that ivory tusks shipped out of the country were at least ten times the amount officially imported," Van Note said. "Virtually none of the tusks generated internally by culling at Kruger National Park are exported whole. That ivory is worked in-country."

Monitor said South Africa was not the only African country where official corruption was deeply involved in the trade in poached ivory and other wildlife products. "Almost all governments in Africa — and many elsewhere — suffer from high-level corruption."

A case in point is "The French Connection" which enabled Emperor Bokassa of the Central African Republic and President Mobutu of Zaire to send planeloads of ivory to France during the era of President Giscard d'Estaing (1974-81). During Bokassa's regime, his country became the largest ivory exporter in Africa. One company, La Couronne (now disbanded), had a monopoly on ivory trading and lifted the volume dramatically until the demise of the empire in 1979. La Couronne said that 79 per cent of its ivory came from Zaire, 20.4 per cent from Sudan, and less than 1 per cent from the Central African Republic. Although the ivory from Sudan and Zaire was obtained illegally, it was always accompanied by full certification and was therefore legal according to the republic's law.

A typical smuggling operation was uncovered on October 10, 1988, when customs officers at the Kazungula ferry border post in Botswana, acting on a tip from a company manager, stopped a twenty-five-tonne truck registered in South Africa. According to its documents, the truck was carrying a load of copper ingots from Zambia to a Mr. A. H. Pong in Pretoria West. The back doors of the truck had Zambian Customs seals affixed to them.

Inside a hidden compartment the customs officers found 104 black rhino horns, about 400 elephant tusks, leopard, pangolin (a long-tailed, scaly, ant-eating mammal) and python skins, ivory bangles, malachite necklaces, bags of zinc and lead, video recorders, and diesel engine parts.

The seizure followed reports of a thriving trade in smuggled ivory, rhino horns, and precious stones through South Africa from countries to the north. The Kazangula ferry crossing over the Zambezi River, the major road link between Botswana and Zambia and Zaire, carries heavy traffic to and from South Africa.

The truck was crewed by two black drivers whom investigators considered were unaware of the real nature of the consignment. The drivers said the truck had travelled from Johannesburg to Lusaka where it dropped off a consignment. It had then continued on a route through Malawi and Zaire before returning to Lusaka. The final leg of the journey would have been from Lusaka to Kazungulu and back to Johannesburg.

Investigators checked the address given for A. H. Pong on the consignment note and could not locate the man or his company. However, they thought the business using the premises could possibly be a cover.

Checks of the transport companies used by A. H. Pong were equally confusing. In July 1988, A. H. Pong had instructed a Botswana company to give his drivers money, ostensibly for fuel. However, the trucks were usually refuelled at this company on account. The manager of the company eventually became suspicious and informed Botswana customs, thus beginning the investigation that led to the seizure of the truck.

Ten consignments were traced between July and October, roughly a week apart, operated by two transport companies. Checks showed that the companies were one and the same and that the persons involved were running at least four bogus transport operations.

Beyond that point the investigations became even more frustrating. "We know who the dealers involved in this trade are," said a South African game park official who gave me details of the seizure, "but so far we have not been able to get enough evidence to convict them."

BREAKING THE POACHING CHAIN

Poachers slay because they can sell. The African conservationist asks, "That pendant you are wearing and that carving on your desk — they're made of ivory, aren't they?"

"Yes, but I'm sure this ivory wasn't poached. I mean, the odds against that would be too great. And besides that, I bought it at a gift shop."

Guess again. As much as 90 per cent of the ivory sold internationally as trinkets, jewellery, and ornaments has been poached. If you have purchased any ivory product within the last decade, almost certainly you have been a silent partner with the poachers. To wildlife preservationists, buyers are no different from the fences or receivers who allow burglars and thieves to prosper.

As for saying, "But my ivory carving comes from Hong Kong or Malaysia or India," such a statement, as we have already seen, is terribly naive.

Like drug dealing, the illegal trade in ivory and rhino horn has high risks for high returns. There are the same clandestine operations, the same furtive meetings, the same internecine wars between rivals scrabbling for money and power. Cargoes, mislabelled or disguised, go by complicated routes to destinations where few questions are asked. Bribes exchange hands. Official eyes close. And life, human or animal, becomes very cheap indeed. "We haven't been able to stop the drug trade," critics might say, "so how do you expect to shut down ivory or rhino horn trafficking?" But drugs are physically addictive. The "need" for anyone to own ivory is based either on an aesthetic appreciation of its beauty or on greed of possession. Both motivations can be resisted.

This foul trade has to be fought at every link in its distribution chain, but two areas presently seem to promise the greatest chances of success — the dealers and the buyers.

Why not with poachers themselves? The chain begins, of course, with the poachers; but starting there to end the trade has not worked to this point. Hundreds more are waiting to take the places of those who are shot or arrested. There are too many of them and — let's face it — they're the small fry.

To be successful, poaching has to be made unprofitable — not only by increasing the risks, but by cutting the profits. The first promising place to do this is at the government level through international cooperation, import controls, and sanctions that will hit the dealers and middlemen.

The late David Sheldrick, who led a vigorous and successful campaign against poaching during his time at Tsavo, also singled out the middlemen as the most likely target and once wrote:

"The [black market] dealers are the weak link in the whole chain. There are comparatively few of them and they are well known. Furthermore, they are very vulnerable while collecting and transporting trophies. What is needed is an incorruptible, dedicated team of investigators to run these people to earth. If dealers can be eliminated, the entire network will be disturbed, and poaching once again reduced to manageable proportions."

The second area of promise is that of the buyer. Through public education programs, the World Wide Fund for Nature and other conservation groups are trying to eliminate the market for poached ivory and rhino horn products.

The big difficulty here is that the small legal trade is a source of income that it is hard to deny some of the poorer countries. However, it gives the middlemen a loophole. Documents can be faked, or obtained by bribery, so that "dirty" products can be laundered through the system.

Nehemiah K. Arap Rotich, the executive director of the East African Wildlife Society, in November, 1988, recommended that people outside Africa support a total ban on trade in ivory and rhino horn products, which, in the case of ivory, should last for at least twenty years.

"A very serious issue with elephants is the fact that they don't start putting on the real bulk of their ivory until after the age of forty — say, between forty and forty-five," he told me. "During their early life, most of their energy goes into their bones and growing.

"If you check the elephants that are being killed now you will find that they are not even forty, they are below that. "The other, more serious thing, is that elephants don't start breeding until about the age of thirty . . . because until then they are not mature enough. If they are killed before they reach that age, there is really no chance.

The way most of Uganda's elephants have gone — to poachers' bullets. Wildlife worker Rick Weyerhaeuser surveys the carnage at Queen Elizabeth National Park. (Photo, Iain Douglas-Hamilton — WWF Photolibrary)

"I have some photographs here of recent poaching" — he spread them out on his desk — "you'll be horrified because what's happening is that they're not just shooting the ones with tusks. Look at this one, it's just the young stuff . . ."

Rotich — and others — would like to see a ban on all ivory and rhino horn sales long enough to restore normal breeding patterns and they appeal directly to buyers to stop supporting the trade.

"If the consumers know they have exterminated a very beautiful animal out in Africa, I think it will make a difference," said Rotich. "I really think so."

This is not just a sentimental or moralistic appeal. The scarcity of ivory and rhino horn has pushed prices so high that unless demand falls poachers will continue their killing until the last of the animals have gone.

In mid-1989 the ivory ban call from Kenya and Tanzania gained a major ally when U.S. President George Bush announced that the United States would ban imports of elephant ivory from all countries. The United States is one of the world's biggest markets for ivory.

The don't-buy campaign could be internationalized by introducing trade sanctions on countries dealing with products from rare and endangered species. Within individual countries, boycotts and protests could target sellers, further reducing the market.

During my time in Africa, several people told me that ban-the-ivory proposals would unfairly penalize suppliers dealing in ivory obtained legally from animals that die of natural causes or are culled in national parks. However, the very existence of "legal" products fuels the illegal trade as well. Painful as it might be, a total ban would be better than what is happening now. Alternatives to ivory and rhino horn do exist, but once the animals are gone, they are gone forever. A ban now that saves the animals can always be renegotiated later.

Individuals can also help by refusing to buy living animals or products from animals that are endangered or threatened. If you want to know what they are, get in touch with the WWF office nearest you (the addresses are listed at the back of this book).

The United States is the wildlife trade's largest single market, representing at least US$1 billion in imports and exports of live animals and animal products from endangered species every year. However, the WWF estimates that as much as one-quarter of the trade could be illegal under U.S. law.

The WWF maintains that in 1986, at least half the belts, purses, and other products made from crocodile skin found in U.S. markets had been imported illegally. As many as one hundred thousand parrots were thought to have been brought in to the U.S. illegally in 1987.

We all need to ask more questions — consumers and retailers — to lessen the possibility of our unwitting contribution to one of the world's most shameful trades.

There is no denying the beauty of this carved ivory on display in Hong Kong, but it is prompting an international cry of outrage. Unless people stop buying such ornaments the elephant is doomed to extinction. (Photo, Jim Thorsell — WWF Photolibrary)

The road over the Caprivi Strip, a finger of Namibia extending north of Botswana, is a route frequently used by poachers and smugglers.

Big tuskers are rich pickings for poachers whose illegal actions ultimately indulge the whims of those who buy ivory ornaments and jewellery.

[1]"Eyewitness Account," *The Weekly Review*, Nairobi, September 9, 1988, p.14.

[2]"African Wildlife Resource," Malcolm Lee, in *Conservation Biology — an evolutionary ecological perspective*, edited by Michael E. Soulé and Bruce A. Wilcox, 1980, p.277.

[3]"Elephant Killings: Bosses Identified," Odongo Odoyo, *The Standard*, Nairobi, October 19, 1988, p.1.

[4]Monitor is a conservation, environmental and animal welfare consortium based in Washington, D.C. On July 14, 1988, it made a statement on U.S. enforcement of the Convention on International Trade in Endangered Species of Wild Fauna and Flora to the Sub-committee on Oversight and Investigations of the House Merchant Marine and Fisheries Committee. The statement was made on behalf of fourteen environmental and animal welfare organizations.

CHAPTER EIGHT
A Place for the Animals

Mount Kilimanjaro sits hunched on the horizon in the pastel dawn, a mantle of orange, yellow, and mauve clouds layered about its pale blue shoulders. The first probings of the sun pick out stubborn streaks of snow along the mountain's highest ridges and set in silhouette the wildebeest and zebra studding the carpet of bleached yellow grass that stretches from its foothills to infinity.

The only sounds in the half-light, as we set up our cameras outside the hut where I had just spent my first night in an African park, are the soft tearings and munchings of grazing animals and the occasional whicker as one of them pauses between mouthfuls or drifts to a more tempting clump. At the back of my mind lurks the knowledge that also out there are predators, but they too are part of the beauty of Africa. But in spite of the inevitability of violence and death, a great sense of peace and purity broods over all. There is a timeless magic in the air — the subtle seduction of Africa.

The early morning breeze is sharpened by the chill that heralds the short rains, the prelude to the true wet season; but by midday the breath of late summer will be sucking greedily at any moisture it can find and sheets of dust will sail before the wind and blanket everything in a grey pallor.

This is Amboseli National Park in Kenya, once regarded as one of Africa's wildlife showpieces, but now recognized as a park in trouble. Amboseli is reeling under a twin assault: its local human neighbours are encroaching on its borders, and a flood of tourists are bringing in much-needed foreign currency but exacting a high price of their own. Amboseli today is a park struggling to avoid becoming a desert.

Far off to the right, the sun flares on a windshield as an early-rising party of tourists heads for a stand of trees and the chance to photograph some elephants. Behind them spirals a plume of dust which hangs in the still air. A short distance away is another miniature tornado and another and another . . . a fifth and a sixth angle in from the side. The drivers have broken one of the park's rules and left the trail to take a short-cut across a flat bed of dried mud. Six mini-bus-loads of tourists hurtling pell-mell across the seared landscape, their drivers trying to get to the best spots first so their clients will get the most interesting pictures and pay the biggest tips.

Several mornings and many kilometres later, a

dragon-like snort awakes me from sleep at Salt Lick Lodge on the fringe of Kenya's Tsavo National Park. Much of the lodge is built on piles and I had fallen asleep to the sounds of animals passing by below me, en route to nearby water holes. But this new sound was like no animal I'd heard before — and it wasn't coming from below, but somewhere above.

Quickly I tugged on my trousers, snatched up my camera, and dashed outside. At first I saw nothing. Then an orange and yellow hot air balloon drifted slowly into view above the roof and angled down to a round concrete pad a few metres away. As it neared the ground, I heard the roaring sound again when the operator fired the propane burner to slow the descent. The passengers waved to someone on the ground and raised their cameras.

Tourists again. Throughout Africa they stalk the animals from motor vehicles, boats, aircraft, balloons — and even on foot in the parks with nature trails. Their presence is tangible proof of the fascination Africa exerts on the rest of the world and is a major source of revenue for some of the poorest nations on Earth. Tourists and animals have a symbiotic relationship in Africa, but it is not a simple one. Do the parks exist for the wildlife or for the tourists? And how do you maintain a balance between the needs of both?

THE "IDEAL" PARK

Various models have been proposed for the "ideal" park. While these models often differ widely from each other, most share three things: a safe refuge for the animals, plants, or protected features; unobtrusive access for tourists; and involvement of local people in wildlife maintenance projects.

In general, an ideal animal park is regarded as being large enough for them to live as normally as possible. During the day, water holes, salt licks, and other attractions entice wildlife to the fringes where tourist facilities such as lodges, trails, and viewing areas are maintained. At night the animals retreat to inner sanctuaries closed off to all humans but park staff.

In some models, a cleared buffer zone, patrolled by armed guards, encloses the entire park. In others, the buffer is provided by farms, private game sanctuaries, tribal lands and projects, all of which are integrated with park activities. The thinking here is that if local people benefit from the park and its wildlife and come

to identify with it, they will no longer see the wildlife as a nuisance or a resource to be used.

Giving them a sense of involvement will, it is hoped, turn them into supporters rather than poachers, opponents, or passive onlookers. "Any project that doesn't involve the local people is unlikely to succeed," comments Hugh Lamprey.

HOW BIG SHOULD A PARK BE?

Of all the land on Earth, we have set aside only 3 per cent for the animals as national parks, reserves, and other protected areas. Generally, this is land we didn't want at the time, but our expanding population is now nibbling relentlessly at the edges of these sanctuaries too.

Nearly all the nations of the Afrotropical Realm[1] have devoted much more than 3 per cent of their land to wildlife reserves — some have even exceeded 10 per cent — but they are now feeling the same pressures as the rest of the world.

The 1985 United Nations list of national parks and protected areas notes that 4.4 per cent of the Afrotropical Realm, or 88 million hectares, is included in 426 parks and reserves. (Another 150 are being considered.) African governments spend about US$150 million on managing these areas and the species they contain.

These protected areas include mountains, forests, deserts, savannas, lakes, and ocean coastline. Some protect mammals, others fish, birds, butterflies, and plants of a variety that almost defies description. Others mark areas of historical or scientific interest and a rare few have been declared Natural World Heritage Sites.

There was an early bias toward savanna areas and larger mammals — possibly an after-effect of the initial interest in game and trophy animals. Now there is a conscious effort to include all land types and cater to a fuller spread of species in protected areas.

It was noted earlier that the ideal park for animals should be large enough for them to live as normal a life as possible. This creates many problems. For a start, what does "large enough" mean? If the park is too big, politicians will complain about wasteful use of land. If it's too small, scientists and conservationists will say that it cannot sustain the plants and animals.

One formula that is used to produce a viable minimum size is to work out the lowest secure population for the various plant and animal species and then estimate the area of land required for each. The requirements of the species most needing protection are then scaled up to the point where a workable compromise is reached for the majority.

If a population level of five thousand is regarded as being acceptable, this can make for some very large "minimum-sized" reserves. Leopards, for example, could be as rare as one every ten square kilometres in a rain forest. This means an impossibly large reserve of five million hectares would be required for the ideal safe population. One of the most common alternatives is to settle for outbreeding leopards by moving them about between different undersized populations.

Another method of determining ideal park size is to study small islands to see what nature has done to produce balanced populations in a limited area. Researchers have found that each island has its point of equilibrium and will usually return to this in spite of artificial tinkering, such as adding or removing species. As a general rule, a tenfold increase in the land area of an island is required to double the population securely.

The island approach is of great interest to African countries because increasingly their reserves are becoming "islands" surrounded by farms and settlements.

The IUCN believes there is still sufficient land area in larger countries to sustain parks of around fifty thousand hectares, but compromise is the rule in smaller countries. For example, reserves can be buffered with areas of partially protected natural

habitat; smaller reserves can be linked by protected corridors; or transfrontier reserves can be formed with neighbouring countries.

The majority of the 426 protected areas in the Afrotropical Realm were established only twenty-five to thirty years ago, often being upgraded from less-developed forms of protected area. But the oldest reserves in Africa are a cluster of three now administered by the Natal Parks Board in South Africa. The Hluhluwe and Umfolozi Game Reserves were proclaimed in 1895 and with the nearby St. Lucia Game Reserve were legislated into existence on April 27, 1897 — one year before what was to become Kruger National Park.

Originally, Hluhluwe and Umfolozi were separate. Now they are linked by a fenced animal corridor, effectively making them one reserve.

A massive extension of St. Lucia was announced recently, and in Niger the newly established Aïr and Ténéré National Reserve covers some 7.7 million hectares.

As impressive as this array of protected areas sounds, Africa is immense, and the parks, reserves, sanctuaries, and conservation areas are collectively little more than a token offering to the animal and plant kingdoms. Some are too small to be viable in a natural sense. In many instances, park boundaries have been established to suit political rather than environmental interests.

Some African countries have highly developed park systems, while in others former wildlife havens lie in ruins after wars, poaching raids, and environmental disasters. There are parks that cover more than a million hectares and there are the tiny pockets of

Wildebeest in the lush setting of Hluhluwe Game Reserve, Natal, South Africa.

specialized reserves that can be travelled in an hour or two. Some are remote and difficult to visit. Others are right in the heart of tourist country and are major contributors to national coffers.

But national parks, whatever country they may be in, are not resources that can be milked indefinitely. They need regular injections of funds if they are to be maintained and developed adequately and if the animals are to be protected from poachers and other human intrusions. The amount of money required is downright scary and most of the African countries either haven't got it, or are spending it elsewhere. This emphasis on tourism makes many conservationists uneasy. "What happens if the tourists stop coming?" they ask. "Will the governments then forget the animals and make other use of the land?"

BIG PARKS COST BIG MONEY

Dr. John Hanks, one of the world's leading authorities on the elephant and rhinoceros, points out that conservation staff in southern Africa believe the minimum annual expenditure for protected area management programs to be effective throughout most of eastern, central and southern Africa is US$200 per square kilometre.[2]

The example he uses to illustrate this point is Zambia, a country with approximately 160,000 square kilometres of protected areas. Using the US$200-per-square-kilometre formula, Zambia's annual expenditure should be in the region of US$32.1 million, a sum clearly far beyond its resources when there are so many human needs to address as well.

Faced with this dilemma, an understandable response is to satisfy the human demands as much as possible and make token payments to the animal causes as a sign of good intent. But it's not that easy. Hanks claims that if the US$200 per square kilometre level is not attained, the chances of failure are high for the token conservation effort and much, if not all, of the funds spent will have been wasted. For the African nations this presents a terrible choice — all, or nothing. Without regular maintenance, even the best of roads, huts, motor vehicles, tools, and other equipment will waste away. Without supervision of the parks, the poachers will have a free hand and the land will be overrun by the local population who will drain away what little nourishment it has for plants or animals.

Hanks maintains this is happening already.

"The required resources of manpower and equipment to protect wild populations have been completely inadequate," he says. "The total financial allocations to wildlife conservation in Africa other than South Africa in 1981 (the most recent figure available) was a mere US$75 million, with about as much again spent in South Africa [Bell and Clarke, 1986].

"The majority of these funds came from national government subventions rather than from external donations. There are now far too many game reserves and national parks in Africa which are inadequately financed, and which do not have anywhere near an adequate complement of trained, equipped, and motivated staff. As a consequence, poaching is out of control, and the basic park or reserve infrastructure and management have collapsed.

Kudu bull at Hluhluwe and the herd he is guarding.

"Both at the national and international level, conservation agencies have seriously underestimated the costs of effective protected area management programs."

Dr. Hugh Lamprey, the WWF representative in eastern and central Africa, supports the US$200 formula and believes that with the exception of South Africa, most of the African nations are spending less than US$20 a square kilometre on their protected wildlife lands.

"There are great variations between the parks," he said, "but nine-tenths of them are run on funding that is between 1 per cent and 10 per cent of what they need to function efficiently. While anti-poaching measures are the number one concern at the moment, there is still a great deal to be done each year to maintain roads and other facilities. Tsavo, I believe, is operating on US$10-20 per square kilometre a year."

But Tsavo is no ordinary park. It is enormous — like the Kruger National Park in South Africa, the Serengeti in Tanzania and Etosha in Namibia, it is larger than many small countries. Working on Lamprey's high figure of US$20 a square kilometre, about US$416,000 is being spent each year on basic maintenance, whereas the formula would indicate that this is only a tenth of what Tsavo needs. The true annual requirement would be more than US$4 million. But Tsavo is only one park in a country with many — each with needs of its own. The total bill soon reaches a horrific level for a country whose financial resources are sorely stretched already.

Clearly, Kenya needs help, but there is a considerable amount of pride in this country, which is held up by many as the great example of democracy in Africa. Kenyans want to be seen to handle their own affairs without interference from outside.

On the other side of the debate, outside aid agencies require assurances that any funds donated to aid wildlife will not only go to that cause in total, but be spent wisely.

Another big problem is how to convince Kenya's people with their many needs that taking care of the animals now will help humans later. In this they are not alone. Although many of the comments following about poverty, lack of resources and forced choices between the needs of wildlife and humans are based on Kenyan experiences, they could just as easily apply to many other African countries. The list of threatened parks at the end of this chapter shows just how widespread the problems are.

Generally, money is so scarce that even working for the government of an African country is not as financially secure as an equivalent post in a Western bureaucracy. For example, Lamprey claims that the wages of a Ugandan game scout today are, in real terms, only 1 per cent of those paid twenty years ago. In Kenya, as elsewhere, many civil servants do not receive a living wage and are forced to look to outside employment to supplement their earnings. Some, inevitably, abuse their positions, getting into conflicts of interest, or even turning to poaching.

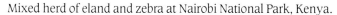

Mixed herd of eland and zebra at Nairobi National Park, Kenya.

Profuse vegetation covers the slopes of the Ngorongoro Crater, Tanzania. One of the most interesting wildlife areas on earth, it is now part of a World Heritage Site.

An obvious tourist is subjected to frequent demands for money in the streets of Nairobi, and major hotels have notices warning about bag and necklace snatchers. I soon learned that when I didn't want to be bothered I should dress and act like a local businessman.

At the international airport, visitors are reminded by other notices and officials that it is illegal to take Kenyan funds from the country. The airport staff regard this law as a windfall and are quick to find ways of relieving travellers of their excess money.

The walk from check-in counter to departure lounge is through an avenue of outstretched palms. Even the departure tax cannot be paid in Kenyan currency or travellers' cheques. The officials demand $20 in U.S. bills, or the equivalent in British currency.

With money in such short supply, conservationists are exerting pressures of their own in the hope of encouraging more efficient use of what funds are available. Among them is Dr. Richard Leakey, chairman of the East African Wildlife Society and director of the National Museums of Kenya. Dr. Leakey cheerfully admits being provocative to get action from the government. He has described the majority of Kenya's national parks and reserves as being "overrun by unplanned and awful roads, sprawling lodges, encroaching cattle and rampant corruption at entry points where vital revenue is lost."[3]

"The authorities are spending some 80 per cent of the available financial resources on personnel costs while these people have totally inadequate equipment to use for road maintenance, anti-poaching and the policing of over-zealous tour guides and drivers," he said.

"As an industry, the wildlife sector is in very serious trouble and it will take great efforts to put things right again."

ON THE ROAD AGAIN

African countries (other than South Africa) may be poor in terms of equipment, but they are rich in manpower. A Westerner who encounters a gang of workmen digging a drainage trench at the roadside would expect to see two or three men with a mechanical digger to do the hard labour and a flagperson or two directing the traffic. In many parts of Africa the digger is often replaced by a long line of men with picks and shovels, each toiling away on a section of the trench.

In the parks, only the most basic work is carried out on the roads and the situation is worsened in savanna areas by drivers who frequently flout the law by driving off the road in pursuit of game to view or photograph. This destroys the fragile grassland and hacks up the countryside with wheel ruts. However, when the land alongside the road looks smoother than the road itself, the temptation to stray is very strong.

In October 1988, we experienced the approach roads to Amboseli National Park in Kenya and decided they were not worthy of the name. The smoother parts were sun-baked washboards that threatened to shake cars and vans to pieces, and many of the potholes every few yards were deep enough to break an axle. It was like driving over the waves of a frozen ocean.

At one stage the bumping and crashing was so bad we didn't notice that our combi's roof hatch had been torn away until several miles after the event. We drove back to look for it and although another driver told us

he had found it in the middle of the road and propped it against the verge, we never saw it again.

Orange dust coiled up behind us and descended in sheets through the hole in the roof whenever the van slowed to negotiate a particularly bad pothole. Several times we had to turn the windshield wipers on to sweep the dust aside like water as it flowed down the front of the van.

Once, after becoming airborne for a metre or so en route to Tsavo, we noticed a new wobble and realized we now had a puncture. That would have been no problem except that the back door of the van had been wrenched so much we couldn't open it to remove the spare.

A happy crowd of Kenyans gathered to lend some sympathy and whatever assistance they could. Among them was a man who said he was a mechanic. With his help we unbolted the back seat and lifted it high enough to drag the spare tire out from underneath. Other helpers scurried about putting rocks behind wheels and pumping on the jack handle. Soon we were ready to continue our lurching progress. Hans tipped our mechanic friend and gave him some extra money to distribute equally among the others.

"What about the old man?" The mechanic pointed to a wiry individual with grizzled hair and a round face split by a gap-toothed grin.

"Give him some too," said Hans. But the mechanic protested. It seemed that by some locally defined right of seniority the old man should get more. Hans handed

over another one hundred shillings, anxious to get on our way again. Eventually we arrived at Kilaguni Lodge in Tsavo soon after dusk, coated bright orange by the dust which had caked the inside of the van and penetrated our luggage and bags of camera gear.

But that wasn't the end of it for me. I had done most of the driving without discomfort, but when I slid out of the van for the last time, my back seized up in terrible pain which lasted for more than a week.

"Amboseli lumbar," said government wildlife adviser, Bill Woodley, as he smiled knowingly the next day. His wife presented me with a spare tube of back rub imported from Britain.

Kilaguni Lodge at Tsavo marked the end of a long and rough journey, but the pay off for me came on my first morning there when I winced over to the dining area around 6 A.M. Tables were set out on a covered verandah overlooking artificial water holes and salt licks designed to lure animals into easy viewing range. I sat spellbound for more than an hour as the sunrise bathed the background hills and the area before me in glowing shades of orange, pink, and red. Way over on the horizon, Kilimanjaro was still present in the thinnest of blue outlines and down at the water holes there was plenty of activity from elephants, buffaloes, gazelles, baboons, and a host of colourful birds. Some of the birds came right up to the verandah in search of sandwich trimmings and kitchen scraps set out for them by lodge staff.

The lodge was about half an hour from the Nairobi-

Mombasa highway which offered prospects of easier driving. However, we soon discovered that the back roads weren't the only ones in poor repair. On long sections of the highway, the paving, which looked as if it had been laid directly on the hard-packed red clay, was crumbling from the edges. In many stretches the highway was barely wide enough to take opposing lanes of traffic.

On some of the steeper climbs, heavy trucks had gouged fifteen-centimetre-deep ruts in the seal. Cars caught in them were held as firmly as wagons on a railroad.

Sometimes the conditions were too tough even for the trucks. It was common to find a broken-down rig with its crew dozing underneath in the shade, awaiting rescue, a few branches plucked from roadside bushes strewn about to warn drivers of the hazard ahead. Also frequent was the sight of trucks that had run off the road and overturned. Some were still smoking from fires that had partially consumed them; others were rusted reminders of past misadventures.

One of the saddest sights of all was the body of a young giraffe lying in a pool of blood at the edge of the road after being mown down trying to cross the highway — a symbol of the conflict between Africa Past and Africa Present.

Fringe-eared oryx group at Tsavo National Park, Kenya.

PRIVATIZING THE PARKS

In 1986, Kenya earned 4,900 million shillings, about US$288 million, from tourism — the major attraction, of course, being the wildlife. That year saw a record high of 614,200 arrivals, and the target announced for 1989 was one million visitors a year.[4] However, exports such as tea and coffee still account for the major portion of Kenya's earnings. In spite of all these assets, in 1987 Kenya recorded a deficit of $US360 million. That debt creates pressure for tourism earnings to be channelled into debt servicing, rather than conservation.

Kenya's population of more than 19 million is growing by a resource-stretching 4.1 per cent a year. The money to provide basic services has to come from somewhere, and a large amount of it appears to be provided by the tourists who come to see the wildlife and sights of more than fifty reserves and protected areas throughout the country. Are the animals earning their keep? Yes, but they're not always the ones to benefit from it. Conservationists in Nairobi believe only about 5 per cent of what is earned from tourism is used to help wildlife.

The generally run-down nature of the parks has caused many conservationists to think back to the days when the parks were administered fairly efficiently under British control. Several have suggested a return to those ways, or at least a revamping of the administrative system.

Leakey, in his role as chairman of the East African Wildlife Society, headquartered in Nairobi, several times advocated the semi-privatization of the management of parks and reserves.

"Let us recognize that the (Kenyan) national parks could be made to work on a profit-earning basis," he said in the society's magazine, *Swara*. "Efficiency, discipline and sound wildlife management could be better done by an authority established by the government but separate from it.

"Such an authority could pay better salaries, regulate prices to match market demand, and provide for more effective management because of its own self-interest. A well-run parks service would attract more visitors, bring in more money, and, in the course of time, pay a useful surplus to the central exchequer.

"The success of the agricultural sector of Kenya's economy is directly tied to the efficient and market-oriented private sector. The government is the beneficiary, directly and indirectly. The management of the very basis of tourism, our wildlife and natural heritage, must improve if tackled in the same way."

In his new role as director of Kenya's Wildlife Department, which has been restructured as a semi-independent body in charge of the parks, Leakey will have an opportunity to test his theories.

Another who expressed concern to us about the way the parks had been administered was conservationist Daphne Sheldrick, foster mother to animal orphans. She was deeply involved in Tsavo's management during the thirty years her husband was warden of Tsavo East and believes Kenya's national parks were operated more efficiently under boards of trustees, a system abolished in 1976 in favour of government control.

"Poaching has got worse and worse every single year," she said. "More and more Somalis are coming in from the north. Greedier and greedier people are getting on the bandwagon. The wildlife department itself has been absolutely ineffectual and has turned to corruption because they have been so starved of funds since the government took over the national parks . . .

"Since then, all the revenue that's generated by the parks — just millions — goes direct to the treasury and very little comes back into the national parks. What does come back only pays salaries.

"In the old days, the colonial days, the headquarters of the wildlife department consisted of fifteen people at the most and then, of course, everyone was out in the field. Do you know how many people are there now? [October, 1988] Four thousand! So there is this huge employment. Everyone is grabbing salaries. There's no money to run the vehicles, no money for maintenance of the roads, no money for field allowances for the anti-poaching forces.

"Morale is so low that these people think, 'Well, my God! If these big boys in the country are making a fortune out of these animals, what about us? We'd better go and get some too because they are not going to last at this rate.'"

SOUTH AFRICA SETS A HIGH STANDARD

The situation is much different in South Africa. In spite of the republic's history of over-hunting and even the extermination of some species, it has a proud conservation record and an excellent parks system.

Today, the IUCN regards South Africa's parks as

being "as good as anywhere in the African continent and better than in many other countries of the world."[5]

It also says that South Africa is in no need of international assistance to manage its protected areas and is ideally placed to provide technical assistance and training to other African nations.

However, the political tensions in Africa are such that I doubt whether this help would be accepted. I can still remember making the mistake of stepping off an aircraft from Johannesburg at Nairobi and being harangued for nearly half an hour by an entry official who accused me of "doing business with the South Africans." He told me he was not going to let me into Kenya.

I said I had already been in twice in the last month on my tour of parks, but he said: "Then you dealt with other people — now you have to deal with me."

The only way I got in this time was by letting him complete his tirades and asking him politely to "repeat the question please." I did it three times before he screamed at me and waved me through. While I am opposed to apartheid, I would also hate to see political differences interfere with the fight to save wildlife.

Politics cannot change the fact that the oldest existent reserves in Africa are administered by the Natal Parks Board in South Africa.

Hluhluwe and Umfolozi are now linked by their corridor, allowing animals to roam from one park to the other in a semblance of free range. However, the complex is one where populations have to be monitored carefully even though the combined area is more than seventy thousand hectares (Umfolozi 47,753 and Hluhluwe 25,091).

But size isn't everything. One potentially misleading argument that is used to excuse low contributions to the big parks is that they are ecosystems large enough to sustain themselves. All the human custodians have to do, it is said, is be prepared to work in with the long, slow cycles of nature which will regulate herd numbers and restore balance in spite of such things as the occasional shocks caused by climate and disease.

There are other factors involved though. In recent years, the Tsavo ecosystem has been invaded by thousands of domestic cattle and goats that are dominating water sources and stripping forage from areas previously reserved for wildlife. As a further blow to the park, roads built for tourists are helping poachers make their raids and getaways. Other parks face similar human interference.

South Africa's Kruger National Park is huge too — 1,948,528 hectares — but much of its water is supplied by feeder rivers which flow into the park from outside and are subject to agricultural and industrial usage and pressures beyond the park's control. Pollution has become a serious problem, and through the years the park has been engaged in a constant search for water supplies of its own.

The lack of water is not the only difficulty facing Kruger. The park has become surrounded by settlements, farms, and other human undertakings which have cut the animals off from traditional migration routes through the region. The park has also been enclosed with eight hundred kilometres of fence strong enough to keep elephants in check. As a result, it has become more of a sanctuary than a park and culling programs have been introduced to keep wildlife numbers in balance. Today problems persist, but an accord is being reached between interest groups in which game-farming ventures are flourishing and some farmers cooperate with park staff to provide private sanctuaries for endangered species.

Dry river bed, Namibia.

215

The 2,227,000-hectare Etosha National Park in Namibia has been mauled by poachers who have plundered ivory, slaughtered animals for meat, and generally contributed greatly to the instability of the area. The park is frequently troubled by droughts, and boundary fences erected primarily to keep domestic animals out have caused serious disturbances to wildlife migratory patterns, particularly among wildebeest. In the last twenty-five years wildebeest numbers have fallen from twenty-five thousand to twenty-three hundred.

Deep gravel pits were dug to provide lime for tourist roads. The pits filled with water after the rains and became infected with anthrax, a disease fatal to herbivores.

In the 5,180,000-hectare Central Kalahari Game Reserve in Botswana, man has taken a terrible toll of wildlife by an expedient which at first seemed more humane than bullets or poison. Domestic stock were considered at risk from foot and mouth disease thought to be carried by wildlife, so the two groups were separated by erecting many miles of veterinary fences.

Not only did the fences keep the wildlife away from the domestic stock, but in times of drought they also cut the wild animals off from their traditional water supplies. Researchers have since reported that wildebeest are required to make round trips of up to one hundred kilometres every time they need to travel from grazing areas to water. Many thousands of them never make it. Some collapse and die in the heat and others get tangled up in the fences in desperate bids for water.

Douglas and Jane Williamson, who began studying the area in 1981, reported densities of wildebeest carcasses at times exceeding fifty per hectare.[6] In 1983, fifty thousand died. Although zebra once grazed in that part of the Kalahari, none have been seen since the late 1960s when the first serious droughts occurred after the erection of the fences.

Besides contributing to the disappearance of zebra and the plight of the wildebeest, the Williamsons believe the fences have kept out species that formerly migrated into the northern Kalahari during times when water was plentiful. Among these they list elephant, rhino, buffalo, roan, sable, and tsessebe. But the final blow in this exercise in futility was that the fences were unable to do what they were intended to do, halt the spread of disease.

"Etosha," meaning "big white place," was the name given by Owambo tribesmen to the ancient dried lake bed, or pan, that is now the dominant feature of the Etosha National Park in Namibia. The pan covers an area 129 kilometres long and 72 kilometres wide in the eastern half of the park and becomes so hot and dry that mirages are common. However, in years of exceptional rainfall, illusion gives way to reality and the pan is covered by water a few centimetres deep, bringing to life the crustaceans and other organisms lying dormant in the usually dry lake bed.

A springbok takes advantage of the slice of shadow offered by a dead tree in a landscape smitten by the lack of water. The Kalahari sands have a low clay content and are so porous that most of the surface water drains away.

The shrivelled remains of a wildebeest provide mute testimony to the perils of straying too far from water. Thousands of animals die every year in regions where livestock fences have cut them off from traditional water sources.

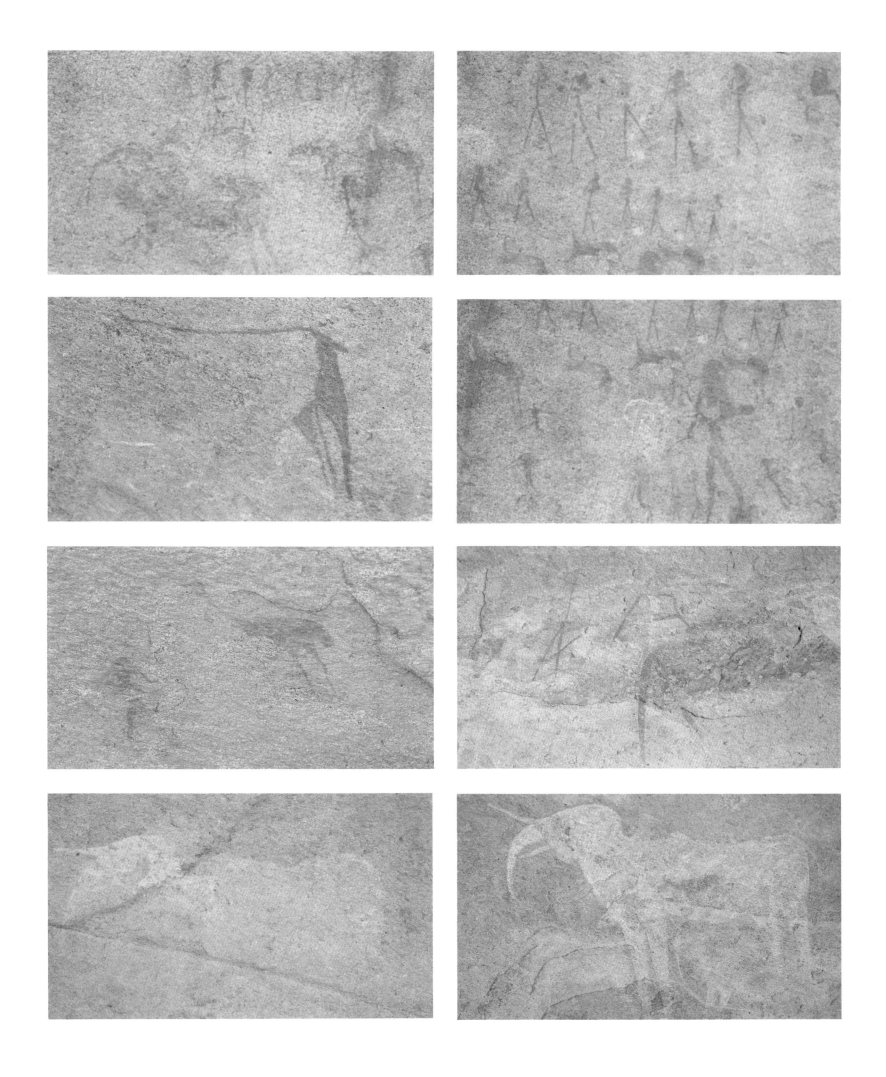

The gemsbok and springbok can go without water for long periods, but in the dry season at Etosha National Park, water is enjoyed wherever it is found.

The animals too await the coming of the rains. Many wildebeest die of thirst each year in Etosha National Park.

Etosha's elephants have smaller tusks than their Central and East African fellows, but this could well be a blessing in disguise. Poaching is not as severe in Namibia as elsewhere, possibly because the ivory is not as rewarding.

The aboriginal people of Australia have a word for it — Dreamtime — that mystical period at creation's dawn, when man was anxiously establishing his place on earth under the watchful eye of temperamental gods. Hans Strohhacker relived part of that experience when he visited a shallow cave that could perhaps be described more accurately as a huge crack in a Namibian mountainside. There, at the deepest part of the cave where the ceiling was too low to allow him to stand, he found these petroglyphs on the ceiling. As he lay on his back, attempting to focus his camera in the semi-gloom, he could not help feeling a kinship with the artists who had wriggled into that same notch in the rock thousands of years ago. The hike to the mountainside and the climb to the cave had taken several hours. By the time Hans arrived, he was hot and tired, so he peeled off excess clothing, stretched out in a cool part of the cave and went to sleep. When he awoke he began to explore. Near the cave mouth, which was about three metres high at the top of its curve, he found some primitive tools which a previous visitor had discovered and left on display. The cave was very wide, but ran only twenty-five metres into the mountainside before petering out in the artists' gallery. Nevertheless, it had been either home or waystation to countless other travellers over the millenia. Hans spent five fascinating hours in the cave, exploring and wondering about these people. Who were they? What was life like for them? Where did they go? The petroglyphs demonstrate the importance of animals in the life of these early hunter-nomads. Presumably, they left the area when it became barren and the game moved to lusher feeding grounds. The view of the outside world through the cave mouth is of a fallen crescent of barren, rocky slopes. But it wasn't always like that. The animals depicted on the cave ceiling once roamed outside in much greater numbers than today. Questions, wonderings, dreams — the cave was a timeless place where the five hours could have as easily been five minutes or five days. There are scores of similar caves in the same area just off the Swakopmund — Okahandja Road not far from Windhoek. Many of them contain similar paintings — perhaps an even more impressive display, but Hans's time in "his" cave is something he will never forget.

THE SERENGETI — AFRICA IN MICROCOSM

Wildebeest are able to thrive on short grasses so low in food value that domestic cattle would struggle to stay alive.

The African park which comes closest to being able to look after itself is also one of those most beset by the pressures of the surrounding human population with its attendant cattle and goats — the 1.4 million-hectare Serengeti National Park in Tanzania. Here the scientific community has been busily engaged at the Seronera Research Centre since 1962 and wildlife champions have fought some of their most stirring battles. So far as tourists are concerned, the Serengeti provides more of the images a visitor expects to see in Africa than just about any other park. Even the name, Serengeti, conjures images of the mysterious and exotic.

The Serengeti is worth singling out for closer study because it is Africa in microcosm — a working model with negative and positive lessons for the other wildlife areas on the continent.

The park began in 1929 when 228,600 hectares of the central Serengeti were declared a game reserve. It became a protected area in 1940 and a national park in 1951. The Serengeti underwent extensive boundary changes in 1959, partly to accommodate pastoral tribes on its borders, and was included with the adjoining Maswa Game Reserve as part of the 2.3 million-hectare Serengeti-Ngorongoro Biosphere Reserve in 1981. That same year it became part of a World Heritage Site. Only the international border to the north separates it from the Maasai Mara National Reserve in Kenya.

Like most parks in Africa, the Serengeti is beset by problems and at times its continued existence has been in doubt, yet it can still provide the most stirring wildlife spectacles on Earth. Among these is the huge annual migration of wildebeest and zebra north to the Maasai Mara in the July-October dry season.

More than two million large animals roam the Serengeti's woodlands and the undulating grassy plains which are its major vegetation. These include wildebeest — about 1.6 million of them — at least two hundred and fifty thousand Thomson's gazelles, many prides of lions, spotted hyaenas and two hundred thousand zebras. Supplementing these is a great diversity of other animals which complete the image of one of the world's greatest wildlife resources.

◁ Grass to the horizon on the Serengeti plains, the flatness broken only by the long necks of giraffes. It is unusual to find the lanky browsers so far from trees.

Until just over thirty years ago, there were no elephants in the Serengeti, but by 1986 it had about two thousand that were believed to have relocated in the park after being forced out of other areas by increasing human activity. The elephants gained some respite, but are still harried by poachers who have also slaughtered the park's black rhinos. In the early 1970s, the Serengeti black rhinos numbered about five hundred, but in 1986 fewer than twenty were thought to survive.

Hunting is prohibited in the park, but meat poachers are rampant. Elephants and rhinos yield their tusks and horns. Wildebeest tails are lopped off to use as fly whisks. Antelopes and zebras are hunted for meat too.

The other big battle for the Serengeti ever since it was declared a protected area in 1940 has been with the pastoralists lining its borders with their cattle, their eyes fixed firmly on the grasslands. The grass is actually not as good as it looks for cattle, but in times of drought it is all there is for the livestock to eat. To start with, African grass is less robust and nutritious than the cultivated strains found on Western farms and certainly far inferior to the pastures of a specialist agricultural country such as New Zealand. Domestic cattle are also not as efficient as wildlife at turning it to meat. Studies conducted in Ugandan parks have shown that a square kilometre of land produces twenty-four to thirty-seven tonnes of wild ungulate meat compared with only three to five tonnes for cattle on the best pastureland in the Kenyan highlands.

To some people this is a clear indication that the future lies not with cattle farming, but in cropping the wildlife. Use the animals best suited to the pasture, they say. This makes sense, but it is an argument fraught with controversy in a society where cattle and land mean wealth.

During the 1960s, scientists were puzzled by the contrast between the grass in the cattlelands surround-

During the February calving season, when herds group for protection from predators, the Serengeti swarms with 1.6 million wildebeest.

ing the park, which was clearly overgrazed, and the same grass inside the park, which fed the huge herds of wildebeest but remained thick and healthy. Something was regulating wildebeest numbers and preventing them from overgrazing.

One of the first suppositions was that predators were keeping herd numbers down, but studies showed this was more a matter of selection than reduction. The predators tended to take the young, very old, lame, or sickly animals, but their influence alone was not sufficient to explain what was happening. There had to be another factor at work as well.

The answer turned out to be something the scientists had long suspected, but had found difficult to prove. The food value of the apparently lush grass fell so much at the height of the dry season that weaker animals succumbed to starvation or became prone to other ills because they were wasting away from what biologists called "under-nutrition" even though they had full stomachs.

This discovery led to an appreciation that the Serengeti's grasslands were a self-sustaining eco-system where the animals, the elements and the grass worked together in perfect harmony. Each animal, each plant species, was perfectly in its place. Here was a rare thing indeed — a big park capable of looking after itself if left alone. But this means that to preserve it for the future, everything must be saved. To tinker with the system is to court disaster.

"It is a failure of the imagination that science is unable to articulate for the rest of us exactly what a sight like this means," said the American zoologist Archie Carr, speaking of the Serengeti in the 1970s.[7] "What you are talking about is the state of order created by nature out of disorder. We can manage only the faintest perception of the beauty in this, the skill and natural selection of nature. Man's closest concept of such processes is his own creation of great art."

A MODEL FOR THE WORLD

One of the Serengeti's contiguous areas, the Ngorongoro Conservation Area, is world famous in its own right. For a start, its 828,800 hectares are based on one of the world's largest unbroken and unflooded remnants of a volcanic crater, which is now home to the densest known population of lions. The conservation area includes palaeontological and archaeological sites which make up one of the world's most important areas for research on the evolution of the human species and many species of extinct animals.

However, the crater area has become almost as famous for the modern developments that are taking place there in an attempt to establish harmony between man, his environment and his animal neighbours.

The Ngorongoro was first established as a conservation area to benefit the Maasai whose sheep and goats grazed up to 75 per cent of the land. The Ngorongoro Conservation Area Ordinance of 1959 was charged with ensuring multiple land use to assist in conserving and developing natural resources, but failed to function because of a lack of rapport between the Maasai and government officials.

A draft management plan was prepared the following year and underwent several revisions before Prime Minister Julius Nyere issued the Arusha Manifesto in 1961. Tanzania is now conducting one of Africa's few pioneer experiments in multiple land use, which attempts to reconcile the interests of wildlife, Maasai pastoralists, and conservation.

Cultivation was banned in 1976 due to incompatibility with wildlife, although it still persists, and forest areas have been established to protect water catchment, soils, and vegetation. In an effort to increase international support for conservation, the Tanzanian Government asked for the Ngorongoro Crater to be put on the list of World Heritage In Danger and it has since been ranked among the most endangered areas.

Today the crater is a specific use zone where only game viewing is allowed, although cattle are permitted controlled access to water in the dry season. As such, it is under close scrutiny from Africa and the rest of the world to see just how the experiment fares.

The Ngorongoro Crater in Tanzania is not only immense, but high. The "floor" averages 2,000 metres above sea level. The lake, which has no outlet from the crater, is unable to flush away the minerals it absorbs from the rocks.

The crater rim rises another 1,000 metres above the floor and is often green to the top.

THE PARKS UNDER ATTACK

Dr. Jim Thorsell, Geneva-based executive officer for the IUCN Commission on National Parks and Protected Areas, has written an article outlining fifty-four threats to protected areas in Africa that were reported in a recent study of twenty-four sites by the Commission and the World Conservation Monitoring Centre at Cambridge.

Chief among these were high poaching levels, livestock conflicts, inadequate management resources, and military and human encroachment.

"No protected area in the world is immune from threats to its integrity," said Thorsell. "A wide range of stresses, such as upstream pollution and civil unrest, inappropriate management, and human disturbances are affecting the natural values for which many areas were established."

There are more than three thousand protected areas on the 1985 UN list of the world's national parks and protected areas, and it is an understatement to say that monitoring the various stresses they face is a demanding task. For three years, IUCN has been compiling a list of seventy-six of the most threatened areas world-wide.

"The intent of the exercise," said Thorsell, "is to create public awareness of the dangers that confront protected areas in all regions of the world and to marshall support for retaining or regaining the integrity of the area. It is not easy to remain popular while compiling such a list; but then, that is not the point of the exercise."

With its diversity of natural biotic features under pressure by expanding human demands and the impacts of technology and changing value systems, Africa is providing many critical test cases of the role of protected areas in society. Despite the large number of parks and reserves, Thorsell claims it is well known that many of them are not managed effectively and thus "have only a tenuous chance of surviving over the long term."

As an illustration, "an example hopefully not to be duplicated," he cites the case of Sudan's Dinder National Park which was established in 1935 and has suffered a gradual loss of biological diversity due to five interrelated pressures.

The first was the progressive loss of the wet season dispersal area for wildlife in the Blue Nile Region of the south to settlement and agriculture.

Second, poaching in the park and heavy hunting pressure in the dispersal area have caused the loss of at least five major species in the last twenty years. Even giraffes have been eliminated (the last one was seen in 1985); and of the once large herds of Sommering gazelle, only a few scattered individuals remain.

A third factor was heavy domestic stock grazing, a problem facing many of Africa's parks. The result in the Dinder has been competition with wildlife, loss of cover, introduction of diseases, excessive trampling and soil erosion. Uncontrolled range fires set by locals exacerbate the problems.

The fourth factor was surrounding land-use pressures on the park which had built up over the years. Thorsell claims the park is now a "desertified island in the middle of a subsistence landscape."

Finally, in spite of early advisory reports from the Food and Agriculture Organization of the United Nations and other wildlife experts, there has been no commitment to implement a management regime in the park. Fundamental park facilities and boundary markers are not in place. Patrols are rare. There are no extension programs to gain the support of local people, and there is almost no tourism.

"Every park has its management problems," said Thorsell. "However, the sad truth of this case is that Dinder's problems are so severe that its viability as a conservation area is being lost and its existence in the twenty-first century is in doubt."

The IUCN's list of the most endangered African parks and reserves, while not comprehensive, makes sombre reading:[8]

Central Kalahari Game Reserve (Botswana): Animal migration routes adversely affected by game fences, mineral prospecting and proposed trans-Kalahari railway.

Makgadikgadi Pan Game Reserve (Botswana): Problems similar to those of the Central Kalahari Game Reserve with fence construction and disruption of migratory game routes.

Manovo — Gounda — St. Floris National Park (Central African Republic): Extirpation of rhinos and poaching of 75 per cent of elephants. Invasion by nomads from Chad and Sudan with large herds of rinderpest-infected livestock.

A herd of domestic goats that has infiltrated Amboseli National Park. In many reserves wildlife now faces serious competition from livestock. ▷

Ouadi Rime /Ouadi Achim Reserve (Chad): Civil unrest.

Tai National Park (Côte d'Ivoire): Illegal settlement, mining, poaching.

Forêt du Day National Park (Djibouti): Continuing degradation by livestock grazing and cutting for firewood. Plans to construct houses for government officials.

Simen Mountains National Park (Ethiopia): Abandonment by staff in 1983 for security reasons.

Ipassa-Makokou Nature Reserve (Gabon): Issue of logging permits, heavy poaching.

Mt. Nimba Strict Nature Reserve (Côte d'Ivoire, Guinea): Poaching, timber removal, mining plans, lack of enforcement.

Shimba Hills National Reserve (Kenya): Poaching of sable and roan antelope, illegal removal of timber, management neglect.

Gorongosa National Park (Mozambique): Military activities, abandonment by staff.

Banhine and Zimane National Parks (Mozambique): Military disturbances and heavy poaching, abandonment by management staff.

Gashaka-Gumti Game Reserve (Nigeria): Expansion of enclaves within reserve, rampant poaching, agriculture in park, inadequate management resources.

Kainji Lake National Park (Nigeria): Poaching, unauthorized fires, domestic livestock grazing, inadequate legislation and enforcement.

Djoudj National Park (Senegal): Radical changes in water regime and lack of water management plan.

Dinder National Park (Sudan): Loss of dispersal area, lack of management, domestic livestock grazing, poaching.

Boma National Park (Sudan): Abandonment by staff due to military disturbances.

Ngorongoro Conservation Area (Tanzania): Inadequate management resources.

Mkomazi and Umba Game Reserves (Tanzania): Takeover by pastoralists, poaching (six species extirpations).

Selous Game Reserve (Tanzania): Drop in elephant population of 50 per cent due to heavy poaching, near extinction of rhino.

Ichkeul National Park (Tunisia): Diversion of 75 per cent of freshwater flow into wetland of park, pollution from agricultural chemicals, grazing pressures, sport hunting.

Garamba National Park (Zaire): Near extinction of rhinos due to poaching.

Lochinvar and Blue Lagoon National Parks (Zambia): Commercial fishing, gypsum mining, military occupation, livestock, and effects of Kafue Dam.

Mosi-Oa-Tunya National Park (Zambia): Rampant poaching, title deeds given for farming inside park.

Many other parks not mentioned on this list are also considered to be in various degrees of difficulty due to the same general causes.

These gerenuk in Tsavo National Park, Kenya, live in a sanctuary that is being threatened not only by poachers, but farmers as well.

Usually, the protected areas are supposed to be sanctuaries for the animals, places where they can cling to a semblance of the life they once knew.

Things aren't working out that way. Having set aside territory for the animals, we keep trying to take it back.

Sometimes the reasons for wanting access to wildlife reserves are compelling and require immediate action. People and their livestock are starving on one side of a fence while on the other there appears to be conditions of plenty. But solving a problem of the moment can create even greater disasters in the long term. Time and time again, environmental scientists have warned that if the forest and animals go, we will not be far behind.

In this sense, the problem is a global one. Africa merely happens to demonstrate some of the principles more clearly; some of the things happening on this continent foreshadow things to come in the rest of the world. In one sense the developed nations have been able to clear their own bush and trees for farms, towns, and cities because there was always a huge reservoir of forests and jungles elsewhere to sustain the global environment. This is no longer true.

In financial terms, we have used up our available capital and are now living on our savings. Unless we can come to terms with our own problems and restore harmony with nature, our account may be closed forever.

[1] The IUCN describes the Afrotropical Realm as being the whole of Africa south of the Sahara, including the island continent of Madagascar, the offshore islands in the Gulf of Guinea, and the oceanic islands of the western Indian Ocean (Mascarenes, Comoros, Aldabra and Seychelles).
[2] "WWF's Continental Strategy for the Conservation of Rhino in Africa," Dr. John Hanks, 1987, p.5.
[3] "A Plea for Urgent Action," Dr. Richard Leakey, *Swara*, magazine of the East African Wildlife Society, Vol. 11, No.5, September-October 1988, pp.6-7.
[4] *The Europa Yearbook*, 1988, Vol. 2, Europa Publications Ltd., London, England, pp.1591-1607.
[5] "Review of the Protected Areas System in The Afrotropical Realm," by IUCN Commission on National Parks and Protected Areas, in collaboration with The United Nations Environment Programme, December 1986.
[6] "Botswana's Fences and the Depletion of Kalahari Wildlife," Douglas and Jane Williamson, *Oryx*, Vol.18, 1988, pp.218-222.
[7] *The Last Place on Earth*, Harold T. P. Hayes, published by Stein and Day, New York, 1977, p.195.
[8] "List of Threatened Parks and Reserves," IUCN Bulletin, Vol.18, Nos. 7-9.

Lions usually hunt at night and spend the day lolling about in the sun or resting in the shade of trees. They may move locations, travelling many kilometres in a single night, but before dawn and at sunset, they establish their presence with roars that can be heard as much as eight kilometres away. These two kings of the beasts survey their diminishing realm from atop a kopje in the Serengeti.

There is a fluid grace about a cheetah even when it is resting. This one is at the Maasai Mara National Reserve in southern Kenya.

231

CHAPTER NINE
Neighbours of the Parks

The pleasant young hotel security guard, who a few minutes earlier had been happily describing his experiences as an extra in the movie *Out of Africa,* studied the wildlife photographs carefully. He nodded and smiled, pointing to a picture of zebras grazing in Amboseli National Park.

"I've seen him," he said. His finger slid across to a wildebeest. "I've seen him too." The next photographs were of elephants and cheetahs. He paused uncertainly. "Is that a leopard?" He shook his head. "I haven't seen him. I haven't seen elephant. I haven't seen rhino or hippo." His eyes brightened. "But I have seen gazelle and giraffe."

Each day he salutes guests arriving at one of the leading hotels in Nairobi, flashes them a brilliant smile, and tells them where to park their cars. The next day, he is there, still smiling, as the tourists leave on their photo safaris and tours.

He is an African and the wildlife which the tourists have come thousands of miles to see is part of his heritage, but the chances are he will never see the animals as tourists do. The cost of staying one night in a lodge is more than he earns in a month. Visitors from small midwestern U.S. towns or European villages will see a greater variety of wildlife in a few days than he has in his life.

His ambition is to save enough money to buy a van so he can drive tourists too.

"To be a driver is a good thing," he said, with his eyes full of dreams. "If I work hard and save my money, I will get two vans and maybe even three. Then I will pay other men to drive for me and I will stay home and be businessman. It is good to be in business."

This is a man who has seen the good life from the outside and has awakened to some of the possibilities. His mind whirls with half-formed entrepreneurial dreams. He believes money is the answer to all his problems. After all, the tourists are rich and most tourists are in business, so he should go into business too.

In such thinking, he is not alone. Through their contact with visitors, hundreds of Africans of all affiliations are learning about the outside world, and they naturally want some of the good life. Many are willing to seek it in their own countries; others are not too proud to ask tourists for help in emigrating. Their reasoning is often naive in the extreme — "Everybody in your country is rich, so I will be rich too."

For many Africans, wildlife represents an opportunity to make money. This is not wrong of itself. The wrongness lies in the approach individuals might take to realize their goals.

One African could make his money as a tour driver who takes tourists to see the animals. Another might produce works of art featuring wildlife. An African cooperative on the border of a park might receive a percentage of the park's income as compensation for lost access rights, or limiting their stock numbers and grazing. Yet another person might turn to poaching.

To some, the parks are good. Others dismiss them as "rich people's playgrounds," or arbitrary lines on a map that prevent them from using their traditional hunting and grazing lands. How can park management make local neighbours into the parks' allies?

LOCAL INVOLVEMENT

An international symposium sponsored by the Endangered Wildlife Trust in Johannesburg, South Africa, late in 1988, focussed on the relationship between local people and their neighbouring game parks, and explored ways of involving them in park activities and goals.

The choice, said the chairman of the symposium, John Ledger, was between a good working relationship with plenty of communication and cooperation, or a bad one where neighbours made managers' lives a misery by entering parks to poach, take firewood, and light fires which endangered the surroundings.

People who were relocated from their traditional homes within park boundaries and were fenced out to keep them from returning usually became bad neighbours, he said. Those who were integrated with the park and actually became part of its management system generally had a good relationship with the administrators and supported park goals. This integration can be as simple a matter as consulting local people on park policies and inviting them to participate in decisions affecting their lifestyles.

"Conservationists have always said, 'If only there weren't so many people . . . It's people outside our parks who are the problem . . . They are the

Maasai settlements are frequently on the fringes of parks, leading to conflict over land use.

poachers,'" said Ledger. "At the symposium we had social scientists — anthropologists actually — saying that those people had legitimate needs and that the aspirations in rural areas needed to be met.

"You can see a spectrum of reactions to that by park managers. In some cases, neighbours are allowed into parks at certain times to harvest thatching grass, poles, and things that they need, such as medicinal plants — all of which are very important to them. It's interesting that those parks generally have good neighbours, whereas the very authoritarian people who say, 'You will not come into my park, otherwise we will arrest you for trespassing,' tend to have bad relationships with their neighbours."

Hard to apply but crucial to the future of the parks is the simple rule that came out of the conference: never consider the needs of the animals in isolation from the needs of the people.

One example of an effective outreach program is the child-education focus of Kenya's National Museums.

"This museum (in Nairobi) has built its reputation on children's education for as long as I can remember," said its director, Dr. Richard Leakey. "The museum has

actually sought to bring school parties from all over the country here. We have enormous numbers coming for guided tours and contact discussion; and it's having a very positive impact throughout the country . . . One would hope that more could be done to make available trips to local parks, film shows, illustrated slide talks and possibly interact with wildlife on nature trails."

In a paper at the 1982 World Congress on National Parks in Bali, Indonesia,[1] Walter Lusigi, then project coordinator for the Unesco integrated project on arid lands, identified one problem facing conservation policies in Africa. The current system of protected lands in Africa was largely imposed by Western countries which failed to recognize the needs, fears, and values of local people.

"In many cases there has simply been no assessment of human needs, and planning still assumes that these countries will develop in the same way as Western countries and that these ideas can be transplanted without modification," he said.

"Despite claims to the contrary, conservation as presented now [1982] remains an alien idea, and the transformation necessary to make it emotionally and intellectually satisfying in its new environment in Africa has not taken place."

"The existence of a human population in a place presupposes a complex of ethnic, social, and biological influences and interactions. If these are not understood and adequately incorporated into conservation plans, the consequences can be serious and even disastrous." He specifically warned that the "bottom-line approach" favoured by Westerners — showing how nature conservation would pay economically — was inadequate.

Living in balance with the environment was an integral component of African cultures, he said. For example, the concentrations of plains herbivores existed only because of a tolerance for wildlife in some African cultures in which the individual was taught to coexist with the natural world and to see himself or herself as part of the system.

"Many traditional African religions referred specifically to the preservation of natural things and made it taboo to kill more than was needed for survival," he said. "Wildlife, which supported life and gave spiritual satisfaction, was hunted for food and clothing, but was also used in tribal ceremonies and rituals. The communal land ownership system was also designed to enhance living in balance with nature . . .

"Through the years, African communities evolved a form of coexistence with the wildlife around them which permitted both to survive. The neglect of these survival strategies is a tragic loss which should be redressed in the future."

The ruins of Great Zimbabwe stand as testament to the many civilizations that have flourished in Africa's past. It was the centre of trade for the powerful state ruled by the Shona people from A.D. 1100 to 1450. Eventually it split into two rival kingdoms and went into decline after the arrival of the Portuguese in the sixteenth century.

Costumed dancers. Many of the African religions and rituals embody a respect for wildlife.

This wall is crumbling now, but it has stood for centuries without the aid of mortar. Ruins can be found over an area with a radius of 160 kilometres, extending into Mozambique. In some areas, attempts have been made to repair the stonework.

The timeless Olduvai Gorge in Tanzania, where fossil finds by Louis and Mary Leakey have revealed much about the origin and development of mankind.

Lechwe feed on grass and water plants and so never stray far from wet areas. However, this has made them easy to hunt and their numbers have dropped by 90 per cent in the last thirty years.

Local involvement has proved an important key to reducing poaching. A case in point is the Kafue Flats wetlands area in Zambia, a region which faced additional threats from hydroelectric dams and over-grazing by cattle. Meat poaching by locals had cut the numbers of Kafue lechwe, an antelope adapted to life on floodplains, from hundreds of thousands to just thirty-five thousand. Government attempts to prevent poaching and reduce over-grazing had had little impact, so Zambia's Department of National Parks and Wildlife set out, with the support of the WWF, to show local people how they could benefit from conservation.

Under an arrangement with local community leaders, the department now sets annual lechwe quotas. The people then decide how many to take themselves and how many to allocate to trophy hunters who are charged US$500 a kill. Poaching is no longer a serious problem — as is evidenced by the lechwe population which has risen above fifty thousand.

The community leaders also advise farmers and the department on cattle numbers, which have been reduced. Local people now strongly support conservation and this, it is hoped, will help persuade the dam operators to control water flows to minimize damage to the flats.

AFRICANS' ACCESS TO THE PARKS

The average cost of a night in a Kenyan tourist lodge in 1988 was 1,200 Kenya shillings per person, or about US$70. A wildlife ranger — even one with the rank of sergeant — could expect to earn a maximum of US$1,701 a year in wages in 1988, plus a monthly housing allowance of US$42 and an US$8-per-day bonus while on safari. The director of the wildlife conservation and management department of the Ministry of Tourism and Wildlife at the time, Dr. Perez Olindo, received a maximum of US$9,240, with a housing allowance of US$198 per month and a field allowance of just under US$24 a day.

Typists and cleaners earning just over US$500 a year have no chance to enjoy the safari holidays arranged for foreign tourists. Kenya is their country, and yet some of its greatest treasures are effectively closed to them.

Yet given the struggle to maintain parks throughout Africa, some commentators have suggested that what is needed is not more tourists but higher entrance fees.

Salt Lick Lodge, a government-operated tourist resort near Tsavo National Park in Kenya.

It is argued that even with fewer tourists — which might not be a bad idea — the revenue would still be at least the same and could well be higher.

While park entrance fees naturally vary from country to country, the ones we paid were usually less than some Westerners would spend during intermission at a movie. These same people are quite prepared to spend US$30 or US$40 a seat at the ballet or a symphony concert and consider it well spent. Would they be prepared to pay the same to see unique animals?

The biggest argument against higher fees is that they would deny many of the country's citizens the right to see part of their national heritage. They simply could not afford to pay such fees, and part of their country would become the exclusive preserve of the visiting rich.

Rwanda has avoided this problem by introducing a two-tier system in the Parc National des Volcans. Foreigners who wish to visit the mountain gorillas in their habitat pay relatively high fees, whereas local people pay only a token amount. This makes the wildlife accessible to the Rwandans and produces revenue from the tourists. A similar scheme exists in Kenya, where nationals pay less to enter the parks.

However, park admission fees are only one source of revenue from tourists. During their visit, they will stay at hotels and lodges, hire cars, charter aircraft, eat meals at restaurants, pay admission fees at other attractions, buy gifts and curios, take package tours, go on photo safaris, and contribute to the country's economy in many other ways.

Most tourists come to see the animals; and if higher park entrance fees reduce their numbers, these other sectors of the industry will suffer. Higher fees might also encourage cheating. It is possible to enter many parks without passing through the main gates. All that's needed is a quick, cross-country drive at a point away from supervision. Once inside, it is unlikely that the driver will be stopped and asked to show proof of having paid the entry fee. In Kenya, poachers have even driven out through park gates with elephant tusks hidden in their vehicles.

Despite these drawbacks, the two-tier system adopted by Rwanda has merit. Those prepared to come half-way around the world to see the animals should not mind paying a higher fee than the locals so long as the rates are explained in advance and don't come as a surprise. If they are happy and keep coming, the other sectors of the tourist industry should not suffer. And it is more than fair that the local residents should get a price break; they have few other advantages compared to what Westerners enjoy.

Clouds heavy with rain overshadow Meru National Park in Kenya, as the dry season nears its end.

CHANGING AFRICAN ATTITUDES

A large percentage of the problems and their solutions lie in how Africans view the animals and the parks that shelter them.

During my research I found one writer (a European) who said somewhat cynically in the 1960s that native peoples had only one word to describe wildlife — "meat." This opinion was repeated by several people in Africa, but there were different points of view. Some native Africans see wildlife as a bounty from the gods — "second cattle" to be used in times of drought and hardship. Then there is the thought that, in a subsistence culture, practicalities will outweigh aesthetic appreciation every time.

Although this "meat-only" view is too general, many people in Africa do indeed have a protein deficiency problem which domestic livestock supplies cannot solve. This has placed greater pressure on the "bushmeat," and, in fact, bushmeat's taste is often preferred to that of domesticated species.

These points were touched upon by Edward S. Ayensu, formerly of the Smithsonian Institution in Washington, D.C., in a keynote paper he delivered at the 1982 World Congress on National Parks in Bali, Indonesia.[2] He asserted that if bushmeat could be rationally exploited on a sustained yield basis in Africa, it could lead to an economic justification for wildlife conservation. It would also give stiff competition to poachers and possibly even make poaching uneconomical.

▷ Signposts at Meru National Park, Kenya. The parks in Africa cater to the lucrative tourist trade, but many Africans cannot afford to stay at the lodges. Ironically, the bird perched atop the signpost is a European roller — another tourist!

Ayensu cited estimates that 50 per cent of the people in Africa south of the Sahara depended on wildlife, including fish, insects, and snails, as an important source of protein. "From my own observations based on extensive visits to African markets, this estimate is very conservative," he said.

In Botswana, rural people eat more than fifty species of wild animals, including elephants, ungulates, rodents, bats, and birds, even though cattle remain the backbone of the national economy.

"Rural communities in the southern states of Nigeria derive 20 per cent of their animal protein from bush-meat, especially in the coastal areas where cattle are susceptible to tsetse flies and other disease vectors," he said. "In Ghana, an estimated 80 per cent of fresh meat consumed is bushmeat."

These figures help Westerners understand one aspect of the complex relationship of Africans to their animals.

When I tried the "Africans-only-see-animals-as-meat" theory on Kenya's Dr. Richard Leakey, the reaction was immediate — and fiery.

"There are many African tribes who don't eat wild meat and never have. You can't make that sort of generalization for an African any more than you can for a Frenchman or an Italian.

BISANADI GATE 9KM
KINNA RIVER 11KM
GARBATULLA 66KM

LEOPARD ROCK

This home in Tanzania is typical of many in Africa — open to the attentions of passing wildlife.

Knowing the elephant's huge daily food requirements, farmers don't always welcome them as neighbours.

"True, if your whole subsistence, your whole livelihood, is based on five acres of land and you have no domestic animals and rarely get meat and you manage to snare a passing antelope and get a square meal a couple of times a year, it's very attractive.

"If your five acres of corn gets flattened by an elephant or a buffalo in the night, reducing you to zero, or below zero, you're hardly likely to have much love. But if you are a middle-class manager and your job is running the local Barclay's Bank, you have children who are at a convent, you have nothing to do on a Saturday afternoon, or have visitors coming from London, then wildlife can be as much a source of pleasure as it can be for someone from New York, or San Francisco, or anywhere else."

As Kenya's free enterprise, capitalistic system produces a larger middle class, support for Kenya's wildlife reserves grows.

"Sadly, the parks themselves are still fairly remote and the hotel accommodation in them is geared for overseas tourism," said Leakey. "It's quite difficult to get space — and when you do get it, to afford it. The sort of money that's being spent in these lodges is prohibitive, even for an affluent Kenyan. But I think there is a recognition of this and some cheaper lodges are beginning to be built. I think it's a very positive development."

An impala herd, part of the abundant wildlife in Hluhluwe Game Reserve, Natal, South Africa.

KINGLY CONSERVATION

There is evidence that many African tribal groupings have practised forms of conservation for generations. For instance, the Zulus set aside areas where no hunting was to take place. One of these was the Emakhosini Valley, south of the White Umfolozi River in what is now Natal. Many tribal leaders lie buried there, and the region is, even today, considered sacred. It is also reverenced as the birthplace of the Zulu nation when the various tribes were welded together in the early nineteenth century by the mighty warrior leader, Shaka.

In almost all cultures, one of the earliest laws established appears to have been that of territorial rights. Whether it was in Africa, Asia, North America, or Europe, groups of people laid claim to land they considered theirs for the purposes of food gathering, hunting, erecting dwellings, and planting crops.

From this came the law of possession, which resulted in the feudal leaders of Europe proclaiming exclusive rights to tracts of land and hunting grounds. Many of these estates evolved in turn into wildlife preserves, because, rightly or wrongly, the original owners were powerful enough to stop the land being carved up for development.

In Africa, Shaka set aside such items as leopard skins, lion claws, and crane feathers for exclusive possession by royalty and established areas where he alone could grant permission to hunt. These royal decrees are described by the Natal Parks Board today as the region's first conservation laws. While some of the restrictions were relaxed by later rulers, Europeans wishing to hunt in Zulu territory had first to obtain the permission of the king, often for a consideration. Whatever the motivation behind them, these ''considerations'' were the forerunners of today's licences and permits used to control the killing or capturing of wildlife.

In spite of this, the history of man's association with the animals of Africa is filled with contradictions and confusions. The native Africans are commonly portrayed as living in harmony with nature and taking no more than they need from the wildlife resources. However, there is plenty of evidence that they have committed their share of thoughtless acts against nature.

On the other hand, it is equally clear that by bringing more sophisticated weapons and tools to Africa, Europeans magnified enormously the ability to kill animals and clear land for farming and other uses. At the same time as they slaughtered the animals and carved up the countryside, they overran the local human populations with superior technology and financial resources. Once the scars of this initial rapacity were evident, the penitent newcomers were able to apply advanced conservation techniques, but now these often run foul of the traditional values of the native peoples.

ANIMAL CROPPING AND FARMING

Writer and wildlife ecologist Norman Myers, who spent twenty years in Africa, working for the United Nations and international conservation organizations, once expressed his wildlife conservation policy this way : "You either use it, or you lose it."[3] Apart from certain key ecological areas where wildlife should be totally protected, he argues that animals should be exploited "for every last nickel" of income.

"The sooner Africans can enjoy gazelle goulash and wildebeest casserole, and the sooner the trade in zebra skins is regulated and expanded rather than decried and suppressed, the sooner a more hopeful era will dawn for African animals," he said in 1981.

In Africa, I was offered such dishes as zebra or topi steaks at tourist lodges; but my standard response was, "I cannot eat an animal I have been admiring all day." While I can appreciate Myers's argument in an intellectual sense, I clearly have some adjustments to make before I can support wildlife with a knife and fork. Eat one now and save two later is an awkward slogan to espouse, even though I can see how it works in theory.

According to Myers, more of the parks should feature not only tourist lodges but canning factories to package meat from excess wild game, as does Kruger National Park in South Africa. The alternative, where culling programs are in force, is to risk wasting a valuable resource.

Myers estimated that at a time when elephants were losing habitat at the rate of as much as 2 per cent a year (1981) an elephant carcass could produce a profit of around US$1,500 from the sale of ivory, hide, and meat.

"Could Africans not devise some way to exploit the 'doomed to die' elephants — those that have nowhere to live — with some of the revenue going to safeguard the future of other elephants?" he said. "In my view, the day when African governments can establish an organization of ivory exporting countries, with strict regulation of the trade, the conservation cause in Africa will take a solid, legitimate step forward."

Myers conceded his approach might appal many committed conservationists in the rest of the world, but said he believed it was possible to adopt a hard-nosed attitude toward conservation while retaining a warm-hearted spirit toward wildlife. "In my view, that is the only pragmatic option available," he said.

During the twenty years he spent in Africa, Myers visited nearly every country south of the Sahara and saw the magnitude of the human problems. He realized that many of the conservation strategies being used were Western imports, based on Western experience. Africans, however, had unique wildlife and human needs that required uniquely African solutions. One of these was to "crop" or farm the wildlife which made better use of the less fertile land than could the prized domestic livestock. This would give the various species economic value and an assured place in the changing Africa.

The terms "cropping" and "farming" are not synonymous. Generally, cropping is regarded as culling excess animals from an area and using the meat and hides, as at Kruger National Park. Farming involves maintaining herds of "wild" animals on farms, often in conjunction with domestic livestock.

When Myers issued his "use it, or lose it" warning, game farming had already begun in southern Africa; in the years since, it has been paying its way for farmers prepared to try something new, be it ostrich farming, raising meat animals, allowing hunting parties on their land, or providing wildlife for tourists to view.

The farming option has been debated for many years and in the process there have been numerous feasibility studies which have demonstrated that many species of mammal wildlife could be domesticated. Particularly favoured are grazing and browsing animals, such as oryx in arid areas, and smaller antelope like springbok and impala.

With many farms devoting only part of their efforts to wildlife, it is difficult to arrive at an accurate figure for the number involved, but in South Africa alone it is tentatively estimated that between seven thousand and ten thousand farmers derive at least part of their income from game.[4]

In Zimbabwe, wildlife has been regarded officially for many years as a renewable resource. The Parks and Wildlife Act of 1975 allows landowners to use wildlife on their land at will and permits them to benefit from such use. Local conservation committees curb any abuses and, if necessary, can be backed up by unilateral action from central government.

The brindled gnu is being considered for game ranching and meat production.

Buffaloes and other grazing forms of wildlife are more efficient than domestic livestock at turning the African grasses into protein. Does this mean the wrong animals are being farmed?

Some conservationists say that putting an economic value on wildlife might be its salvation.

HUNTERS VERSUS KILLERS

No discussion of the economics of wildlife can overlook hunting. South Africa allows surplus, aged, and other close-to-death big game animals to be moved from parks to private land, where trophy hunters are permitted to stalk and shoot them for substantial fees. Part of the proceeds are then used to benefit other wildlife. The argument here, as with culling, is that the animals are going to die anyway so their deaths should be used to benefit their fellows.

Kenya has banned hunting altogether; but before it did so, hunters contributed 6-7 per cent of the annual revenue from tourism. The argument is still used that professional safari operators (who cater to gun and camera shooters) have a vested interest in preserving wildlife so their businesses can continue to operate successfully. If the animals disappear, so does their livelihood.

Hunters in South Africa also told me that they believed their armed presence in game areas helped keep poachers at bay. This doesn't mean the hunters would do battle with the poachers, but that professional hunting safari groups, able to defend themselves, could act as spotters for rangers and other anti-poaching units.

However, history suggests that European hunters went gun-crazy in Africa during the nineteenth century and first half of the twentieth. In trying to understand why this happened, it helps to remember that most of them came from countries where the best hunting grounds had been closed off as private preserves for generations. Alternatively, if they were from the privileged classes, they were used to taking what they wanted and might even have considered it their right.

Not only did the rich and powerful in European countries close off forests, fields, and waterways to the common people, they installed gamekeepers to make sure that trespassers were kept out. For the rich, the hunting grounds provided sport. To the poor, they were larders with doors now bolted shut. Nevertheless, in 1831, one-sixth of all the criminal convictions in England were for poaching.

Thus, the European discovery of Africa must have seemed to be a rediscovery of Eden. Here, from horizon to horizon, was an apparently boundless hunting ground seething with game animals and not a gamekeeper in sight. The fact that there were already human inhabitants with prior claims to the land passed almost unnoticed. Here was a chance to live for a while as the rich lived, or perhaps to even become one of the rich and privileged in this new land.

What the Europeans wanted, in most cases they took. The shooting and the clearing of land for farms began on a scale never before seen in Africa. But by the end of the nineteenth century, the first warning voices had been raised. The impossible was happening. The continent had limits after all; and it was possible to hunt, farm, or crowd certain species to extinction.

In Zululand, for instance, C. D. Guise, a noted sportsman, petitioned the governor to introduce greater preservation measures for wildlife in general and for the white rhino in particular. The outcome was the establishment of five reserves on April 30, 1895, three of which still exist today — St. Lucia, Umfolozi, and Hluhluwe.

The rich, the royal, the (in)famous, and the adventurous continued to hunt in the twentieth century. Denys Finch Hatton (one of the central figures in the movie *Out of Africa*) arrived in 1910 from England to make his home in East Africa and eventually became one of the most respected safari guides of his day. Among his clients was Edward, Prince of Wales, destined to become King Edward VIII.

In his later years, Finch Hatton turned from his rifle to his camera. At least part of his reason was his increasing revulsion at the wholesale slaughter that had replaced the hunt.

On May 23, 1929, Finch Hatton wrote to *The Times* in London, protesting the habits of certain Americans who prowled about Tanganyika in cars, shooting game indiscriminately. Earlier he had written an article for *The Times* on photographing African game, which had prompted a letter of support from a Mr. Andries Pienaar who disgustedly described American parties that raced animals down by car before shooting them. One group had shot thirty-seven buffaloes in this way — "bulls, cows and youngsters were killed indiscriminately."

Another party of Americans had killed twenty-one lions from their car. The same group once left camp with the words "Let us shoot at every living thing we can find today and see what bag is possible in one day."

"And," Pienaar wrote, "what shall we say of the two gentlemen who entered the Serengeti by motor car and

An impala herd stays close to the protective cover of a clump of trees in the Maasai Mara National Reserve, southern Kenya.

Some animals in protected areas, such as this old lion in Kruger National Park, South Africa, no longer run for cover when they see an approaching human.

killed between them eighty lions? Can one think of anything more nauseating? No, worse than that, these men find circles abroad where they are admired. They figure in magazines as 'Famous Big Game Hunters'. The party who had the thirty-seven buffaloes filled the American magazines with their pictures and tales of prowess for weeks on end. They had never been in Africa before, but a single safari sufficed to raise them to the first ranks as the greatest hunters.''

Finch Hatton went on to accuse the Tanganyikan authorities of doing nothing to enforce the game laws. Douglas Jardine, chief secretary to the Government of Tanganyika, denied the charge, but the irrepressible Finch Hatton scathingly itemized the government's failures in trying to stem "this quite exceptional orgy of slaughter."

The professional hunters I met in Africa share his abhorrence and argue that it was not hunting at all, but killing for the joy of killing.

Termite hills vary enormously in shape, size and texture, but nowhere could we find one to match this six-metre skyscraper near Lake Bogoria, Kenya.

The countryside surrounding the lake has other surprises, such as these hot springs, evidence of dormant volcanic activity along an escarpment which extends from Ethiopia to Zimbabwe.

Flamingoes fringe the emerald waters of beautiful Lake Bogoria in Kenya.

WESTERN "INTERFERENCE"

Do Westerners have the right to interfere in Africa, especially since conservation is an internal political issue? In addition to meddling, is it not also hypocritical?

Some Africans argue perceptively: "You Westerners come here preaching conservation, but where are your forests? How healthy are your lakes and rivers? Where is your wildlife?"

In other words: "You have plundered your own environment and become rich, so why should you try to stop me doing the same? If you have used up your own wild places, killed all your wild animals, and dug or drilled all the wealth out of your ground, why should you now try to take ours, or prevent us from using it?"

My answer is that Westerners are not hypocrites. While our own conservation record is still far from perfect, we have learned from our experience. We are trying — not in a patronizing or paternalistic way — to help others avoid the same mistakes. It is not necessary for others to stumble along the same paths.

Quite simply, humankind no longer has forever to decide how we are going to save the world from ourselves. We will all literally sink or survive together. Africa's resources are part of the global treasure. Western knowledge and experience is also part of that global treasure. Both should be used together.

We can work together because the differences in attitudes to conservation which seem to exist between many African people and the rest of the world are not really differences of attitude, but differences in time. The various parts of the world are at different stages of development.

Outsiders who seek to help Africans need the wisdom to recognize this. Most of the problems I have highlighted in Africa either exist or have existed in every developed country. For outside helpers, humility is a most useful virtue.

For their part, Africans must accept that if advisor countries have experienced and worked through many of these problems already, the counsel they offer is all the more valuable. Listening to the advisors then becomes a matter of common sense rather than loss of pride.

ARGUMENTS AGAINST CONSERVATION

Those who are dismayed at the alarm of conservationists have several concerns that deserve to be addressed. Do conservationists lack a balanced perspective? Are they exaggerating both the problems and the solutions? As I have argued hard and persuasively for my own perspective in the preceding chapters, I feel that it is only fair to acknowledge these questions and attempt to provide reasonable answers.

The most compelling argument against greater conservation efforts is that of self-preservation. It is argued that human beings come first; that when people are starving, food and resources should go to them rather than to wildlife. Further, human beings should not have to suffer even a marginal existence while resources that could contribute to their health and well-being are being committed to wildlife conservation.

Close behind the plea for human needs to take precedence over wildlife comes the argument of evolution and survival of the fittest. A superior species will always take precedence over a secondary species, it says. Human beings therefore have a right to claim whatever territory they need, and inferior species must accommodate those decisions.

In answer to this, it must be asked if mankind's claim to superiority can be separated from its moral responsibility which enjoins on us the necessity of preserving other forms of life.

We have great needs. There is no doubt that millions of people are starving throughout the world. There is no doubt that our environment is in a mess. There is also no doubt that species have died out because they could not adapt to change quickly enough, or could not beat the competition. Remember the dinosaurs?

We live in a world where at least 730 million people do not eat enough to satisfy their basic requirements; 1,200 million lack safe drinking water; 2,200 million live on less than US$400 a year, and the plight of the poorest is worsening. The problem here is just as much one of distribution as supply. The resources exist, but they are often in the wrong places.

But killing animals to make more room and resources for ourselves will not get us out of our troubles. It will merely postpone the reckoning. We made our own problems and should face them and beat them with minimum harm to our neighbours. If we have neither the energy nor the will to do this, why should we drag the animals down with us? If we brush them aside in an attempt to save ourselves without tackling the basic inequalities and injustices in the world, the animals will have died for nothing and we will have lived in vain.

There are those who say that it is all very well to look at the long term, but what about the here and now — shouldn't we forget the animals and help people first? There is no simple answer. Each one of us should do whatever we can to relieve suffering where we find it, but this could be fruitless if we don't have a master plan. In an earlier chapter, Dr. John Hanks argues that without cooperation and a coordinated plan, wildlife conservation efforts will fail. Is this any different from the human situation? What benefit is winning a skirmish if we lose the war?

Complicating the issue of wildlife conservation in Africa is the need for a higher standard of living. Africans' desire for a better life for themselves and their children is one with which everyone can identify.

I do not condemn the emerging African middle class for aspiring to the standard of living portrayed as the norm in movies, books, magazines, and television. Such desires, will, I hope, be balanced against the risks of losing local culture and becoming a clone of the West. There is no rule which says that achieving a better standard of living and preserving one's ethnic values are mutually exclusive.

A hippo herd frolics in the clear waters at Mzima Springs not far from Tsavo National Park in Kenya. The flow from the springs is piped to Mombasa and eventually becomes part of the city's supply of drinking water.

Dr. Richard Leakey, a third-generation African, resents the suggestion that newly independent African nations have made a mess of their countries since taking over from former colonial administrators.

"The colonial authorities managed perfectly well to bring these countries into what seemed to be a reasonably civilized state," he said, "but they did so by making sure that the majority of citizens couldn't aspire to that standard of living.

"What has happened since independence is that everybody, ultimately, would like to have two cars and a refrigerator and a deodorant to spray under their arms. When you take the numbers involved in that lifestyle and the fact that politically it's reasonable for everybody to be given a chance to get there, then the carrying capacity of some of these fragile ecosystems puts it into a very grave context. That's part of the problem.

"A lot of people make the comment that if you had been here thirty years ago things were beautiful. They were beautiful except for the people. We mustn't forget that. It's very easy for a Westerner to say 'Good Lord! It's a pity these countries got independence, because look what a mess they're making.' Well, if those colonial powers had tried to achieve the same level of advance for every indigenous man, woman and child, they would have very quickly gone into the same situation.

"That's the problem. You can't create wealth overnight in a population of 20 million [Kenya]; and until you have, they are going to be dependent on the land and they are going to abuse the land in the short term."

The ambition of most African countries in scrambling to catch up with the developed nations is understandable, but they should take the time to learn from the mistakes of others. Indeed, the catch-up period can be shortened and made less painful by using the outside world's hindsight wisdom to avoid pitfalls. Progress can and must be achieved without continuing the assault on wildlife and the environment.

In the meantime, in many little ways we continue to demonstrate a carelessness for other species that may one day return to haunt us. Let me illustrate:

In the late 1970s, elephant experts Oria and Iain Douglas-Hamilton were engaged in a research project in Tanzania's Selous Game Reserve when a series of shots brought them running from their tent. A game scout had emptied his rifle at an elephant near the camp. The elephant, bleeding from its wounds, tottered to the bank of a nearby stream while the scout went to get a small gun to finish the task.

Oria Douglas-Hamilton described the elephant's last moments with these words[5].

"He was standing looking at the water, waiting with us for death, when the gun arrived. Iain walked up to him, lifted the gun to his heart, said, 'Sorry, old chap,' and pulled the trigger. Instantly, his legs folded and he collapsed. No one moved. The birds were still, there was no sound now except the trickling stream. It was the saddest sight I ever saw.

"The scout was standing nearby. 'Why did you shoot?' I whispered.

"'Because he was touching the ropes of my tent,' he answered."

In contrast, consider these words uttered by Seattle, an American Indian chief, in 1854:

"What is man without the beasts? If all the beasts were gone, men would die from a great loneliness of the spirit. For whatever happens to the beasts soon happens to man."

Seattle's perceptive comments were those of a man who lived close enough to nature to observe the effects of change on his environment and was able to perceive the interrelationship of all living species. It doesn't matter that he lived half a world away from Africa. Truths of this magnitude are universal and within them lies one of the greatest motivations for preserving animal life on Earth — companionship.

HOPE FOR THE FUTURE

We must recognize, too, that many of the attitudes needed for African animals to coexist with their human neighbours are already in place. Though much of the pressure and funds for conservation work comes from outside Africa, the tendency to assume that most of the caring also comes from outside Africa, too, is not fair.

A more balanced picture comes from unrelated studies conducted in Rwanda, Tanzania, Brazil, and the U.S.A., which indicate that there is little difference in attitudes about conservation and wildlife between the peoples of the so-called undeveloped and developed countries.[6]

In Rwanda, despite its population pressures and continual demand for more farmland, 49 per cent of the farmers polled near the Parc National des Volcans opposed breaking up the park and said they saw some

The striking colours of young sable antelopes provide vivid contrast with the more subdued tones of their elders.

utility in the protected forest. This generally matched the figures returned in similar polls in the other countries. However, in a second Rwandan survey conducted four years later, after a conservation education program in the region, the support rose to 81 per cent.

The big differences in attitudes to wildlife between Africa and the outside world (education programs apart) lie in circumstances and priorities.

In the industrialized West, conservation is a popular and relatively inexpensive social cause. Almost anyone can espouse it with whatever degree of fidelity they choose. They can even ignore it altogether and go to a football game.

In Africa's subsistence economy, strapped closely to the environment, the margin between life and death is very slender. Conservation is not a hobby, but a technique for staying alive. Long-term survival depends on husbanding an already limited resource today so that it can also be harvested tomorrow. But this takes great discipline when you are still hungry or thirsty. Conservation also takes a bigger bite out of disposable income in poor countries.

Species have always become extinct as they have failed the test of evolution and lost ground to more "successful" life forms. But the competition now is far from fair.

We have swarmed across the Earth with almost complete disregard for the well-being of our companion species. As masters of all we survey, we have forced our planet into the twin roles of boundless larder and bottomless garbage dump.

Now there is the possibility that we, too, will face disaster as the effects of this unwise dominion work against us.

[1]"Future Directions for the Afrotropical Realm," Walter J. Lusigi, published by the Smithsonian Institution Press, Washington, D.C., 1984. (Proceedings of World National Parks Congress, Bali, Indonesia, 1982.)
[2]Keynote Address: "The Afrotropical Realm," Edward S. Ayensu, Smithsonian Institution Press, Washington, D.C., 1984.(Proceedings of World National Parks Congress, Bali, Indonesia, 1982.)
[3]"A Farewell to Africa," Norman Myers, *International Wildlife* magazine, Vol. 11, No.6, 1981, pp. 36-47.
[4]"Game Farming in South Africa as a Force in Conservation," Richard Luxmoore, *Oryx*, Vol.19, No.4, 1985, pp. 225-231.
[5]"Africa's Elephants, Can They Survive?", Oria Douglas-Hamilton, *National Geographic*, November 1980, pp. 571.
[6]Cited in "Public attitudes to Wildlife and Conservation in the Third World," A. H. Harcourt, H. Pennington and A. W. Weber, *Oryx*, Vol. 20, No.3, July 1986, pp. 152-154.

The floodwaters of the Umfolozi River in Natal, South Africa. Man's meddling along the course of the river has caused silting at the river mouth, endangering birds and fish in St. Lucia National Park, one of the oldest wildlife conservation areas in Africa.

This book uses the African conservation situation as a model for the rest of the world. But comparisons can be drawn in other areas too. For example, just as the world's food and wealth are shared unequally, so is Africa's precious water. In some areas, such as the sand dunes of Namibia, wildlife and humans die of thirst, while in others there are huge concentrations of water. The Victoria Falls, the world's most spectacular display of water power, are less than two hundred kilometres from the eastern fringe of the Kalahari Desert. A big temptation for man is to redress the water imbalance, but this is fraught with hidden perils.

CHAPTER TEN
How Can We Help?

We live in a world threatened by pollution, acid rain, holes in the ozone layer, a jostling, ever-increasing crowd of humanity, and a never distant prospect of nuclear war. Now yet another writer is carrying on about saving the animals! Haven't we got enough problems already?

Opponents of wildlife conservation extend the current population trends into the future and see the need for tightly managed food and water production on a planet much too crowded to have room for animals. In this view, any attempt to preserve wild spaces and wild animals is sheer romanticism.

The situation is indeed serious. This is not a science-fiction picture of an urbanized Earth, but straight-line predictions for two or three decades of trends that are already in full spate. The population in Kenya, for example, is increasing by 4 per cent a year. This means that a country which had about nine million citizens when it achieved independence in 1963 will have forty million by the end of the century and, according to demographers, has the potential to peak around seventy million.

Female common waterbuck. Only males of this species have horns. This herd is at Samburu National Reserve in central Kenya, on the banks of the Ewaso Ngiro River, the only source of year-round water in that part of the country.

These people will need homes, jobs, schools, hospitals, and land. With the better regions taken up, the only tracts of land left are the less fertile areas occupied by the animals.

Even South Africa, the most technologically advanced of the African nations, is feeling the pressures of a soaring population. In 1900, the population was about five million, but by 2000 it will have risen to fifty million. South Africa's present rate of growth is about 1,900 people a day; each year jobs have to be found for 210,000 new workers. Besides jobs, resources have to be found. Chief among them is water.

A Natal Parks Board pamphlet discussing the pressure on resources cites a United Nations study which found that industrialized countries require ten thousand litres of water to produce twelve eggs, five hundred litres for an orange, three thousand litres for one kilogram of beef, and four hundred and fifty thousand litres to produce one automobile.

Such everyday requirements are enormous and place constant pressure on the environment. In the Natal region of South Africa, parts of the magnificent wilderness area of the Umfolozi Game Reserve are being directly threatened with inundation by at least one major dam as the struggle to meet the water demands of a growing population continue.

Food demands are increasing just as quickly. Each year an average of twenty million people die of starvation or malnutrition around the world. By the year 2000, the amount of land cultivated per person will have been cut in half and the population will have reached six billion. While three hundred million extra hectares of land will have been cultivated, three hundred million will have been lost to urbanization and three hundred million to soil degradation. The net loss to wildlife conservation will be nine hundred million hectares.

The Earth's population is not just growing, but growing faster every year. At the time of Christ, the world's population is thought to have been around three hundred million. It took until 1830 to reach the first billion. One hundred years later, in 1930, the population reached the two billion mark. Then in thirty more years, it was three billion and just sixteen years later, four billion. Robert McNamara, president of the World Bank from 1968-81, once described the accelerating population growth as, in many ways, a more dangerous threat to the world than thermonuclear war.

"Unless governments, through appropriate policy action, can accelerate the reduction in fertility," he said, "the global population may not stabilize below eleven billion. That would be a world none of us would want to live in."

Yes, we have plenty of challenges. But the human spirit is such that we have always met them in the past. The electric light seemed the pinnacle of achievement; then along came lasers and fibre optics. We have all heard the analogy of the first computers that were so big they filled rooms and we have smiled as we thought of the ones on our office desk or the calculators in our pockets. As soon as an apparent barrier is reached someone finds a way around it. Much of the technology we have today would have been almost incomprehensible as recently as 1969, the year man reached the moon.

Trends need not continue, either. More efficient food production, better medicines, environmentally benign products, changes in political leadership and thinking, twinges of the conscience — all of these and more have the power to change our direction.

The key to it all is the will.

The baobab tree in Central Africa achieves great girth, the diameter of the trunk sometimes reaching ten metres. However, it takes its time in growing — two thousand years or more. Such trees were young at a time when Julius Caesar ruled the Roman Empire. They have lived through the times when wildlife swarmed across Africa, when Europeans came with machines and economic power, and they will still be there centuries from now. Will the animals still be there too? Will man?

ANSWERING THE CALL

The most common response among people who previewed the information in this book was one of horror. They found it hard to believe that human beings could be so selfish, unthinking, and uncaring.

At first they didn't want to believe it. Then, from somewhere in the darker recesses of their minds came the whispers that none of us like to acknowledge — the awareness of what groups of people have done to their own kind over the ages. If we do not even respect our own species, then why should the extermination of other species for pleasure or — even more "justifiably" — for profit, seem unthinkable?

Suddenly anything was possible. The horror gave way to outrage and invariably, their next words were: "What can be done about it?" Some of them personalized the question by saying: "What can I do about it?"

The purposes of this book, as Hans Strohhacker declared in his foreword, are to help awaken the rest of the world to what is happening in Africa and to strengthen the international cooperative effort to save its wildlife. If people of good heart can be persuaded to raise their voices against what is happening and lend their energies to the cause, there is real hope at last. While scientists and academics have been sounding the alarm for years, their messages often don't get beyond their immediate circles or are not understood by the general population. The academics need our backing so that together we can convince our political leaders there is a desire for change. The combined influence of a caring general population the world over is vital if the slaughtering of animals and ravaging of the Earth are to be halted before it is too late. This issue goes far beyond national boundaries, ethnic differences, and political philosophies.

Hans and I set out to argue convincingly that for better, or for worse, humans and animals are in this together, because neither group can survive without the other — or a balanced and healthy environment. Much more than aesthetic appreciation of wildlife is involved. We are part of the same macrocosm and our destruction of the forests, plants, and animals is nothing less than self-mutilation.

But given the complex and confused nature of the problem, what can really be done? Human beings are notoriously short-sighted. After all, CITES, the World Wide Fund for Nature, and others have sought for years to first sound the alarm and then coordinate relief efforts among the hundreds of other groups, projects, and concerned individuals. At first glance, their successes seem insignificant, but we must armour ourselves against the despair, cynicism, and sense of futility that can erode the strongest of resolves and lead to surrender.

Dr. Hugh Lamprey still has a voice of optimism. "We don't know what animals our grandchildren are likely to see in Africa," he said. "It depends on whether our [conservation] efforts today are successful or not."

He discards the straight-line projections downward to extinction. "You can never suppose things are going to stay the same. Things are always going to change. Anybody who just continues trends is crazy."

In the case of the statistically probable extinction of the elephant and rhinoceros he says, "We hope that won't happen. We don't expect it."

Dr. Richard Leakey is another who champions change instead of continuation. He believes the growth of an affluent black African middle class in Kenya and other areas will mean support for conservation in ways that weren't possible ten years ago.

"Today, critical action is possible," he said. "I feel very strongly that if one keeps that in mind the thing can be turned around. I think there are probably more rhinos in Kenya today than there were six months ago. It's the first time in a hundred years that Kenya can say, 'We have more rhinos than we had six months ago.'

"Of course, we may only have five hundred as opposed to five hundred thousand, but we now appear for the first time ever to have reversed that trend. If we can continue to reverse that trend, even modestly, year by year, then things are possible . . .

"I think one's got to be very careful not to always stress the pessimism if there's an opportunity for some optimism."

Such optimism is far from blind. When we take on the long, perhaps lifelong, task of preserving and nurturing an endangered species, we also need to nurture our own courage. We need to celebrate the removal of the southern white rhino from the IUCN's list of endangered species. For the first time ever, a major African animal listed in the Red Data book has escaped extinction. Our task is now to keep the white rhino out of the book forever and to prove to the world that extinction is not the only alternative for a listed species.

Africa's white rhino has struggled back from the brink of extinction, but unless people stop buying rhino horn products, its end may merely be postponed. If we truly are a superior species, we must demonstrate it by exercising superior judgement and exterminating poaching instead.

Thanks to the efforts that have been made already, we know many of the core issues in Africa:

- We must work against the loss of wildlife habitat, particularly the draining or pollution of waterways and the destruction of forests.
- We must eliminate the international market for ivory and rhino horn.
- Simultaneously, we must crack down on poaching and eliminate middlemen and dealers in this trade.
- We must find better ways of dealing with the population explosion and demand for land.
- We must upgrade poor or inappropriate agricultural techniques.
- We must help Africans succeed in achieving a better standard of living.
- We must reinforce national governments in their efforts to eliminate political corruption.
- We must manage the perils of emerging industrialization.

- We must find ways to reduce national debt.
- We must develop land-use planning and national conservation strategies.
- We must eliminate ignorance of environmental issues and ensure that due regard is always given to the full implications of any action.
- We must protect Africa against the danger of exploitation by multi-national businesses and richer nations.

This is not meant to be an exhaustive list, but to distill the most immediate concerns. Many of the issues are interrelated, such as the loss of wildlife habitat, the human population explosion, and the desire for land. Such relationships make them more complex but also hold out hope that improvements in one sector will improve others as well.

Some argue that there are really only three issues: poaching, loss of wildlife habitat, and the human desire for a better standard of living. But whether there are three or twelve issues, they all grow out of the same soil: human greed. It is this single human failing that could well provide the biggest battle of all.

A THREE-LEVEL APPROACH

The World Wide Fund for Nature, in its twenty-fifth anniversary yearly review in 1986, looked ahead to the tasks facing the world's conservation movement.

"The first challenge of the next twenty-five years is to achieve the objectives of the next five or ten," the review said. "If present rates of habitat destruction, pollution, species loss and desertification continue, we will not have another twenty-five years in which to fulfill our aims.

"The resources available to conservation groups are meagre. On one hand, they can be used for matters such as conservation education in the widest sense, as part of a long-term strategy to influence all types of decisions. On the other, those resources can be used immediately and achieve something specific but limited. It is always easier to raise funds for the second option, but it tends to produce short-term results.

is a universal human characteristic. The same responses could be developed among any people.

A network of wildlife clubs is springing up throughout Africa. These clubs bring children into contact with wildlife and expose them at an early age to many of the issues that will affect their future.

While they are only part of the greater awareness effort, they are one of the most promising of all in the long term. Exchanges of information are proving extremely helpful.

Allied with them in mission are the numerous conservation societies and wildlife societies, primarily for adults, that address local issues and make people think more carefully about their relationships with the environment and responsibilities to wildlife. Here too, information exchanges are important.

Similar organizations exist outside Africa — the concerns they are designed to address can be found everywhere there are great concentrations of people.

"It is now becoming clear that conservation will only really succeed if investment is made in the long-term approach."

For this reason, the WWF has adopted a three-pronged approach to the challenges of the future — through awareness, training, and education.

AWARENESS

Awareness is the first step. Solving many of the world's conservation problems will require positive political decisions which, in turn, means increasing public and institutional awareness.

This often begins with simple exposure. Dr. Leakey says that the fascination of visiting tourists for wildlife

However, as a species we need to develop a concern for events far removed from our immediate surroundings. In a global sense, Africa is our back yard.

TRAINING

Training comes next, because developing countries are potentially the hardest hit by conservation problems. Their efforts are often under-funded and inadequately serviced. Training opportunities are few and limited; but without training in all types of conservation skills from land management to fund-raising, conservation groups remain ineffective.

"Only by building strong local institutions devoted to the pursuit of ecologically sustainable development will rapid progress be possible,'' says the WWF in its anniversary review. ''Conservation, in short, cannot be imposed from above. It has to have grass roots support and capability.''

Programs in different parts of Africa concentrate on training park staff, wardens, rangers, and management. Perhaps the best known of these is the College of African Wildlife Management established at Mweka, on the Tanzanian slopes of Mt. Kilimanjaro, in 1963. The college has trained technical staff from many anglophone African countries and is regarded as the pioneer training institution of its type in the world. The campus site was chosen for the advantages of its location near various types of parks, reserves, and game-controlled areas. These include the savanna grasslands of the Serengeti, the plateau area of the Ngorongoro highlands, the montane forests and alpine moorlands of Kilimanjaro and Meru, the alkaline lakes of the Rift Valley, and the marine resources of the Indian Ocean.

EDUCATION

By ''education'' the WWF means shaping the attitudes of the next generation. The planet is facing increasingly intense competition for living space and resources, not just within, but also among, nations. How well our natural life-support systems and biological resources survive such competition will depend largely on how today's young people are educated. To this end, the WWF seeks to introduce conservation principles into educational systems, hoping in the next decade to ''extend its influence and more than double its strength . . .

''The future ecological health of the planet will determine not just the quality of life, but Man's basic ability to grow crops, to harvest fish from the seas, and to use fresh water for drinking,'' says the anniversary review. ''Only a determined conservation effort will secure that future. The challenge which faces WWF and other conservation groups and agencies is immense.''

There is no other protected area training institution that operates in such a variety of life zones, ranging from glaciers at fifty-nine hundred metres to coral reefs.

Facilities are fairly extensive (including residential, administrative, and teaching buildings; vehicles; and field equipment) and the training program is directed toward middle-level managers. Most of its graduates achieve posts as assistant or senior field officers.

However, Mweka has little in the way of secure, long-term funding and needs constant support from the international aid and conservation agencies. Besides the Tanzanian government, at least six foreign countries, three United Nations agencies and five non-governmental organizations have assisted with funding or teaching staff in the past.[1]

Out of education grow national and international conservation policies that plan a future containing African animals. But often the groups and individuals contributing to national conservation strategies have to challenge traditional concepts and confront almost overwhelming public opposition — waging a constant battle in education. A case in point is the situation in Botswana where cattle are wealth and wildlife is seen as an obstacle to expanding herds of domestic livestock. The task here involves changing public opinion and convincing the population that wildlife can also make a meaningful contribution to the economy.

The early morning light blends sky and horizon into a misty foreground, leaving a flock of flamingoes suspended between earth and sky at Lake Manyara National Park, Tanzania.

INTERNATIONAL COOPERATION

Another development occurring throughout Africa is the drafting of national conservation strategies, which often involve the conservation societies mentioned earlier. Some, like the East African Wildlife Society, which developed from the Kenya Wildlife Society established in 1955, now operate in several countries. Others are specific to a single country or region.

In developing their own conservation strategies, most countries try to at least reach accommodations with neighbouring states on issues such as wildlife migration and poaching controls. Such an approach is common sense. The problems faced are often regional in nature and go-it-alone policies are less likely to be successful.

In urging greater international cooperation and assistance for Africa, I do not wish to imply that little is being done at present. Africa has received a tremendous amount of aid from the rest of the world already. Unfortunately, the problems facing Africa are huge by any measure. There are other difficulties as well.

Outside organizations wishing to assist conservation causes in African countries frequently get bogged down in local politics and experience difficulties or delays as they deal with national and local governments. Aspects of national pride are involved too. The cry: "We can look after our own affairs and don't need your patronage" has diminished in recent years, but the issue is still sensitive. Certain diplomatic niceties must be observed if projects are to run smoothly.

For example, Leakey suggests bringing African leadership into the business of conservation in other parts of the world.

"I think the WWF could have done more to involve President Kaunda [of Zambia] in a dialogue with the Brazilians over what's happening to the rain forest and the implications of carbon dioxide build-up," he said. "There has been a conscious development of a sort of Western/European/Caucasian club and the thinking that 'these other people don't understand, they've got too much on their hands and we've got to go around and tell them.'

"I think you could get far stronger sympathy at the political level if African leaders are involved on a global basis in dealing with some of these issues. The loss of rain forest in Brazil is as much a concern to Kenya as it is to Canada. Why aren't Kenyans being asked to participate in these discussions? Why aren't the leaders of African states being asked to take a weekend off a year to commit themselves to an international issue such as toxic dumping at sea? There are many cases that can be brought up — whales, seals — there are lots of issues and I think it would help."

Leakey's proposal has merit. As Africans become part of the solution to global problems centred elsewhere in the world, it will become obvious that the global community has an interest in helping to solve African-centred problems.

Another example of successful international cooperation that could do with many imitators is the story of the San Diego Wild Animal Park and its role in helping save the white rhino. A sister facility of the world-famous San Diego Zoo, the park is situated on a 730-hectare site in California's San Pasqual Valley and contains microcosms of Africa and other exotic environments from around the world.

Early in 1971, a shipment of twenty prized white rhinos left Durban in South Africa, bound for the park. After twenty-five days at sea and a journey by train and truck, the rhinos were released in the fifteen-hectare enclosure that was to be their new home. The big question then was whether they would breed.

Because the new herd's males were sexually immature, a designated sire was transferred, rather nervously, from the San Diego Zoo. During his nine years at the zoo, Mandhla hadn't shown the slightest interest in his female companion. However, in the wide-open spaces of the park he sired fifty-nine calves during the next thirteen years. Eventually he was shipped to another zoo to make room for a new bloodline, but it was a triumph for the park and rhinos-in-the-bank for the rest of the world.

INDIVIDUAL ACTION

Hundreds of millions of good-hearted people will never see Africa or its animals in person, but they still care about wildlife and understand how the issues affect their children as well. What specifically can these people do?

Craig Sholley, the American-born director of the mountain gorilla project in Rwanda, recommends that people begin by becoming more knowledgeable on wildlife matters.

"There's benefit from finding out as much as possible about other areas of the world," he said. "Once people become attuned to the problems in the world, then certainly they can spread the word and their monetary support is much needed and appreciated.

"I think it behooves everybody to find out what the good [conservation] organizations are. There are a lot of conservation organizations that profess to be doing tremendous things. I think if people do their research they'll find there are a few good ones that really use money wisely. Once you've researched the appropriate organizations and once you find a species or habitat area that is worth your monetary support, then donate some funds to that particular organization and I believe it will be used wisely."

As part of this education effort, Sholley believes that anyone who works in Africa on wildlife projects should return to their home countries periodically and speak about their personal experiences to raise the general awareness level.

The number of people in this category is rather small, but the point Sholley is making can be extended to include people who visit Africa. The same principle also applies within our home countries, where we can tell others about what we have discovered or learned about our own conservation problems.

Sholley recommends doing some research to discover the better conservation groups and projects worthy of our support. Information of this type is no further away than a telephone directory and the neighbourhood library. Newspapers, too, are a good source of information and there are many specialized magazines that can be obtained at newsstands or by subscription.

Patterns of financial support received by aid agencies vary, but the WWF reports that well over half its income is provided by the general public in the form of membership contributions, donations, collections, and legacies. Millions of supporters throughout the world make regular contributions to the WWF, but there are hundreds of millions more who could help too.

Perhaps the most visible organization working for Africa's animals, the WWF is the world's largest private international nature conservation organization. It has more than three million supporters and twenty-six affiliate and associate organizations on five continents.

The WWF has been involved with African aid projects since it was founded in 1961 and has a commitment to stay there and help establish a pool of skilled native-born conservationists.

"We don't want to find that when the WWF moves out the effort collapses," observes Hugh Lamprey. "We recognize that we are going to have to be there for a long time, or else hand over to another agency."

Although the WWF has had many successes in Africa since the 1960s, Lamprey says there is a vast leap between its usual US$100,000-$200,000 projects and the massive undertakings of international aid organizations such as USAID whose projects tend to start around US$2 million and perhaps reach as high as US$20 million.

Among the WWF's aims is the fostering of new parks. In spite of the difficulties being experienced in caring for the present parks in Africa, Lamprey argues that more are needed, even if only on the basis of "if we don't get them now, we never will."

As a case in point, he said the WWF was struggling to obtain recognition for a richly forested region in the Uzungwa Mountains in Tanzania, about 240 to 320 kilometres inland from Dar es Salaam and slightly to the south. The mountains themselves are noteworthy, too, as they contain some of the most ancient rock in Africa.

"It is the longest unbroken high-altitude range of forest in East Africa, going from three hundred to twenty-four hundred metres, and is incredibly rich in plant and animal species which occur nowhere else," Lamprey said. However, the fringes of the region are being settled already; and agriculturalists, timber pirates, and poachers are encroaching on forest lands. Because of the unrest in the area and the presence of soldiers, conservationists have found it extremely difficult to do a proper assessment of what the forest offers.

The WWF has adopted an interesting concept as part of its fund-raising — "debt-for-nature" swaps. A conservation organization buys part of a developing country's foreign debt at a discount. This acquired debt is then redeemed for its original value in local currency, local currency bonds, or dollar bonds, and used for conservation purposes. When the discounted debt is redeemed in local bonds that pay a high rate of interest, debt-for-nature agreements can multiply by a factor of six or more the funds that the WWF applies to conservation in developing countries.

A typical transaction was one in which the WWF purchased US$1 million of Ecuador's external debt from U.S. banks for nearly US$355,000, or thirty-five cents on the dollar — a rate that tripled the value of the investment made by members and other donors.

Individuals who have positions in corporations or are in a position to influence corporate policy could encourage them to support such organizations as the WWF. Some corporations have donated goods and services to the WWF. Others have paid for the privilege of using WWF symbols on product wrappings. Invariably the response from customers in terms of sales of WWF-endorsed products has been dramatic and rewarding.

The reason? People really do want to support the conservation of natural areas and appreciate corporations with sensitivities to this aim.

EXPRESS YOUR OPINIONS

If we have opinions about such issues as the destruction of wildlife habitat and the hounding of elephants and rhinos to extinction we should voice them — loudly.

We must speak up and write up a storm that will goad our leaders into action as we become aware of conservation issues. Amnesty International encourages an international campaign of letter writing to countries that have jailed what it terms "prisoners of conscience." We can extend that principle and write letters for wildlife.

The letter writing need not even be on an international level. We can ask our elected political representatives to add their voice to party concerns about conservation issues within our own neighbourhoods and countries as well as Africa. After all, we are all in this together.

Letters and telephone calls to politicians, newspaper editors, and other community leaders may seem ineffective ways of lodging a protest and awakening public interest, but they do work, particularly if the numbers are sufficiently large.

Dr. Leakey, in Nairobi, told me: "I have a feeling that a really major campaign of letter writing on this issue [poaching in Kenya] could have an impact. If the Kenyan Government received three hundred thousand letters on the issue of elephant poaching, there would be much more attention given."

Conservation-minded individuals in many fields can add their expertise to the efforts to save wildlife diversity and the environment. Such "outside" experts as doctors, lawyers, writers, heads of business and trade organizations, scientists, politicians, legislators, and law enforcement officers can all play a part, but the efforts needs to be coordinated through international agencies such as the WWF, United Nations, and the IUCN — whichever is appropriate for the circumstances.

At the next meeting of your professional organization, ask if its parent body has a policy about such issues. If no policy exists, encourage the formation of one, perhaps working in conjunction with similar organizations in Africa and elsewhere.

On an individual basis, put your money or your talents where your mouth is by donating services to

Buffaloes can be extremely aggressive as loners, but collectively err on the side of caution. Left, the famed stare as they spy the camera. Right, a dignified departure.

conservation organizations. They are unlikely to turn away skilled volunteers because they need all the help they can get. Again telephone directories and library reference departments and magazine racks will be an enormous help.

If all else fails and you can find no organization willing to express your concerns, do what countless others have done before you and form your own.

Members of the public can also praise instances of environmental responsibility by big business. We are quick to condem those who err, but we should be just as swift to praise companies and organizations that demonstrate a respect for the environment. Often we can achieve more if we make friends of big business, rather than enemies. Dialogue, not diatribe, is the best policy.

And perhaps most importantly, ordinary citizens can support a total ban on products of endangered species. Don't buy any ivory item. Don't buy anything made of rhinoceros horn. Make a point of not buying smuggled plants, live animals, or animal products. Protest when you find them for sale. Organize boycotts. Ask for stricter enforcement of existing legislation, and work for stronger laws.

Increasingly, there are signs that the message is getting through. For example, the West German piano manufacturer, Steinway, announced in 1989 that it would discontinue using ivory keys once its existing stocks were exhausted. For many people throughout the world, the music will sound even sweeter.

THE ''MORAL'' ISSUE OF WEALTH

Do the richer nations of the world have a moral responsibility to bear a larger share of the costs involved in having African nations serve as caretakers of such a significant part of the world's wildlife heritage?

Suggestions that African countries should not exploit their environments have often drawn ''it's all right for you to talk'' responses from the Africans. They point out that the West has already exploited its own resources and has amassed considerable wealth in the process. Should not they be allowed to do the same?

The Government of Cameroon suggested in 1971 that the West should either share its wealth, or at least reduce its own onslaught against nature to allow developing countries to take up the slack.

It is not unreasonable to ask the rest of the world to play a greater part in meeting the costs of preserving the wildlife heritage in Africa. To a certain extent, we do it already through financial assistance to recognized World Heritage Sites. However, there is room for assistance on many more levels. International banks and financial agencies, foundations, churches, and trusts could increase their already significant contributions to a larger fraction of the total costs.

The Earth's resources, financial and otherwise, could be shared far more equitably. For example, one of the first things I saw when I returned home to Canada was a recently logged hillside, littered with the debris of smaller logs that didn't make the grade. How the fuel-poor Africans would love to put this ''waste'' to use. On an international scale, the possibilities of more equitable distribution are enormous. Agricultural surpluses could be regarded in the same light.

CONCLUSION

Human beings have scaled the pyramid of life and stand dominant at the very top. But it is a lonely and isolated existence. And as long as we insist on retaining that position at the cost of subjugating, suppressing, and destroying all other species, it is very insecure. We are on a course now that is eroding it away beneath our feet.

If we continue, our own extinction is only a matter of time. Without the forests of the land and the plankton of the ocean there will be a great gasping for breath. We will be alone in an empty Eden. But only for a very short while.

If we respond to the challenge and meet it; if we attain harmony not only between nations, but with our animal companions and nature itself, that Eden will not be lonely and could last forever.

---

[1]''Training Protected Area Personnel: Lessons from the College of African Wildlife Management,'' G. T. Mosha and J. W. Thorsell, published by the Smithsonian Institution Press, Washington, D.C., 1984. (Proceedings of the World National Parks Congress, Bali, Indonesia, 1982.) Countries cited in the paper include Canada, U.S.A, Germany, U.K., Denmark and Kenya. Organizations include African Wildlife Leadership Foundation, Rockefeller Brothers Fund, IUCN/WWF, Franfurt Zoological Society, and the Ford Foundation. If the wildlife sanctuaries are to survive, it is vital that Africa has a continuing supply of trained park and reserve staff. To achieve this, the colleges need continued financial support.

We each face personal challenges in our journey through life. Sometimes we feel hemmed in on all sides by the problems of the world and the way ahead seems obscured. Sometimes we ask ourselves what one person can do to make things better. Can one person really make a difference? The message of this book is that we can. We must cut away the side issues so that the simple things, the important things, stand revealed. The way ahead then becomes very clear. We must save our wildlife. We must use our environment efficiently. If we don't, we will die. In producing this book we have not sought for profit, but to make a healthy difference in attitudes to wildlife and the environment. This is one way of helping African wildlife. There are many others. The following pages contain a list of conservation groups that would welcome your support, either financially, or as a member. Make your stand now and help save a priceless part of the world's heritage.

List of Conservation Organizations

The two wildlife organizations mentioned most frequently in this book are the International Union for Conservation of Nature and Natural Resources (IUCN) and the World Wide Fund for Nature (WWF).

They work together closely and even share a joint world headquarters in Gland, Switzerland.

Brief descriptions of both organizations (taken from their own sources) appear below.

The IUCN

The IUCN is a network of governments, non-governmental organizations (NGOs), scientists and other conservation experts, joined together to promote the protection and sustainable use of living resources.

Founded in 1948, IUCN has more than five hundred member governments and NGOs in over one hundred countries. Its six commissions consist of more than three thousand experts on threatened species, protected areas, ecology, environmental planning, environmental policy, law and administration and environmental education.

The IUCN is an independent, international non-profit organization entirely without political or other partisan affiliation. At the head of its list of duties, IUCN puts the monitoring of the status of ecosystems and species throughout the world.

Allied functions involve planning conservation action, both at the strategic level through the World Conservation Strategy and the program level through its conservation efforts for sustainable development.

The IUCN also promotes similar action by governments, intergovernmental bodies and NGOs. Wherever possible it provides assistance and advice necessary to achieve these goals.

International Union for Conservation of Nature and Natural Resources:
Avenue du Mont-Blanc,
CH-1196, Gland,
Switzerland.
Telephone: (022)647-181.
Telex: 22-618 iucn ch.
Telegrams: IUCNATURE, Gland.

The WWF

Founded in 1961, the WWF is the largest world-wide private nature conservation organization. It has national affiliates and associate organizations on five continents.

For the first twenty-five years of its existence WWF was known in English as the World Wildlife Fund, though in other languages it has been known as the World Nature Fund.

Since 1986, although it has retained its legally registered name, the WWF has referred to itself as the World Wide Fund for Nature, in order to better reflect the scope of its activities.

Its prime aim is to conserve the natural environmental and ecological processes essential to life on Earth. In pursuing this, WWF pays particular attention to endangered species of plants and animals and to natural habitats which are of benefit to man.

WWF aims to create awareness of threats to the natural environment, to generate and attract on a world-wide basis the strongest possible moral and financial support for safeguarding the living world, and to convert such support into action based on scientific priorities.

Since its founding, WWF has channelled over US$110 million into more than four thousand projects in some 130 countries. These projects have saved animals and plants from extinction and helped to conserve natural areas all over the world.

During the past thirty years, WWF's work has evolved from conservation of single species to the more global conservation of habitat and environment.

In this work, WWF has served as a catalyst for conservation action and brought its influence to bear on critical conservation needs by working with and influencing governments, NGOs, scientists, industry and the general public alike.

It now has more than three million supporters world-wide.

World Wide Fund for Nature:
WWF — International,
Avenue du Mont-Blanc,
CH-1196, Gland,
Switzerland.
Telephone: (022)647-181.

WWF Affiliate Organizations

WWF — Australia:
Level 17, St. Martin's Tower,
31 Market Street,
Sydney, NSW 2001,
Telephone: (02)297-572.

WWF — Austria:
Ottakringerstr. 114-166/9,
Postfach 1,
A-116-2 Vienna,
Telephone: (0222)46-1463.

WWF — Belgium:
608 Chaussee Waterloo,
B-1060 Bruxelles.
Telephone: (02)347-3030,
or 347-3570.

WWF — Canada:
60 St. Clair Ave. East,
Suite 201,
Toronto, Ontario M4T 1N5.
Telephone: (416)923-8173.

WWF — Denmark:
Osterbrogade 94,
DK-2100 Copenhagen 0.
Telephone: (01)38 20 00.

WWF — Finland:
Uudenmaankatu 40,
SF-00120 Helsinki 12.
Telephone: (080)64 45 11.

WWF — France:
14 Rue de la Cure,
F-75016 Paris.
Telephone: (01)4527-5802.

WWF — Germany:
Sophienstrasse 44,
D-6000 Frankfurt a/M90.
Telephone: (069)77 06 77.

WWF — Hong Kong:
10/F, Wing On Life Building,
22 Des Voeux Road,
Central Hong Kong.
Telephone: (5)26 44 73.

WWF — India:
c/o Godrej & Boyce Ltd.,
Lalbaug, Parel,
Bombay 400 012.
Telephone: (22)9131361.

WWF — Italy:
Via Salaria 290,
I-00199 Rome.
Telephone: (06)85 24 92.

WWF — Japan:
Dai 39 Mori Building,
2-4-5 Azabudai,
Tokyo 106.
Telephone: (03)434-2221.

WWF — Malaysia:
P.O. Box 10769,
Kuala Lumpur.
Telephone: (03)255-4495.

WWF — Netherlands:
Postbus 7,
NL-3700 AA Zeist.
Telephone: (03404) 22-164.

WWF — New Zealand:
P.O. Box 6237,
Wellington.
Telephone: (04)731-758.

WWF — Norway:
Rosenkrantzgate 22,
N-0160 Oslo 1.
Telephone: (02)42 43 15.

WWF — Pakistan:
P.O. Box 1312,
Lahore.
Telephone: (42)63 30 62.

WWF — South Africa:
P.O. Box 456,
Stellenbosch 7600.
Telephone: (02231)72892/3.

WWF — Spain:
6 Santa Engracia,
E-Madrid 10.
Telephone: (01)410-2401/2.

WWF — Sweden:
Ulriksdals Slott,
S-171 71 Solna.
Telephone: (08)85 01 20.

WWF — Switzerland:
Postfach 749,
CH-8037 Zurich.
Telephone: (01)44 20 44.

WWF — United Kingdom:
Panda House, 11-113 Ockford Road,
GB-Godalming,
Surrey.
Telephone: (04868)20-551.

WWF Associate Organizations

Argentina:
Fundacion Vida Silvestre,
Defensa 245 51 6 Piso,
(1065) Cap. Federal.
Telephone:
30-3778/4086 331-4864.

Ecuador:
Fundacion Natura,
Av. 6 de Diciembre 5043,
y El Comercio,
Casilla 243,
Quito.
Telephone: (02)249-780.

Thailand:
Wildlife Fund Thailand,
255 Soi Asoke,
Sukumvit 21,
Bangkok 10110.
Telephone:
(02)258 3004/6000-3.

Other Useful Organizations

Center for International
Environment Information,
345 East 46th Street,
New York, NY 10017,
United States of America.

CITES,
rue du Maupas 6,
1004 Lausanne 9,
Switzerland.

Flora and Fauna Preservation
Society,
8-12 Camden High Street,
London, NW1 0JH, England.

Food and Agriculture Organization
of the United Nations,
Via delle Terme di Caracalla,
00100 Rome, Italy.

Frankfurt Zoological Society,
Alfred Brehm Platz 16,
6000 Frankfurt am Main,
West Germany.

Friends of the Earth,
124 Spear Street,
San Francisco, CA 94105,
United States of America.

International Centre for
Conservation Education,
Greenfield House,
Guiting Power,
Cheltenham, Glos. GL54 5T2,
England.

International Council for
Bird Preservation,
219c Huntingdon Road,
Cambridge, CB3 0DL, England.

National Audubon Society,
950 Third Avenue,
New York, NY 10022,
United States of America.

National Wildlife Federation,
1412 16th Street, NW,
Washington D.C. 20036,
United States of America.

New York Zoological Society,
The Zoological Park,
Bronx, NY 10460,
United States of America.

Peoples Trust for Endangered Species,
19 Quarry Street,
Surrey, GU1 3EH, England.

San Diego Wild Animal Park,
15500 San Pasqual Valley Road,
Escondido, CA 92027 - 9614,
United States of America.

Sierra Club,
Office of International Affairs,
777 United Nations Plaza,
New York, NY 10017,
United States of America.

The Nature Conservancy
International Programme,
1785 Massachusetts Avenue NW,
Washington D.C. 20036,
United States of America.

Unesco,
7, Place de Fontenoy,
75700 Paris, France.

United Nations Environment
Programme, (UNEP)
P.O. Box 30552,
Nairobi, Kenya.

U.S. National Park Service,
Department of the Interior,
P.O. Box 37127,
Washington D.C. 20013-7127,
United States of America.

World Conservation Monitoring
Centre,
219c Huntingdon Road,
Cambridge CB3 0DL, England.

Zoological Society of San Diego Inc.,
P.O. Box 551,
San Diego, CA 92112,
United States of America.

Organizations in Africa

African Wildlife Foundation,
Embassy House, Harambee Avenue,
P.O. Box 48177,
Nairobi, Kenya.

(U.S. address:
1717 Massachusetts Avenue NW,
Washington D.C. 20036, U.S.A.)

College of African Wildlife
Management, Mweka,
P.O. Box 3031,
Moshi, Tanzania.
(Trains anglophone Africans.)

East African Wildlife Society,
P.O. Box 20110,
Nairobi, Kenya.

Elsa Wild Animal Appeal,
P.O. Box 4572,
North Hollywood, CA 91607,
United States of America.
(Funds educational projects
affiliated with wildlife clubs in
Kenya and elsewhere.)

FAO Regional Office for Africa,
P.O. Box 1628,
Accra, Ghana.

FAO Regional Office
for the Near East, P.O. Box 2223,
Cairo, Egypt.

Kalahari Conservation Society,
P.O. Box 859,
Gaborone, Botswana.

Natal Parks Board,
P.O. Box 662,
Pietermaritzburg, South Africa.

School for the Formation of
Wildlife Specialists,
P.O. Box 271,
Garoua, Cameroon.
(Trains francophone Africans.)

Wildlife Conservation Society
of Zambia,
P.O. Box 30255,
Lusaka, Zambia.

Wildlife Clubs of Kenya,
P.O. Box 40658,
Nairobi, Kenya.

List of Wildlife Parks and Protected Areas

KEY TO PARK STATUS ABBREVIATIONS

BoR	Botanical Reserve	GS	Game Sanctuary	S	Sanctuary
BR	Biosphere Reserve	HR	Hunting Reserve	SA	Safari Area
BRC	Biosphere Research Centre	HZ	Hunting Zone	SF	State Forest
CA	Conservation Area	IF	Integral Forest	SNR	Strict Nature Reserve
CaR	Catchment Area	INR	Integral Nature Reserve	SR	Special Reserve
CF	Classified Forest	IR	Integral Reserve	TA	Tourist Area
FoR	Forest Reserve	NFR	Natural Forest Reserve	WA	Wilderness Area
FR	Faunal Reserve	NP	National Park	WAR	Wildass Reserve
FS	Flamingo Sanctuary	NR	Natural Reserve	WHS	World Heritage Site
GMA	Game Management Area	P	Park	WR	Wildlife Reserve
GMR	Game Management Reserve	PR	Partial Reserve	WRA	Wilderness Research Area
GPA	Game Production Area	R	Reserve	WS	Wildlife Sanctuary
GR	Game Reserve	RP	Recreation Park	WUA	Wilderness Utilization Area

ALL PARK AREAS ARE SHOWN IN HECTARES.
100 HECTARES EQUALS 1 SQUARE KILOMETRE
1 HECTARE EQUALS 2.42 ACRES
640 ACRES EQUALS 1 SQUARE MILE

ANGOLA

1	Amboin	PR	50 000
2	Bandeira	PR	40 000
3	Bikuar	NP	790 000
3a	Buffalo	PR	40 000
4	Chela	PR	80 000
5	Humbe	PR	25 000
6	Iona	NP	1 515 000
7	Kameia	NP	1 445 000
8	Kangandala	NP	60 000
9	Kisama	NP	996 000
10	Luando	IR	828 000
11	Luiana	PR	840 000
11a	Mavinga	PR	595 000
12	Mocamedes	PR	445 000
13	Mupa	NP	660 000
14	Techipa	PR	40 000

BENIN

1	Atakora	HZ	175 000
2a	Djona	HZ	225 000
2	Pendjari South	HZ	200 000
3	Pendjari North	NP	275 500
4	W du Benin	NP	568 500

BOTSWANA

1	Central Kalahari	GR	5 180 000
2	Chobe	FoR	240 000
3	Chobe	NP	998 000
4	Gemsbok	NP	2 480 000
5	Kasane	FoR	120 000
6	Kazuma	FoR	12 800
7	Khutse	GR	244 000
8	Mabuasehube	GR	179 200
9	Maikaelelo	FoR	30 000
10	Makgadikgadi Pan	GR	414 000
11	Moremi	WR	180 000
12	Moselesele (Proposed)	SA	1 215
13	Nxai Pan	GR/NP	259 000
14	Sibuyu	FoR	101 824

BURKINA FASO (Upper Volta)

1	Arly	FR	206 000
2	Bontioli	FR	12 700
3	Dida	CF	{ 56 000
4	Deux-Bales	CF	{
5	Diefoula	CF	{
6	Koflande	CF	{
7	Kourtiagou	FR	51 000
8	Nabere	FR	36 500
9	Pama	FR	223 500
10	Po	NP	155 500
11	Sahel	FR	1 600 000
12	Singou	FR	192 800
13	W du Burkina Faso		235 000

BURUNDI

1	Bururi (Proposed)	FR	1 500
2	Kibira (Proposed)	NP	37 870
3	Kigwena (Proposed)	FR	360
4	Lake Rwihinda (Proposed)	NR	425
4a	Rumonge (Proposed)	FR	400
5	Rusizi (Proposed)	NR	5 235
6	Ruvubu (Proposed)	NP	43 630

CAMEROON

1	Babules	FoR	50 000
2	Bafia	FR	42 000
3	Banyang-Mbo		40 000
4	Benoue	NP/BR	180 000
5	Bone-Paupa	FoR	50 000
6	Bouba Ndjidah	NP	220 000
7	Campo	GR	330 000
8	Dendeng	FoR	60 000
9	Dibombe Mabobe	FR	40 000
10	Dja	FR/BR	500 000
11	Douala-Edea	FR	160 000
12	Doume	FoR	40 000
13	Edea Ngambe	FoR	40 000
14	Ejaham	FoR	50 000
15	Faro	NP	330 000
16	Fusgom	FoR	50 000
17	Kalamaloue	NP	4 500
18	Kalfou	FR	4 000
19	Keingke Sud	FoR	20 000
20	Korup	GR	83 675
21	Lake Balembi	FR	10 000
22	Lake Lobeke	FR	43 000
23	Lake Oku (Kimbi River)	GR	5 625
24	Lake Ossa	FR	4 000
25	Mangambe	FoR	20 000
26	Mbamba	FoR	45 000
27	Mbam-et-Djerem (Proposed)	NP/GR	421 000
28	Mone River	FoR	40 000
29	Mozogo Gokoro	NP	1 400
30	Mta-Ali	FoR	35 000
31	Nyong/Kelle/Kribi	HR	60 000
32	Nyong River	FR	80 000
33	Pangar Djerem	GR	480 000
34	Rumki Hills	FoR	75 000
35	South Bakunda	FoR	40 000
36	Takamand	FoR	60 000
37	Waza	NP/BR	170 000

CENTRAL AFRICAN REPUBLIC

1	Andre Felix	NP	170 000
2	Aouk-Aoukale	FR	330 000
3	Avakaba Presidential Park		175 000
4	Bahr-Oulou (Proposed)	FR	320 000
5	Bamingui-Bangoran	NP	1 070 000
6	Basse-Lobaye	BR	18 200
7	Bongos Sanctuary (Proposed)		265 000
8	Gribingui-Bamingui	NP/FR	438 000
9	Koukourou-Bamingui	FR	110 000
10	Manovo-Gounda-Saint Floris	NP	1 740 000
11	Nana-Barya	FR	230 000
12	Ouandjia-Vakaga	FR	130 000
13	Vassako-Bolo	SNR	86 000
14	Yata-Ngaya	FR	420 000
15	Zemongo	FR	1 010 000

CHAD

1	Aboutelfan	FR	110 000
2	Bahr Salamat	FR	2 060 000
3	Binder Lere	FR	135 000
4	Fada Archei	FR	211 000
5	Manda	NP	114 000
6	Mandelia	FR	138 000
7	Ouadi Rime-Ouadi Achim	FR	8 000 000
8	Siniaka-Minia	FR	426 000
9	Zakouma	NP	300 000

CONGO

1	Conkouati	FR	300 000
2	Lefini	FR	650 000
3	Lekoli-Pandaka	FR	68 200
4	Mboko	FoR	90 000
5	Mont Fouari	FR	15 600
6	Mont Mavoumbou	HR	42 000
7	Nyanga North	FR	7 700
8	Nyanga South	FR	23 000

9	Odzala	NP	126 600
10	Tsoulou	FR	30 000

CÔTE D'IVOIRE

1	Azagny	NP	17 000
2	Banco	NP	30 000
3	Comoe	NP/WHS	1 150 000
4	Diefoula	CF	60 000
5	Divo R	BOR	50 000
6	Haut-Bandama	FR	123 000
7	Iles des Erotiles	NP	20 000
8	Marahoue	NP	101 000
9	Mt. Nimba	SNR/WHS	5 000
10	Mt. Peko	NP	34 000
11	Mt. Sangbe	NP	100 000
12	N'Zo	FR	73 000
13	Tai	NP/WHS	330 000

DJIBOUTI

1	Day	NP	3 000

EQUATORIAL GUINEA

1	Mont Alen	PR	95 000

ETHIOPIA

1	Abijatta-Shalla Lakes	NP	88 000
2	Awash	NP	72 000
3	Awash West	WR	100 000
4	Bale	WR	150 000
5	Bale Mts	NP	220 000
6	Chew Bahar	WR	200 000
7	Gambella (Proposed)	NP	200 000
8	Gash Setit	GR	100 000
9	Gewane	WR	400 000
10	Harrar	WS	400 000
11	Mago	NP	150 000
12	Mille Sardo	WAR	1 000 000
13	Nakfa	GR	250 000
14	Nechisar	NP	70 000
15	Omo	NP	345 000
16	Simen Mts.	NP/WHS	22 500
17	Tama	WR	
18	Yavello	WS	150 000
19	Yangudi Rassa	WAR/NP	200 000
20	Yob	GR	150 000

GABON

1	Ipassa-Makokou	SNR	15 000
2	Lope-Okanda	NP	358 000
3	Minkebe		400 000
4	Moukalaba	FR	100 000
5	Petit-Louango	FR	200 000
6	Wonga-Wongue	HR/NP	358 000

GAMBIA

1a	Abuko	NR	113
1	Delta du Saloum	NP	2 000
2	Gambia River	NP	627
3	Kiangs West	NP	10 000

GHANA

1	Ankasa	GPA	20 736
2	Bia	GPA	22 810
3	Bia	NP	7 776
4	Bomfobiri	WS	7 258
5	Bui	NP	307 360
6	Digya	NP	312 595
7	Gbele	GPA	32 400
8	Kalakpa	GPA	32 400
9	Kogyae	SNR	32 375
10	Mole	NP	492 100
11	Nini-Suhien	NP	10 427
12	Owabi	WS	5 184
13	Shai Hills	GPA	5 443

GUINEA

1	Massif du Ziama	BR	116 170
2	Mt. Nimba	SNR	13 000
3	Tomine		250 000

KENYA

1	Aberdare	NP	76 619
2	Amboseli	NP	32 206
3	Arawale	NR	53 324
4	Bisanadi	NR	60 600
5	Boni	NR	133 900
6	Buffalo Springs	NR	33 915
7	Central Island	NP	500
8	Chyulu Hills		30 000
9	Dodori	NR	87 739
10	Hell's Gate	NP	6 800
11	Kakamega Forest	NP	9 698
12	Kerio Valley	NR	10 000
13	Kiunga	BR	60 000
14	Kora	NR	178 780
15	Lake Bogoria	NR	10 705
16	Lake Naivasha		20 000
17	Lake Nakuru	NP	20 000
18	Lambwe Valley	NP	12 000
19	Losai	NR	180 680
20	Maasai Mara	NR	151 000
21	Maralai	GS	20 000
22	Marsabit	NP	{ 208 842
23	Marsabit	NR	{
24	Meru	NP	87 044
25	Mt. Elgon	NP	16 923
26	Mt. Kenya	NP	58 800
27	Mt. Kulal	BR	700 000
28	Mwea	NP	6 803
29	Nairobi	NP	11 721
30	Nasolot	NR	92 500
31	North Kitui		74 500
32	Ol Doinyo Sabuk	NP	1 842
33	Rahole	NR	127 000
34	Ras Tenewi Coastal Zone	NP	35 000
35	Saiwa Swamp	NP	192
36	Samburu	NR	16 500
37	Shaba	NR	23 910
38	Shimba Hills	NR	19 251
39	Sibiloi	NP	157 085
40	South Island	NP	3 880
41	South Kitui	NR	183 300
42	South Turkana	NR	109 100
43	Taita Hills	GS	11 340
44	Tana River Primate		16 807
45	Tsavo	NP	2 082 114

LESOTHO

1	Sehlabathebe	NP	6 805

LIBERIA

1a	Cape Mount (Proposed)	NR	10 000
1	Cavally (Proposed)	NR	10 000
2	Cestos Sankwen (Proposed)	NP	145 000
3	Loffa-Mano	NP	230 000
4	Mt Nimba (Proposed)	NR	29 000
5	Sapo	NP	130 700
6	Wonegezi (Proposed)	NR	40 000

MADAGASCAR

1	Ambatovaky	SR	60 050
2	Ambohijanahary	SR	24 750
3	Ambohitantely	SR	5 600
4	Analamerana	SR	34 700
5	Andohahela	INR	76 020
6	Andranomena	SR	6 420
7	Andringitra	INR	31 160
8	Anjanaharibe	SR	32 100
9	Ankara	SR	18 220
10	Ankarafantsika	INR	60 520
11	Berenty Private Reserve		205
12	Bemarivo	SR	11 570
13	Betampona	INR	2 228
14	Bora	SR	4 780
15	Cape Sainte Marie	SR	1 750
16	Foret d'Ambre	SR	4 810
17	Isalo	NP	81 540
18	Kalambatritra	SR	28 250
19	Kasijy	SR	18 800
20	Lokobe	INR	740
21	Mangerivola	SR	800
22	Maningozo	SR	7 900
23	Manombo	SR	5 020
24	Manongarivo	SR	35 250
25	Marojejy	INR	60 150
26	Marotandrano	SR	42 200
27	Mont d'Ambre	NP	18 200
28	Nosy Mangabe	SR	520
29	Perinet-Analamazaotra	SR	810
30	Pic d'Ivohibe	SR	3 450
31	Tampoketsa d'Analamaitso	SR	17 150
32	Tsaratanana	INR	48 622
33	Tsimanampetsotsa	INR	43 200
34	Tsingy de Bemaraha	INR	152 000
35	Tsingy de Namoroka	INR	21 742
36	Zahamena	INR	73 160

MALAWI

1	Chimaliro	FoR	
2	Chongoni	FoR	
3	Dedza-Sailima	FoR	
4	Dzalanyama	FoR	
5	Kasungu	NP	231 600
6	Kaningina	FoR	
7	Lake Malawi	NP	9 400
8	Lengwe	NP	88 700
9	Liwonde	NP	54 800
10	Majete	GR	78 400
11	Malasa Complex	FoR	
12	Mangochi	FoR	
13	Matipa Complex	FoR	
14	Mehinji	FoR	
15	Mt. Mulange	FoR	
16	Musisi	FoR	
17	Mwabvi	GR	10 400
18	Namizimu	FoR	
19	Nkhota/Kota	GR	180 200
20	Nyika	NP	313 400
21	South Viphya Complex	FoR	
22	Thombani	FoR	
23	Thyolo/Chiradzulu	FoR	
24	Vwaza Marsh	GR	100 000

MALI

1	Asongo-Menaka	FR	1 750 000
2	Badinko	FR	193 000
3	Banifing-Baoule	FoR	13 000
4	Bossofola	FoR	12 000

5	Boucle du Baoule	NP	350 000
6	Elephant	FR	1 200 000
7	Faya	FR	80 000
8	Fina	FR	136 000
9	Kenie-Baoule	FR	67 500
10	Kongossambougou	FR	92 000
11	Nafadji	FoR	43 000
12	Sounsan	FR	37 600
13	Talikourou	FoR	13 900

MOZAMBIQUE

1	Banhine	NP	700 000
2	Bazaruto	NP	15 000
3	Chimanimani (See Zimbabwe)		
4	Gile	R	210 000
5	Gorongosa	NP	375 000
6	Maputo Reserve		90 000
7	Marromeu Reserve		1 000 000
8	Pomene Reserve		10 000
9	Rovuma (Niasaa)	NP	1 500 000
10	Zambesi	WUA	1 000 000
11	Zinave	NP	500 000

NAMIBIA

1	Cape Cross Seal	R	650 000
2	Caprivi	GR	530 000
3	Daan Viljoen Park	P	3 953
4	Etosha	NP	2 227 000
5	Fish River Canyon	NR	46 100
6	National West Coast	T.A.	
7	Namib/Naukluft	P	4 976 800
8	Omaruru	NR	1 000
9	Skeleton Coast Park	P	1 639 000
10	Tsaobis-Leopard	NR	35 000
11	Waterberg Plateau	P	40 500

NIGER

1	Air and Tenere (Proposed)	NR	7 736 000
2	Gadabedji	FR	76 000
3	Tomou	NR	76 000
4	W du Niger	NP	220 000

NIGERIA

1	"A"	GR	
2	Akpaka	GR	
3	Alawa	GR	
4	Anambra (Proposed)	GR	29 620
5	Ankwe River Complex	GR	
6	"B"	GR	
7	Chingurmi-Duguma (Proposed)	GR	35 400
8	Dagida GR	GR	29 422
9	Damper (Proposed)	GR	
10	Ebba/Kampe	GR	11 730
11	Falgore	GR	
12	Gashaka-Gumti (Proposed)	GR	636 300
13	Gilli-gilli	GR	36 200
14	Iri-Ada-Obi	GR	
15	Kamuku (Proposed)	GR	120 000
16	Kogin/Kano	GR	60 000
17	Kwiambana	GR	261 000
18	Lake Chad (Proposed)	GR	36 800
19	L Kainji	NP	534 082
20	Lame/Burra	GR	205 967
21	Obudu (Proposed)	GR	72 000
22	Ohosu (Proposed)	GR	47 000
23	Okomu (Proposed)	GR	123 800
24	Opanda	GR	110 000
25	Old Oyo	GR	
26	Ologbolo-Emu-Urho	GR	19 440
27	Omo	BR	460
28	Pai River	GR	
29	Pandam	GR	22 400
30	Sambisa	GR	68 600
31	Sapoba	FoR	49 200
32	Stubbs Creek	GR	
33	Udi Nsukka	GR	5 600
34	Udo	GR	5 400
35	Upkon	FoR	
36	Upper Ogun	GR	110 000
37	Wase Sanctuary	GS	115 300
38	Yankari	GR	224 000

REPUBLIC OF SOUTH AFRICA

1	Addo	NP	8 879
2	Alexandria	SF	23 566
3	Andries Vosloo Kudu Reserve	NR	6 493
4	Anysberg/Klein Swartberg	CA	58 785
5	Augrabies Falls	NP	9 415
6	Bathurst	SF	5 315
7	Bloemhof Dam	NR	22 072
8	Blouberg East & West	NR	11 298
8a	Bonte Bok	NP	2 786
9	Blyde River	NR	22 664
10	Borakalalo	NP	7 380
11	Cape of Good Hope	NR	7 675
12	Chelmsford Public	NR	6 845
13	Commando Drift	NR	5 983
14	De Hoop	NR	17 846
15	Doorndraai Dam	NR	7 229
16	Dornkloof	NR	8 765
17	Drakensberg State Forests	SF	190 000
18	Dukuduku (Part)	FR	15 055
19	Gamka Mt	NR	9 428
20	Gamkapoort	NR	8 000
21	Giant's Castle	NR	34 638
22	Golden Gate Highlands	ND	6 241
23	Groendal	WA	25 047
24	Groot Swartberg/Swatberg East	CA	121 002
25	Groot Winterhoek Mt.	CA	81 188
26	Hans Merensky	NR	5 282
27	Hawequas Mt.	CA	115 910
28	Hluhluwe	NR	23 067
29	Hester Malan	NR	6 576
30	Hottentots Holland Mt.	CA	84 936
31	Itala	NR	25 896
32	Kalahari Gemsbok	NP	959 103
33	Karoo	NP	27 011
34	Karoo	NR	14 000
35	Kouga/Baviaanskloof	FoR	172 208
36	Kruger	NP	1 948 528
37	Knysna	CA	44 230
38	Langeberg (East)	CA	71 300
39	Langeberg (West)	CA	77 096
40	Lekgalameetse	NR	18 125
41	Loskop Dam	NR	14 800
42	Manyeleti	GR	22 772
43	Matroosberg Mt	CA	95 259
44	Mkuzi	GR	25 091
45	Mountain Zebra	NP	6 536
46	Ndumu	GR	10 117
47	Ntendeka	WA	5 230
48	Otterford	SF	11 467
49	Oviston	NR	13 000
50	Outeniqua Mt.	CA	158 515
51	Pilanesberg	NP	50 000
52	Pirie	FoR	5 239
53	Pongola	NR	6 222
54	Riversonderend Mt.	CA	69 453
55	Rooiberg Mt.	CA	25 344
56	Royal Natal	NP	8 856
57	St Lucia	GR	36 826
58	St Lucia Park	NR	12 545
59	Sandveld	NR	3 624
60	Sederberg Mt.	CaA	126 375
61	Serala	SF	21 998
62	Sodwana/Cape Vidal	SF	57 954
63	Soetdoring	NR	6 173
64	Storms River	NR	13 700
65	Suikersbosrand	NR	13 337
66	Suurberg	SF	21 121
67	Tembe Elephant Reserve	NR	29 878
68	Tsitsikamma Forest and Coastal	NP	3 318
68a	Tsitsikamma	IF	15 615
68b	Tsitsikamma Mts. Forest Region	FR	80 000
69	Tsolwanna	CP	7 557
70	Tussen-die Riviere	NR	22 000
71	Umfolozi	NR	47 753
72	Verloren Valei	NR	6 055
73	Verwoerddam	NR	11 237
74	Walker Bay	SF	7 118
75	Weza State Forest	SF	9 000
76	Willem Pretorius	GR	12 005
77	Woodbush/De Hoek	SF	6 626

RWANDA

| 1 | Akagera | NP | 250 000 |
| 2 | Volcanoes | NP | 12 000 |

SENEGAL

1	Basse-Casamance	NP	5 000
2	Delta du Saloum	NP	73 000
3	Djoudj Nat. Bird S.	WHS	16 000
4	Ferlo (North)	FR	487 000
5	Ferlo (South)	FR	633 700
6	Kalissaye Bird Reserve	R	16
7	Langue de Barbarie	NP	2 000
8	Ndiael Bird Reserve	R	46 550
9	Niokolo-Koba	WHS	913 000

SIERRA LEONE

1	Gola East	FoR	22 800
2	Gola North	FoR	45 000
3	Gola West	FoR	6 200
4	Kangari Hills	FoR	12 950
5	Loma	FoR	
6	Mamunta-Mayoso Swamp	NR	1 500
7	Nimini	FoR	
8	Outamba-Kilimi	NP	98 000
9	Sherbro		
10	Tama	FoR	16 200
11	Tingi	FoR	
12	Western		17 870

SOMALIA

1	Angole-Farbiddu	NP	
2	Arbowerow	NP	
3	Arbowerow	WR	
4	Boja Swamps	WR	
5	Daalo Forest	NP	
6	El Chebet	WR	
7	El Hammure	WR	
8	Far Wamo	WR	
9	Gaan Libaax	NP	
10	Haradere-Awale Rugno	WR	
11	Harqan-Dalandoole	WR	
12	Hobyo	WR	

#	Name	Type	Area
13	Jowhar-Warshek	NP	
14	Lack Badana	NP	
15	Lack Dere	NP	
16	Lack Dere	WR	
17	Las Anod	NP	
18	Ras Guba	NP	
19	Ras Hajun	WR	
20	Taleh	GR	
21	Zeila	GR	
	SUDAN		
1	Ashana	GR	90 000
2	Bandingiru	NP	
3	Bangangai	GR	17 000
4	Bire Kpatuos	GR	500
5	Boma (Proposed)	NP	2 280 000
6	Boro	GR	150 000
7	Chelkou	GR	550 000
8	Dinder	NP/BR	650 000
9	Dinder Buffer Zone		227 300
10	Imatong		
11	Jebel Marra	FR	
12	Juba	GR	20 000
13	Kidepo	GR	450 000
14	Meshra	GR	450 000
15	Mbarizunga	GR	1 300
16	Mongala		
17	Nimule	NP	41 000
18	Numatina	GR	210 000
19	Radom	NP	1 250 970
20	Rahad	GR	
21	Shambe	GR	62 000
22	Shambe ext		
23	Southern	NP	4 481 970
24	Zeraf	GR	970 000
	SWAZILAND		
1	Hlane	GR	14 164
2	Malolotja	NP	18 000
3	Mlawula	NP	12 000
4	Mlilwane	WS	4 545
5	Ndzindza	NR	5 500
	TANZANIA		
1	Arusha	NP	13 700
2	Biharamulo	GR	130 000
3	Burigi	GR	220 000
4	Gombe	NP	5 200
5	Ibanda	GR	20 000
6	Katavi	NP	225 300
7	Kilimanjaro	NP	75 575
8	Kizigo	GR	400 000
9	Lake Manyara	NP/BR	32 000
10	Lake Natron	FS	
11	Mahale Mtn. (Proposed)	NP	161 300
12	Maswa	GR	220 000
13	Mikumi	NP	323 000
14	Mkomazi	GR	100 000
15	Moyowosi	GR	600 000
16	Ngorongoro	WHS	828 800
17	Ruaha	NP	1 295 000
17a	Rubondo Island	NP	45 700
18	Rumanyika	GR	80 000
19	Rungwa	GR	900 000
20	Sadani	GR	30 000
21	Selous	WHS	5 000 000
22	Serengeti	WHS	1 476 300
23	Tarangire	NP	260 000
24	Ugalla	GR	500 000
25	Uluguru Mts. (Proposed)	PA	
26	Umba	GR	150 000
27	Usambaras Mts. (Proposed)	PA	621 300
28	Uwanda	GR	500 000
29	Uzungwa Forest (Proposed)	NP	100 000
	TOGO		
1	Fazao-Malfakassa	NP	192 000
2	Fosse aux Lions	FoR	9 000
3	Keran	HR	9 550
4	Keran	NP	170 000
5	Togodo	R	35 000
	UGANDA		
1	Ajai	GR	15 800
2	Bokora Corridor	GR	205 600
3	Budongo	NR	1 041
4	Bugungu	GR	52 000
5	Bwindi (Impenetrable)	FR	31 000
6	Dufile	S	48 900
7	Entebbe	S	5 200
8	Jinja	S	800
9	Karuma	GR	82 000
10	Katonga	GR	20 800
11	Kidepo Valley	NP	134 400
12	Kibale Forest Corridor	GR	56 000
13	Kigezi	GR	33 000
14	Kyambura	GR	15 700
15	Lake Mburo	NP	53 600
16	Malaba	S	20 700
17	Matheniko	GR	160 000
18	Mt. Kei (See Dufile)	S	
19	Murchison Falls (Kabalega)	NP	384 000
20	Otze (See Dufile)	S	
21	Pian-Upe	GR	231 400
22	Queen Elizabeth (Ruwenzori)	NP/BRC	197 800
23	Toro	GR	55 488
24	Gorilla	NP	2 900
25	Zoka Forest Elephant	S	20 700
	ZAIRE		
1	Bombo-Lumene	GR	240 000
2	Bomu	NR	
3	Garamba	WHS	492 000
4	Kahuzi Biega	WHS	600 000
5	Kundelungu	NP	760 000
6	Lomako Yekokora	GR	
7	Luki	FoR	33 000
8	Maiko	NP	1 083 000
9	Salonga North	NP	{3 656 000
10	Salonga South	NP	{
11	Shaba Forest Elephant	GR	
12	Upemba	NP	1 173 000
13	Yangambi Flora Reserve	FR	250 000
14	Virunga	WHS	780 000
	ZAMBIA		
1	Bangweulu	GMA	657 000
2	Blue Lagoon	NP	45 000
3	Chambeshi	GMA	62 000
4	Chibwika-Ntambu	GMA	155 000
5	Chisomo	GMA	339 000
6	Chizera	GMA	228 000
7	Isangano	NP	84 000
8	Kafinda	GMA	386 000
9	Kafue Flats	GMA	517 500
10	Kafue	NP	2 240 000
11	Kalaso-Mukoso	GMA	67 500
12	Kansonso Busanga	GMA	778 000
13	Kasanka	NP	39 000
14	Kaputa	GMA	360 000
15	Mweru-Wantipa	NP	313 400
16	Lavushi Manda	NP	150 000
17	Liuwa Plain	NP	366 000
18	Lochinvar	NP	41 000
19	Luano	GMA	893 000
20	Lower Zambezi	NP	414 000
21	Luambe	NP	25 400
22	Lukusuzi	NP	272 000
23	Lukwakwa	GMA	254 000
24	Lumimba	GMA	450 000
25	Lunga Luswishi	GMA	1 334 000
26	Lupande	GMA	484 000
27	Lusenga Plain	NP	88 000
28	Luwingu	GMA	109 000
29	Machiya Fungulwe	GMA	153 000
30	Mansa	GMA	207 000
31	Mosi-oa-Tunya	NP	6 600
32	Mulobezi	GMR	342 000
33	Mumbwa	GMA	337 000
34	Munyamadzi	GMA	330 000
35	Musalangu	GMA	1 735 000
36	Musele-Matebo	GMA	370 000
37	Namwala	GMA	360 000
38	North Luangwa	NP	463 600
39	Nsumbu	NP	202 000
40	Sandwe	GMA	153 000
41	Sichifula	GMR	360 000
42	Sioma-Ngwezi	NP	527 600
43	South Luangwa	NP	905 000
44	Tondwa	GMA	54 000
45	West Lunga	NP	168 400
46	West Petauke	GMA	414 000
47	West Zambezi	GMR	3 807 000
	ZIMBABWE		
1	Bangala	RP	2 800
2	Charara	SA	169 000
3	Chegutu	SA	71 597
4	Chete	SA	108 100
5	Chewore	SA	339 000
6	Chimanimani Eland S.	NP	17 100
7	Chipinga	SA	26 100
8	Chirisa	SA	171 300
9	Chizarira	NP	191 000
10	Dande	SA	52 300
11	Deka	SA	
12	Doma	SA	76 400
13	Gonarezhou	NP	505 300
14	Hwange (Wankie)	NP	1 465 100
15	Inyanga	NP	28 900
16	Kazuma Pan	NP	31 300
17	Lake Kyle	RP	18 000
18	McIlwaine	RP	55 000
19	Mana Pools	NP	219 600
20	Manjirenji	RP	3 500
21	Matetsi	SA	292 000
22	Matobo	NP	43 200
23	Matusadona	NP	137 000
24	Mt. Selinda	RP	3 500
25	Mushandike	S	12 900
26	Ngezi	RP	5 800
27	Sapi	SA	118 000
28	Sengwa	WRA	37 300
29	Tuli	SA	41 600
30	Umfuli	RP	6 000
31	Umfurundzi	SA	76 000
32	Urungwe	SA	287 000
33	Zambesi	NP	56 400

Index

Hundreds of mammals, reptiles and birds are mentioned in *The Empty Eden*. However, only those that feature prominently are included in the index. Where the listing refers to a photograph, the page number is shown in bold type.

For a more comprehensive guide to the wildlife of Africa, the following publications are recommended:

A Field Guide to the Mammals of Africa — including Madagascar, Theodor Haltenorth and Helmut Diller, published in English by William Collins (original German title, *Saugetiere Afrikas und Madagaskars*, BLV Verlagsgesellschaft mbH, Munchen).

A Field Guide to the Larger Mammals of Africa, Jean Dorst and Pierre Dandelot, published by William Collins.

Roberts' Birds of Southern Africa, revised by Gordon Lindsay MacLean, published by The Trustees of the John Voelcker Bird Book Fund, Cape Town.

An excellent overview of Africa's parks and protected areas can be gained from two IUCN publications. They are:

IUCN Directory of Afrotropical Protected Areas, prepared and published by IUCN in collaboration with the United Nations Environment Programme and with the financial support of the World Wide Fund for Nature and the United Nations Environment Stamp Conservation Fund.

Review of the Protected Areas System in the Afrotropical Realm, prepared by the IUCN Commission on National Parks and Protected Areas in collaboration with the United Nations Environment Programme.

Copies of both books can be obtained from IUCN Publications Services, 219c Huntingdon Road, Cambridge CB3 ODL, United Kingdom, or Avenue du Mont-Blanc, CH-1196 Gland, Switzerland.

Savanna, 88, 89, 207.
Savimba, Jonas, 201.
Seattle, North American Indian chief, 250.
Sebungwe, 51.
Secretary bird, 166, **170.**
Selous Game Reserve, Tanzania, 229, 250.
Serengeti National Park, Tanzania, 210, 223-226, **222.**
    Serengeti grasslands, 89.
Serengeti-Ngorongoro Biosphere Reserve, 223.
Shaka, Zulu leader, 241.
Sheldrick, Daphne, 13-14, 28-29, 36-41, 48, 52, 214.
Sheldrick, David, 14-15, 203.
Shimba Hills National Park, Kenya, 229.
Sholley, Craig, Director of Mountain Gorilla Project, 60, 62, 64-66, 68-69, 73, 260-261 (see "gorilla, mountain species").
Simen Mountains National Park, Ethiopia, 229.
SMA Goldcap S26, 14.
Somalis, 195, 198.
South Africa, 33, 50, 201-202, 209, 242, 254.
South America, 15.
Spotted hyaena, **97,** 223.
Springbok, 106, **124, 216,** 242.
Steinbok, 106.
Steinway, 263.
Sudan, 57, 202.

T

Tai National Park, Côte d'Ivoire, 229.
Taita Hills Lodge, Kenya, 22.
Tanzania, 19, 51, 201, 204, 210, 223-226, 259.
Termite hill, **246.**
Terrapin, **163.**
Thomson's gazelle (see also Gazelle), 89, 223.
Thorsell, Dr. Jim, 228.
Topi, 89, **97,** 106, **116, 119.**
Tortoise, **163.**
Tourists, 73, 207, 211, 236-237, 240, 242, 244.
Trees, 77.
Trophy hunting, 20, 50, 74, 91, 196, 236, 244-245.
Trypanosomiasis, 37.
Tsavo National Park, Kenya, 14, 16, 22, 28, 35-37, 40, 89, 195-196, 198, 207, 210.
Tsetse fly, 37, 50-51, 74, 81, 239.
Tsessebe, 106.

U

Uganda, 35, 51, 57.
Umfolozi Game Reserve, Natal, 45-46, 50-51, 208, 215, 244, 254.
Umfolozi River, **59, 252.**
Umba Game Reserve, Tanzania, 229.
Unesco, integrated project on arid lands, 233.
United Nations, 207.

V

Van Note, Craig, 200-201.
Victoria Falls, **252.**
Virunga, the Passion of Dian Fossey, book by Farley Mowat, 60.
Virunga Mountains, **71.**
Virunga National Park, Zaire, 60.
Visoke (in Virungas), 66.

W

Wagtails, 169.
Wart hog, **156-157.**
Water,
    effect of new sources, 75
    lack of in Kruger National Park, 215
    wildebeests dying of thirst, 216.
Waterbuck, 93, 106, **120-121, 254.**
Water leguaan, **162.**
Weaver birds, **184-185.**
Wetlands, 80, 84-85, 236.
White Umfolozi River, 241.
Wild dog, 81, **81, 146-147.**
Wildebeest, **74,** 89, **104-105,** 106, **132-136,** 206, **208,** 216, **216-217, 223-225,** 223-224.
Williamson, Douglas and Jane, 216.
Wilson, Roger, 69.
Woodley, Bill, 198, 213.
World Congress of National Parks, 1982, 233, 238.
World Conservation Monitoring Centre, 82.
World Heritage Sites, 58, 263 (see also footnote 3, 59).
World Wide Fund for Nature, 16, 52, 57, 66, 82-87, 199, 203-204, 258-262. (See also Lamprey, Hugh)

Z

Zaire, 19, 51, 201-202.
Zambezi River, poaching activity, 52.
Zambia, 19, 51-52, 201-202, 209.
Zimbabwe, 19, 33-35, 52, 57-58, 195, 201, 242.
Zebra, 21, 93, **99, 104-105, 138-140, 179, 210,** 223, 242.
Zulus, 241.
Zululand, 50, 241, 244.